The Tudors

ABOUT THE AUTHOR

Richard Rex is Director of Studies in History at Queens' College, Cambridge and reader in Reformation History at the University of Cambridge. He has written and researched extensively on Tudor England and his other books include: *Elizabeth I: Fortune's Bastard?*, *Henry VIII: The Tudor Tyrant*, *Henry VIII & the English Reformation* and *The Lollards*. He lives in Cambridge with his wife and whichever of his six sons happen to be at home.

The Tudors

RICHARD REX

AMBERLEY

This edition first published 2012

Amberley Publishing
The Hill, Stroud
Gloucestershire, GL5 4EP

www.amberley-books.com

British Library Cataloguing in Publication Data.
A catalogue record for this book is available from the British Library.

ISBN 978-1-4456-0700-9

Typesetting and Origination by Amberley Publishing.
Printed in Great Britain.

CONTENTS

GENEALOGY OF THE HOUSE OF TUDOR

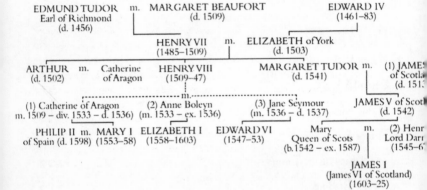

EDMUND TUDOR   m.   MARGARET BEAUFORT   EDWARD IV
Earl of Richmond   (d. 1509)   (1461–83)
(d. 1456)

HENRY VII   m.   ELIZABETH of York
(1485–1509)   (d. 1503)

ARTHUR   m.   Catherine   HENRY VIII   MARGARET TUDOR   m.   (1) JAMES
(d. 1502)   of Aragon   (1509–47)   (d. 1541)   of Scotla
                                                    (d. 151

                             m.

(1) Catherine of Aragon   (2) Anne Boleyn   (3) Jane Seymour   JAMES V of Scot
m. 1509 – div. 1533 – d. 1536)   (m. 1533 – ex. 1536)   (m. 1536 – d. 1537)   (d. 1542)

PHILIP II   m.   MARY I   ELIZABETH I   EDWARD VI   Mary   m.   (2) Henr
of Spain (d. 1598)   (1553–58)   (1558–1603)   (1547–53)   Queen of Scots   Lord Darr
                                        (b. 1542 – ex. 1587)   (1545–6

JAMES I
(James VI of Scotland)
(1603–25)

PREFACE

There have been countless books on the Tudors published in the last century and, in whatever form publishing develops over the next century, there will doubtless be countless more: biographies, histories and textbooks; monographs on specialised aspects of politics, social life, religion, economics and culture; collections and editions of original sources. Nobody could even hope to read them all. Yet while the Tudors are among the most familiar, they are also among the most interesting of England's ruling dynasties, and an author is therefore entitled to hope that another book on the Tudors can be added to the heap without much special pleading. That said, there have not been many books like this one, and this one will certainly be rather different from previous books of the same kind.

For this is not a history of Tudor England. Still less is it an attempt to conform to current historical fashion as a history of 'Tudor Britain': as the kingdoms and lordships of the British Isles were neither all 'Britain' nor all 'Tudor', it is difficult even to describe, let alone to write, a history of the entire British Isles in this period. Worthwhile though both those endeavours certainly are, this book simply has a different scope. It aspires to retell a familiar story in an unfamiliar way. It sets out to explore the reigns of the five Tudor monarchs very much from the royal perspective. This might sound a little old-fashioned – but the point is precisely to avoid the old-fashioned confusion between the history of kings and the history of their kingdoms. This book is meant as a series of essays in brief political biography, a study of the public lives, rather than of the 'private lives', of the Tudors. Indeed, one might say that, as monarchs, the Tudors did not have private lives. The monarch was, as such, a public person, and the most intimate details of his or her life were matters of acute public interest. So the emphasis in these pages is on the politics of personal monarchy. The idea is to give a brief narrative of the politics of England from the point of view of the central character in the political system, the monarch, and to show how the personal character and concerns and beliefs of the monarchs affected the ways in which they acted within contemporary institutions and interacted with other political figures.

It is customary to preface a book with long lists of names of those who have helped or advised the author along the way, a secular litany at times as remorseless as the thanks at an awards ceremony. Large numbers of scholars have contributed to this book through their publications on Tudor history, which have shaped my own understanding of the period. As this book is meant for readers rather than for scholars, and has been written rather than 'researched', I have dispensed with the traditional array of footnotes and bibliographical references. Most of the factual information is common knowledge. Uncommon knowledge is mostly derived from my own work, but where I am conscious of depending on the findings and insights of others, I have tried to acknowledge my debts in a general way in the guide to further reading at the end of the book. But that aside, the book is a solo effort, so the usual polite reminder that 'all the mistakes are my own' is hardly worth making. I have no one else to blame.

Nevertheless, I should like to thank three people who have contributed to the writing of this book in more general ways. First of all, I should like to thank David Starkey for reminding us that, whatever else history might be, it is about people and it is for people. Here it is. I hope people enjoy reading it. Secondly I should like to thank my son Henry for his constant encouragement ('Good luck with the Tudors!', 'Have you finished the Tudors yet, Dad?'). Yes, I've finished. Sorry it took so long. And finally I should like to thank my father, Peter Rex, himself a historian, for... for too many things really, but perhaps these will do: interesting me in the past, and teaching me two of the things every historian needs to learn – when to believe, and when to doubt. Thank you.

Richard Rex
Queens' College, Cambridge

1

HENRY VII

ACCESSION

Henry Tudor was one of the unlikeliest men ever to ascend the throne of England. Royal blood ran thin in his veins – drawn ultimately from illegitimate origins and filtered through the female line – and he was one of the few men in late medieval England with absolutely no claim to the throne whatsoever: his Beaufort ancestors, John of Gaunt's bastards by Catherine Swynford, had been legitimised by an Act of Parliament, but had subsequently been specifically excluded from the succession. Nevertheless, this trickle of Lancastrian blood was a valuable political asset in that intermittent series of dynastic struggles we call the 'Wars of the Roses', especially once the blood of the last direct heir of the House of Lancaster, the young Prince Edward, had been spilled on Tewkesbury Field in 1471.

After that final and catastrophic defeat for the Lancastrian cause, Henry's powerful and ambitious mother, Lady Margaret Beaufort, had spirited him away from England. For the next dozen years he was sheltered in the relative security of the court of Brittany, over which presided Duke Francis, a prince almost independent of his notional sovereign, the king of France. The insecurity of Henry's early life, measured out in plot and intrigue, left a permanent mark on him. By the time he launched what would turn out to be his triumphant bid for the throne in 1485, he was for all the world a sorry figure, a nobleman long separated from his domains, a refugee who knew more of France than of his native Wales or of the England he hoped to rule. His accession owed less to the innate strength of his claim or of his position than to the staggering ineptitude of his predecessor, Richard III, in dissipating within just a couple of years the legacy of political consensus which Edward IV had painstakingly accumulated for the Yorkist dynasty.

For all the trouble Henry took to bolster his dubious legitimacy, his reign was always overshadowed by the fact that he was little more than a noble adventurer who got lucky: the first dozen years of his reign were spent scheming and fighting against pretenders whose claims were only slightly more ridiculous than his own.

Henry VII was haunted by an awareness of the political realities of his own success, as we can see in the suspicion, verging at times on paranoia, with which he viewed the governing class of his own country.

The family name of Tudor was of course Welsh, and the male line which Henry represented was of princely descent. After the destruction of the Glendowers (thanks to their disastrous revolt against Henry IV), the Tudors became the focus of the almost messianic political hopes and dreams (still preserved in a mass of bardic literature) with which the Welsh compensated themselves for military defeat and political impotence. Henry's Welsh ancestry, though of doubtful worth in English politics, was to prove invaluable in his bid for power in 1485. It was no accident that Henry landed in Milford Haven, and that Welshmen were numerous in his army. The troops brought to his banner by his uncle, Jasper Tudor, and by the Welsh magnate Rhys ap Thomas were the core of the force which faced Richard III at Bosworth Field. Indeed, much of the general success of the Tudor regime in Wales can be attributed to the Welsh origins of the new dynasty, and this loyalty, subsequently bolstered by the twin processes of union with England and religious reformation, was maintained under the Stuarts. Welsh troops were a major factor in the Wars of the Roses, and Henry's Welsh ancestry certainly helped him recruit the support of this crucial military constituency. Much later, Welsh troops were to be the core of Charles I's army in the first English Civil War, from the recourse to arms in 1642 to final defeat at Naseby in 1645.

Welshness was less of a recommendation to Henry's English constituency, although the evergreen Arthurian legends provided a useful way of bridging the cultural gap. 'Arthur' was a well-chosen name for his eldest son. Thomas Malory's hugely popular *Morte d'Arthur* had recently revived the Arthurian cycle's appeal to an English audience. Nor, thanks to his long exile, did Henry in fact bring with him the sort of personal following of Welsh hangers-on that might have offended English sensibilities in the way that James VI and I's band of Scottish freeloaders and carpetbaggers managed in the early seventeenth century. All Henry brought with him was a handful of English exiles.

Richard's reckless squandering of the political resources carefully built up by his brother opened the door to Henry. His first raid, launched from Brittany in 1484, achieved nothing more than to cause Richard to pursue his elimination through diplomatic manoeuvres. Henry had to flee Brittany for France. But in 1485 he had another go. His mother, whose various marriages had brought her a huge personal fortune along with a vast web of useful family connections, had negotiated an informal agreement with Edward IV's widow, Elizabeth Woodville, by which elements of the Yorkist connection would support Henry Tudor on the understanding that he would take Edward's daughter, Princess Elizabeth, as his wife. Encouraged at least by the evident lack of enthusiasm for Richard's regime, Henry set sail with a small band of loyal friends and mercenaries.

Landing in Milford Haven on 7 August 1485, Henry moved north and east through Wales, calling upon the Tudor connection in Pembrokeshire but also recruiting from the clients of the late Duke of Buckingham (executed by Richard III in 1483) and eventually securing the allegiance of the powerful Welsh magnate Rhys ap Thomas, who held Carmarthen Castle. His large Welsh force came together at Shrewsbury and then marched across the Midlands, encountering Richard's predominantly northern army near Market Bosworth in Leicestershire. Although most of the English peerage refrained from committing itself to either side, two large forces from the north also converged on this area: Yorkshiremen and Borderers under Henry Percy, Earl of Northumberland, and men from Lancashire led by Thomas Lord Stanley (Margaret Beaufort's third husband and thus Henry Tudor's stepfather). In the ensuing battle, Stanley's decision to support Henry was no great surprise. Percy's refusal to commit himself to Richard was the decisive moment. It cost not only the king's but also his own life. Four years later the Earl of Northumberland, left conspicuously undefended by his own retainers, was lynched at Topcliffe in Yorkshire by a mob protesting against tax assessments. The underlying bitterness of the north against his betrayal of a man who, for all his faults, was certainly a northerners' king fuelled both the rage of the mob and the indifference of the retainers.

Richard III's death in action (outcome of a characteristic recklessness) made Bosworth Field a decisive battle. Henry took possession of London, summoned Parliament, and backdated his reign to the day before Bosworth: a legislative sleight of hand which enabled him to pass an 'act of attainder' against those who had opposed him. (An act of attainder was a statute declaring named individuals guilty of treason, and subjecting them to a range of penalties, most importantly the confiscation of all their property and goods.) The vast majority of the peerage had studiously held aloof from the Bosworth campaign. The Wars of the Roses had taught them that the risks of fighting on the losing side outweighed the benefits of fighting on the winning side. But they now thronged to demonstrate their loyalty by attending Henry's coronation on Sunday 30 October 1485.

Throughout his reign Henry was anxious to establish continuity with both of the preceding dynasties, the Yorkist as well as the Lancastrian. His marriage to Elizabeth of York, celebrated on 18 January 1486, sealed the loyalty of many of those Yorkists who had supported him against Richard III. More importantly, it added considerably to the perceived legitimacy of their children. The reconciliation of Lancaster and York in Tudor through this royal marriage was a recurring note of Tudor propaganda, vividly expressed in the full title of Edward Hall's chronicle, *The Union of the Two Noble and Illustre Famelies of Lancastre and York*, and ultimately canonised in Shakespeare's history plays.

Henry also emphasised his affiliation with the Lancastrian house by encouraging the cult and canonisation of Henry VI (who, like Charles I after him, was far more esteemed after his tragic death than he had ever been in his lifetime: bad kings make good martyrs, and the incessant stream of miracles reported by his hagiographer, John Blacman, contrasts strangely with Henry's lifetime record of passivity and detachment). Indeed, the story was put about that when the young Henry Tudor was paying a visit to Henry VI's court, the saintly king prophesied that one day the

A drawing of Henry VII by a French or Flemish artist.

boy would wear the crown. Perhaps the most remarkable feature of Henry's own presentation of his claim to the throne was that it was principally founded not upon his genetic, but legally questionable, descent from John of Gaunt through his mother, Lady Margaret, but upon a more tenuous family connection with an altogether more impressive royal figure, Henry V, through his father, Edmund Tudor. For Edmund was the son of Owen Tudor, a Welsh gentleman, by Queen Catherine de Valois, the daughter of Charles VI of France, the widow of Henry V, and the mother of Henry VI. Henry VII liked to refer to Henry VI as his uncle, which was strictly true (his father was Henry VI's half-brother), but tended to suggest a blood link to the Plantagenets through the male line – which was not true.

Henry devoted enormous energies to buttressing his flimsy dynastic status. Right of conquest, or at least trial by battle, constituted his initial title to the throne, and this violent foundation was at once glossed over and indirectly acknowledged in the declaration of his first Parliament that his reign had commenced the day before Bosworth Field. The fact that Parliament was the recognised organ of national consent thus lent further weight to his claim. At the same time, Henry sought sanction from the highest accessible authority. If God's decision had been given in battle, the decision of his vicar on earth, Pope Innocent VIII, was deemed almost equally valuable, not least in securing the obedience of the clergy, who still commanded considerable landed wealth and thus the political power which accompanied land in medieval society. Henry's appeal for papal confirmation of his title, incidentally, though far from an acknowledgement of the more extreme formulations of papal

Papal support for Henry VII publicised in an official broadside, probably issued when Perkin Warbeck landed in Cornwall in 1497. Innocent VIII and Alexander VI had formally confirmed Henry VII's right to the crown, and this notice summarises their decree of excommunication against his enemies and their grant of indulgences to his supporters.

authority which still commanded some theoretical support in the papal curia, is nevertheless a more than adequate answer to those who, despite two generations of modern research, still insist on the outdated notion that medieval England resented and where possible resisted the claims of the papacy.

But Henry also had to convince his own people that he was their rightful king, and one of the traditional means of doing this was by displaying the king in person before his people on a royal progress. So on 10 March 1486 he set off on the first, and perhaps the greatest, Tudor royal progress. The first leg took him up to York, roughly following the line of the Great North Road, and calling at most of the major towns on or close to that route, such as Cambridge, Stamford, Lincoln, Nottingham and Doncaster. The second leg swept down across the Midlands to Bristol, by way of Nottingham, Birmingham, Worcester and Gloucester. The third and final leg took him across the country down the Thames Valley to London, by way of Abingdon. He was back at Westminster by June. The receptions in the greater towns were an opportunity for his new subjects to demonstrate their loyalty, and for the king to give earnest of his goodwill by confirming civic privileges and offering redress to grievances. They were also an opportunity for the king to make a timely demonstration of his power. In April 1486, Viscount Lovel and two gentlemen named Humphrey and Thomas Stafford, who had availed themselves of ecclesiastical sanctuary after fighting on the wrong side at Bosworth, broke out and tried to raise Yorkist support against Henry in Yorkshire and Worcestershire. Henry spent a good few days at both York and Worcester on his tour. Finally, visits to shrines en route saw him set up many votive candles in thanksgiving for his victory at Bosworth and in hope of the safe delivery of his wife, who was already pregnant with their first child.

LAMBERT SIMNEL AND PERKIN WARBECK

The peerage which had turned out in force for the coronation was less eager the following year, when Henry faced his first serious challenge: the appearance of a youth purporting to be Edward, Earl of Warwick (the son of Edward IV's brother

George, Duke of Clarence, by Isabel Neville), but better known to us as Lambert Simnel. The real Earl of Warwick was a prisoner in the Tower, where he would spend virtually his entire life. In the early stages of this plot, Henry tried to take the wind out of its sails by parading Warwick through the streets of London, to prove that the pretender in Ireland was nothing but a fraud. It is possible that Simnel bore some physical resemblance to Warwick, although it is difficult to credit the Earl of Kildare, who induced the Irish Parliament to recognise the youth as their rightful king, with enough naïvety to have taken this pretence seriously.

The real leader of the rebels in 1487 was John de la Pole, Earl of Lincoln. He actually had a credible claim to the throne in his own right, as the eldest son of Elizabeth (the sister of Edward IV) by the Duke of Suffolk. But he had made his peace with Henry soon after Bosworth, and was actually one of the king's councillors when the Simnel plot began. However, while Henry was on an Easter pilgrimage in East Anglia in April, news reached him of Lincoln's flight to Flanders, where he was raising mercenaries. Having hastened to Walsingham to make his vows at the great shrine of Our Lady, Henry rushed back to London via Cambridge, and then headed towards the Midlands to prepare against the threat of invasion. The great stronghold of Kenilworth was chosen as his base, and became the virtual seat of government for the summer. Meanwhile, Lincoln took his mercenaries to join the rebels in Dublin, and was present at Simnel's coronation as Edward VI on 24 May. He led the Yorkist forces across the Irish Sea early in June, and faced Henry VII at Stoke (near Newark) on 16 June. Had he proven victorious he would doubtless have dealt with the wretched Simnel rather more harshly than Henry VII did, and pursued his own claim instead. But Lincoln and his henchmen fell in battle while Simnel was captured and treated with unwonted clemency for a Tudor rebel: put to work in the king's kitchens.

After the victory at Stoke, Henry made a second royal progress, this time through the northern heartlands of Yorkist sentiment, in another attempt to defuse or deter potential opposition. He went by way of Nottingham, Pontefract and York to Durham and Newcastle, and spent a couple of weeks in the far north-east before returning to London by way of Raby Castle (the great stronghold of the Nevilles), Richmond, Ripon, Pontefract, Newark, Stamford and Leicester. His decision later that year to have his wife, Elizabeth, formally crowned as queen may have been a further attempt to garner support among old Yorkists.

The second impostor to trouble Henry's uneasy settlement was Perkin Warbeck ('Perkin' was a diminutive form of 'Peter'), who, for much of the 1490s, was to tour the capitals and courts of neighbouring countries as the figurehead for Yorkist conspiracy against the Tudors. Once again, the trouble started in the old Yorkist stronghold of the Irish Pale. Warbeck, who came from the Low Countries, was apparently selected for his role on the basis of his good looks. He had arrived in Ireland as a servant to a merchant clothier who, among other things, used him to parade his fine wares around the ports they visited – Perkin seems to have been one of history's first recorded male models. He caught the eye of Yorkists on the look-out for a suitable mannequin, and it was decided that he should masquerade as Edward

Perkin Warbeck, the man whose claim to be Edward IV's second son, Richard of York, plagued Henry VII for a decade. The portrait helps explain not only his early career as a male model but also the success of his pretence: there is a certain resemblance to Edward IV.

IV's second son, Prince Richard – a part he had to learn English in order to play. The cause of the pretender was eagerly taken up by England's enemies in 1492, first by James IV of Scotland and then by Charles VIII of France. The peace of Étaples, which brought to an end Henry's phoney war against France in 1492, forced Perkin to abandon France for the protection of the Yorkist matriarch Margaret, Dowager Duchess of Burgundy, in the Netherlands. (It was fortunate for Henry and the Tudors that Margaret, the widow of Duke Charles the Bold, had no children of her own to challenge for the English crown.) Burgundian support for the impostor led to a trade-war between England and the Netherlands, but it is typical of Henry VII that in his supreme caution he considered no more direct action than that.

A complex web of Yorkist conspiracy and Tudor espionage was spun over the next few years, with a full tally of defections, arrests and executions – most notably of Sir William Stanley, brother-in-law of the king's mother, a man who had fought for Henry at Bosworth. The plotting culminated in Warbeck's attempt to land at Deal in Kent on 3 July 1495. But Henry's effective counter-espionage had already drawn the teeth of the plan. When Warbeck's advance party was ignominiously defeated by local levies – a defeat doubly bitter in a county which was both notoriously unstable and traditionally Yorkist – he kept to his ship and made for Ireland, where he tried in vain to take the port of Waterford. Failing there, he took refuge over winter in Scotland at the court of James IV, who treated him royally enough and arranged his marriage to a Scottish noblewoman. In the meantime, the spinning of the wheel of fortune in European affairs had made the Burgundians anxious for English friendship, which in turn caused them to cut off Warbeck's support in the Low Countries. Despite the lack of European backing, James IV launched an invasion of England on Warbeck's behalf. Although James soon retreated (on realising that the English troops coming to meet him were intending to greet him as an invader rather than as a liberator), Henry decided on a retaliatory expedition against Scotland. Over the winter of 1496–97 he raised loans and secured an ample grant of taxation from Parliament. A substantial force was gathered in the north, with Lord Daubeney, one of Henry's former companions in exile, at its head.

The great invasion, however, was frustrated by events farther south. The levy of taxation for war in the north excited the resentment of the south-western counties of England, whose men saw no reason to pay for the protection of their distant compatriots in the northern Marches. Initially stirred up by the oratory of a lawyer, Thomas Flamank, and led by a blacksmith, Michael Joseph, the revolt soon spread from Cornwall into the nearby counties. A local magnate, Lord Audley, put himself at its head and led the force in a march eastwards, by way of Winchester and the pilgrims' way to Kent. But Kent proved as unresponsive to the Cornishmen as it had to Warbeck, so the rebels camped on Blackheath, overlooking London, uncertain of their next move. Henry, having recalled Daubeney and his men from the borders, waited until he had a massive superiority in numbers before moving against them, which he did, to decisive effect, on Saturday 17 June 1497. Executing only the ringleaders, he pardoned most of the rebels, though whether out of clemency or for fear of pushing his luck is far from clear. Meanwhile, hoping to take advantage of the disorder in England, Warbeck sailed for Cornwall by way of Cork, and James once more led his troops across the border. But James was beaten back by a force raised by the Earl of Surrey, Warden of the Marches, while Warbeck, having been hounded out of Ireland, finally set foot upon English soil for the first time in Cornwall. He found that the miserably armed men who rallied to his standard were no match for the walls and guards of Exeter (a city traditionally stout in self-defence), and as the forces of Daubeney and Henry converged on the peninsula, he first took flight and then threw himself upon the king's mercy.

The Perkin Warbeck affair was not yet over. In June 1498 he briefly slipped the leash, only to find himself, after recapture, immured more securely in the Tower of London. There he made the acquaintance of the Earl of Warwick, and the final act in his tragicomedy commenced. A conspiracy began, or so we are told, to seize control of the Tower and challenge Henry from the very citadel of his power. If not complete fiction (for revealingly few records survive of this obscure affair), then the conspiracy was at best the work of informers and *agents provocateurs*. The upshot was a series of show trials in November 1499, resulting in the executions of Warbeck and a handful of accomplices. More usefully, it gave Henry a welcome pretext to remove a far more threatening figure from the scene. The Earl of Warwick, foremost among his potential rivals for the throne, was beheaded for alleged involvement on 29 November 1499.

THE PROBLEM OF TRUST

Given the sequence of risings and plots which Henry faced, and indeed the way in which he himself had come to the throne, it is hardly surprising that suspicion and insecurity are the keynotes of his reign (indeed suspicion, though not usually insecurity, was arguably the keynote of the entire dynasty). Henry was the first king of England to feel the need for a personal bodyguard. He founded the Yeomen of the Guard, who, sporting something like their original costume, still preside over the Tower of London. But suspicion and insecurity went far beyond mere concern for immediate personal safety. They affected every aspect of Henry's government – finance, law and order, the nobility, and the Church – and made his style of politics very different from the traditional kingship of medieval England. This new style of governance has been subjected to sharply contrasting assessments. Generally it has been seen as 'new monarchy', as a policy deliberately and wisely setting out to replace the unstable baronial politics of late medieval England with a more centralised and elevated monarchy. But reassessments of late medieval politics (barons were not antisocial megalomaniacs who would rip the country to pieces unless restrained by the firm hand of the king, but were the king's most natural supporters, having more invested in the security of the social order than anybody else) have resulted in a radically different view of his methods as unwise, ill-considered and even downright incompetent.

Henry did trust some people – mostly those whose loyalty and service to him dated back to Bosworth or beyond. For the most part, they were not from the peerage, but from the gentry and the clergy. The men whom Henry brought with him to England on his bid for the throne in 1485 were led by John Morton, the Bishop of Ely, whose loyalty was soon rewarded with appointment as Lord Chancellor and translation to the see of Canterbury (respectively in March and December 1486), and for whom he eventually secured the award of a cardinal's hat (1493). The most direct insights we have into the cardinal come from the pen of Thomas More, who served in his household as a young boy. Morton is known in folklore from the eponymous 'Morton's fork', a sort of Parkinson's law of tax collection. The story goes that, in advising those who had the duty of assessing people's capacity to contribute to a 'benevolence' (a kind of goodwill loan to the king), he posed the following dilemma. If people had an extravagant lifestyle, then they were obviously wealthy and could afford to give generously, and if they lived frugally, they were obviously stashing their money away and so were equally able to give. The dilemma is credited to Morton by Francis Bacon, writing a hundred years later, but More's anecdotes about his former master show us a witty and intelligent man, hardly likely himself to have formulated such a policy. An earlier version of the story, told by Thomas More to Erasmus, credited it to Henry's other great clerical minister, Richard Fox. The story itself is doubtless *ben trovato*, but it does not belie the reign which produced it. Henry and his advisers had a shrewd idea that there was a great deal more money out there than people wished to let on. They were right.

Richard Fox had also been with the king in exile, and proved one of his most effective servants. He became Lord Privy Seal in 1487, and was rewarded with a succession of ever wealthier bishoprics. Among the secular power-brokers of his reign, many had also joined Henry in exile. John de Vere, Earl of Oxford, was the foremost in rank, and was granted one of the highest military appointments as Admiral of England. Early companions from exile or from the days of the Bosworth campaign provided several of the 'men of business' whose activities in law and finance would underpin Henry's tight regime. Men such as Edward Poynings, Reginald Bray, Thomas Lovell and Giles Daubeney dominated the first ten or fifteen years of the reign. But only Daubeney was promoted to the peerage as a reward. The second generation of his servants, including the notorious Richard Empson and Edmund Dudley, were the kind of men who flourish under intensely suspicious conditions: ambitious, unscrupulous outsiders without strong ties among the families of the élite, working and answering directly to the king. Henry's most favoured lay servants tended to earn knighthoods, in many cases the supreme form of knighthood represented in the Order of the Garter. The Garter, in fact, served as the ultimate accolade under Henry. Most of his leading lay supporters or servants were in time recruited to it, including his own mother, Lady Margaret.

ROYAL FINANCES

It has long been acknowledged that finance was one of Henry VII's governmental priorities. His legendary attention to detail is illustrated by the fact that he personally audited and signed every page of his 'chamber accounts'. These were the income and expenditure record of the king's 'chamber' or immediate personal household. It is characteristic of Henry that he preferred to channel royal finances through this institution, which was under his direct and everyday supervision, rather than through the more formal, more impersonal and above all more distant Exchequer. This attention to detail has been rather mistakenly erected into a standard of royal competence by some modern historians, as though a king were some kind of exalted civil servant, to be assessed by promptness and precision in the despatch of paperwork. In fact, medieval kings were not conceived of as glorified clerks or accountants. If the personal engagement of this king in the nitty-gritty of government tells us anything, it is that he did not even trust his closest servants, but felt it necessary to keep them under intensive and intrusive scrutiny.

What really matters about Henry VII's financial policy is the way in which he set about raising revenue. More than any king before him, he was a victim of the baronial myth that the king should 'live of his own', that is, that under normal circumstances the king should pay for his court, household, central administration and costs of governance out of his 'ordinary' income, rather than by drawing on the common purse of the nation through direct taxation. This myth had first been aired in the context of the deposition of Richard II and the usurpation of Henry IV in

1399. In order to appease the nobles whom he had bounced into acknowledging his claim to the throne, Henry IV had undertaken precisely to 'live of his own', turning a short-term and short-sighted slogan into a constitutional principle. Although Henry V had broken free of this constraint thanks to his stunning success in war (the contingency of war was recognised as a justification for direct taxation), the slogan haunted governments throughout the fifteenth century. The only thing which made the principle that the king should 'live of his own' remotely feasible was the increase in the acreage and value of the Crown lands over the same period. First the Lancastrians and then the Yorkists extended the Crown lands by adding to them the massive hereditary estates of their houses. And the extinctions and attainders of noble families who chose the wrong side at one time or another in the Wars of the Roses provided further gains. Once Henry VII had taken the throne, the Crown lands were worth some £40,000 a year. Unlike most previous kings, he showed no intention of using this massive endowment to refill the depleted ranks of the English nobility. Instead, he clung on to it with both hands.

The only form of taxation on which kings could count as a regular source of income was the levying of customs duties on imports and exports. Although even customs revenues depended upon parliamentary grant, it had become traditional for these duties to be granted to each king for life in the first Parliament of the reign. Perhaps a House of Commons already tending to be dominated by the landed gentry was happy to grant the king taxes which, at least in appearance, weighed on merchants and tradesmen rather than on themselves, and perhaps the merchants were only too well aware of how closely their prosperity depended on the favour and protection of the king. At any rate, the customs were granted to Henry VII as usual, and formed a crucial part of his budget. As customs duties were levied upon quantities rather than upon prices (in other words, like modern UK petrol duty rather than like VAT), they tended to rise only with the volume of goods traded, not with prices. Given the slow pace of technological change and economic growth (when there was any – markets then were even more volatile than now), there was not much that the king could do to increase the yield of the customs (nor indeed of the Crown lands), other than to raise the rates on unit volume. This was always contentious, though Henry actually managed to impose a new book of rates in 1507. Not until 1558, after half a century of massive inflation, would the customs duties be revalued again, and then only under the pressure of paying for an unsuccessful war. The impact of Henry's revaluation was worthwhile. Early in his reign the customs yielded about £33,000 a year on average; by the end, about £40,000 a year.

The third main component of the king's 'ordinary' revenues comprised the fruits of his 'prerogative', namely the 'profits of justice' and 'feudal incidents'. It was here that the king looked to squeeze extra income out of his kingdom. The 'prerogative', that bundle of rights and powers which belonged to the king under English law by virtue of his office, became a subject of particular interest in Henry VII's reign precisely because of the vigour he showed in exploiting it. Fines (after the deduction of various costs) eventually made their way into the king's coffers, and Henry was especially keen not only on collecting these fines, but also on adding to the range of offences which were punishable by fines. Indeed, it has been suggested that for all his apparent concern with law and order, he was for the most part only bothered about enforcing those laws which brought financial returns.

'Feudal incidents' were payments which the king received by virtue of his position at the pinnacle of the social pyramid. Landowners whom the law classified as 'tenants-in-chief' were deemed to hold their lands directly from the king in return for feudal duties (mostly military service) owed to the king. Tenants-in-chief were obliged to pay fees ('entry fines') to the king when they came into possession of their lands by inheritance. In addition, because heirs under the age of twenty-one and female heirs or widows were unable to perform military service, when the lands fell into their hands, the king drew the profits until their death, marriage or majority. The increasingly fragmented results of the land and marriage market, combined with the political disorders of the fifteenth century, had tended to reduce the value of these feudal incidents to the Crown. At first under Edward IV, and then with a vengeance under Henry VII, the Crown set about reclaiming its feudal rights. Assisted by rising lawyers with an eye for royal favour and Crown office, the extent of the royal prerogative was pushed outwards by fair means or foul – hence the increasing attention paid to the prerogative in lectures at the Inns of Court (which at that time were the institutions where England's lawyers were taught and trained).

The moment of inheritance was the point at which much landed wealth came for a moment within the king's grasp. 'Inquisitions post mortem' ('investigations after death') were held whenever a landowner died, with a view to establishing how much land, if any, he held from the king. Royal commissioners were appointed to pursue the king's claims, and the line between investigation and intimidation was easily and often crossed. Sworn juries were induced to favour royal claims, and there was a tendency to define more and more of a person's land as held directly from the king. Where landowners, heirs or widows infringed regulations or failed in their feudal obligations, inordinate fines were levied upon them (or their heirs). Thus, the Duke of Buckingham was mulcted of a stupendous £2,000 because his widowed mother had omitted to seek royal permission before remarrying. The exaction of fines and dues under the royal prerogative became a major industry under Henry VII. Towards the end of the reign, his average income from wardship was over £9,000 a year, and a new royal official, the Surveyor of the King's Wards, was established in 1503 to manage it more efficiently. His income from feudal fines and the other profits of justice was probably even greater, but is harder to calculate. The exploitation of prerogative income culminated in 1508 with the creation of another new officer, the Surveyor of the King's Prerogative, to supervise and co-ordinate the business – and to ensure that the collection and handling of the monies were kept closely under the eye of the king. Henry VII's notorious officials, Richard Empson and Edmund Dudley, were the men most closely associated with the exploitation of the royal prerogative. This earned them arrest and execution in the next reign, and it is from notes left by Dudley that we know many of the details of their activities.

For all its morally and even legally dubious aspects, Henry VII's financial policy was, in purely financial terms, a success: Henry wiped out royal debt and accumulated a legendary treasure. Unfortunately, its scale is literally legendary: we do not know for certain just how much he had in chests in his private apartments. Francis Bacon, writing over a century later, claimed on the basis of documents now lost that it was upwards of £2 million. Although his figure has been discounted for some time, there is a possibility that he was right. For the best figures available regarding Henry VIII's wars in the first years of his reign show an enormous gap between income and expenditure which can only have been bridged by the treasure his father left. Henry VII died in cash terms probably the richest king England has ever known.

This cash surplus has long been regarded as one of Henry's greatest achievements. However, in a compelling challenge to the general consensus on his success as a king, Christine Carpenter has questioned what use this surplus could possibly have been, given that it was far in excess of his ordinary expenditure needs, yet unequal to the burdens of a foreign war (the main extraordinary call upon revenue) – even had he had any intention of fighting one. She is certainly right to see his overflowing treasury as an index of his vulnerability and poor credit. Henry clearly never felt safe enough to run up debts or raise taxes in the manner of more secure kings. Moreover, the range of dubious fiscal expedients to which he and his agents resorted in order to fill the treasury had a huge political cost in terms of unpopularity and especially aristocratic grievance. Several earlier kings who had pursued similarly extortionate policies had met with the wrath of their barons, for such policies offended not only their vested interests as landowners but also their sense of justice – the maintenance of which was generally recognised as a king's primary responsibility before both God and man.

So was Henry's financial policy worldly wisdom or inexplicable folly? Granted that even his treasure was inadequate to the costs of foreign war, was it a pointless gain made at intolerable political risk? In fact, given Henry's character and circumstances, a case can be made, if not for the wisdom, then at least for the utility of his policy. It can be explained even if it cannot be justified. His greatest fear was that he would fall victim to just such an attempt on his throne as he had himself launched against Richard III. While it might be argued that he should have relied on the basic loyalty to the ruler prevalent in England, he could see for himself the increasing reluctance of the nobility to fight on either side in a dynastic conflict. One thing that an ample treasure certainly could do was to underwrite the costs of a single campaign at home. If Henry should ever have faced a coup like his own, at least he had the wherewithal to raise large numbers of troops very quickly. This rationale was not, of course, offered by the king. But that this may have been the purpose of his treasure is suggested by a passage in Thomas More's *Utopia*, so much of which commented or reflected on the recent history of his own country. For More included among his reports of fictitious transatlantic societies a reference to one in which the king was limited by law as to the scale of treasure he could accumulate: it was to be just enough to permit him to overcome a rebellion, but not so much as to encourage him to rule tyrannically over his own people or strive after foreign conquests. Given More's youthful service with Cardinal Morton, this is the sort of idea which might well have been current in the governmental circles around Henry VII. But even if security rather than almost aimless accumulation explains Henry's huge treasure, it does not justify the political cost at which it was gathered. Thomas More's comments suggest that he saw Henry VII as having overstepped the mark. The two risks he points out, of tyranny at home and vain aggression abroad, might well be reflecting on the latter years of Henry VII and the early years of Henry VIII.

HENRY VII AND THE NOBILITY

Henry's relationship with the English aristocracy has elicited historical judgements as diverse as has his fiscal policy. On the one hand, he has been praised for humbling the nobility, for destroying those 'overmighty subjects' who had plagued the late medieval polity. On the other, he has been pilloried for cold-shouldering the nobility and magnates who were his natural allies, councillors and supporters in the regions. The one thing which is almost universally agreed is that his policy towards the nobility was very different from anything which England had ever seen before. Why, and with what effect, are more contested questions.

His new approach was most evident in his reluctance to restore or create noble titles. While the reign of Edward IV had been generous in this regard (he created or restored thirty-five noble titles), and the reign of Henry VI positively profligate in its inflation of the titled nobility, Henry VII was niggardly with his grants and restorations. His immediate relatives and closest supporters from 1485 received the bulk of these. His mother, Lady Margaret Beaufort, was restored as Countess of Richmond in her own right, while her third husband, Thomas Stanley, became Earl of Derby. His uncle, Jasper Tudor, was restored as Earl of Pembroke and later promoted Duke of Bedford. But as Henry himself was Margaret's heir, and Jasper Tudor had no children, these grants were essentially short-term. John de Vere's attainder was reversed, and he was restored to the earldom of Oxford. Giles Daubeney received a peerage. However, of those peers who lost their titles as a result of fighting against Henry at Bosworth or of treason thereafter, few were restored. Thomas Howard, Earl of Surrey and heir to the duchy of Norfolk, was restored to his earldom in 1489, but paid for it through ten years of loyal service mostly in the northern Marches. He had to wait until the reign of Henry VIII to regain the duchy for his house. The English peerage remained depleted throughout Henry VII's reign. Of 138 individuals attainted in his reign, only forty-six secured restoration in his lifetime. The peerage itself numbered fifty-five in 1485, but had shrunk to forty-two by 1509.

The motive for this grudging policy was, once again, suspicion. Henry VII simply did not trust the nobles and magnates, and had no wish to swell the ranks of those he seems to have viewed as potential rebels rather than as pillars of his regime. His fiscal policy converged with his suspicion of the nobility in the extent to which he used legal and penal sanctions to keep them under his thumb. Fines levied for offences real, imaginary, alleged or foreseen became not only a source of revenue but a political weapon, especially when suspended for the duration of good behaviour. 'Bonds and recognisances' were imposed on nobles (and on many others) by which they were obliged to perform or refrain from specified actions on pain of enormous fines, of which certain portions sometimes had to be deposited as guarantees. More than half of the peerage was bound over in this way at some stage of Henry's reign, and only about a quarter of the peerage remained entirely free from attainder, punitive fines, or bonds throughout that period. One way or another, the vast majority of the peerage found itself firmly under Henry's thumb. They certainly did not like it, but it severely curtailed their freedom of action and thus their potential to oppose the king.

The offences for which nobles and others could become liable to fines or subject to bonds were themselves evidence of the king's distrust. For example, the practice of 'retaining' was central to the operation of the late medieval polity. Nobles and others 'retained' men as advisers, servants and muscle in order to fulfil their household, local, regional and even national obligations (in the extreme case, raising armed men to serve the king in war). While this practice was indispensable, it was obviously open to abuse, and fifteenth-century kings legislated to regulate it. But Henry VII put this regulation on a wholly new footing by securing a judicial interpretation which in principle made retaining for almost anything other than household purposes illegal (an interpretation he enshrined in statute in 1504). As it was virtually impossible for nobles to avoid breaching this law, it became a happy hunting ground for a regime keen to impose bonds and recognisances. The most notorious bond of the reign, in the sum of £100,000 on George Neville, Lord Abergavenny, was imposed in the wake of an offence against this measure. There were many such prosecutions early in the reign, and thereafter many nobles and gentry compounded or undertook bonds in order to avoid prosecution. From one point of view, given the way Henry VII treated them, it is surprising that his nobles did not rise up against him. But from another point of view, the ruthless control which Henry set about imposing upon them from the start was precisely what whittled away their will and power to resist. Henry was, in short, following the course of action which, a generation later, Machiavelli would recommend to other 'new princes': ruling by fear rather than by love. Not that Henry needed Machiavelli to teach him what to do: on the contrary, Machiavelli could have taken his correspondence course.

Henry's reduction in the power of the peerage led generations of historians accustomed to thinking of the barons as the rivals of the king and the bane of his subjects to conclude that his reign represented an important stage on the highroad of law and order towards modern civil society. Growing recognition of the central role of the nobility in late medieval and early modern English government has caused this traditional wisdom to be questioned in two ways. Some have argued that there was no reduction in the power of the peerage, but this looks like a triumph of hope over evidence. By 1509 there were fewer peers, with less landed wealth, less able to raise troops in their own name, and more strictly subject to royal supervision. There can be no doubt that their power, individually and collectively, was reduced during this reign. More realistically, questions have been asked as to whether a reduction in noble power was the same as an increase in law and order. Evidence has been found from the north and in the Midlands which suggests that the weakening of the customary control of a region by a powerful local magnate led to an increase in feuding among the gentry and to a reduction in the ability of the gentry (lacking magnate leadership) in their turn to repress banditry and disorder. Such evidence is hard to interpret, but what can certainly no longer be maintained is that Henry reduced the power of the nobility in order to improve law and order. He was probably worse placed even than us to assess the impact of his policy on law and order, but would probably have pursued the same policy irrespective of that impact. Quality of governance for the common people simply did not figure on his political agenda. His objective was to ensure that the nobility were not in a position to mount a challenge to his rule, and in this he succeeded.

JUSTICE AND PEACE

Law and order, or, as Tudor writers would have put it, justice and peace, are notoriously difficult to assess even today, in an age of detailed crime statistics and relatively effective policing. Making judgements of this kind about the Tudor age on the basis of such patchy court records as have survived the last 500 years is hazardous to say the least. And if it is difficult for us to assess today, it was probably even more difficult at the time, when the difficulties would have been less readily appreciated, and the relationships between reporting, policing, trying, punishing and deterring crime were even less well understood than they are now. In fact, the quality of justice and of law and order then, as now, was perhaps more a matter of perception than of reality. A just king was a king who was thought to be just, much as today a strong Home Secretary is one who is thought to be strong. In these terms, Henry VII certainly made a show of concern for justice. One thing his reign made clear was that nobody was too powerful to be subject to royal justice. If the Duke of Buckingham could be fined £2,000, then nobody was above the law. That was perhaps as much an advance for the law as the possible deterioration of order in some regions was a setback for it.

The main instrument for local justice and administration was the 'commission of the peace'. For the most part organised on a county basis, the commission of the peace consisted of a number of wealthy local gentlemen, perhaps assisted by bishops, abbots or peers – the 'nobility' in the very broadest sense. These justices of the peace (JPs) were responsible for punishing lesser crimes (more serious crimes went before touring judges from London in judicial sessions known as the Assizes) and for responding to crime and disorder on an executive level. Their numbers and their responsibilities expanded fairly constantly throughout the Tudor period and beyond, but it is revealing to note that the first handbook for JPs, the *Book of the Justice of the Peace*, was published in 1506. We should not see this as an 'official publication', but the mere fact of the book's appearance is evidence for the growing importance of the JP in society. Henry VII's particular contribution to the development of the system was the placement on these county commissions of a number of representatives of his own interests. Thus he placed Cardinal Morton on every commission in the country, and Morton's successors as Archbishop of Canterbury and Lord Chancellor also found themselves on the commissions of a number of counties they probably never saw. A number of other household men and trusted clerics and officeholders (for example Jasper Tudor, Reginald Bray, Giles Daubeney and Richard Fox) were also deployed in this way.

The purpose of this initiative is not immediately apparent, as few of these men can ever have attended the Quarter Sessions of the commissions to which they were appointed. But on examination, Henry's policies, though often unconventional, rarely belie that 'politic wisdom in governance' which his contemporaries saw in him. In this case, his aims seem to have been chiefly symbolic, to emphasise the responsibilities which the commissions owed to the king at the centre, and to lend prestige to the commissions in the localities by associating their members with statesmen of the highest rank. In a society which set great store by rank and connection, the practical impact of these symbolic acts should not be underestimated. In addition, the placing on commissions of those household agents, such as Reginald Bray, who were responsible for the dubiously legal measures which made up Henry's 'fiscal feudalism' may have helped to defuse the possibility of legal interference with their work.

Henry also made much of his concern for law and order through legislation. His Parliaments passed twenty-one statutes concerning JPs and their work, giving them jurisdiction over matters ranging from riot and unlawful retaining to weights and measures and alehouses. In one early statute Henry castigated the tendency of JPs to abuse their powers to favour their friends and harm their enemies and inferiors. No doubt they did. For all the humbug about justice (then, as now, everybody was in favour of justice), in practice litigants, whether plaintiffs or defendants, treated the law as a means of promoting their own interests, if necessary at the expense of competitors. Henry VII's ruthless exploitation of the law for his own ends can have done little to discourage this. All this legislative activity was not accompanied by sustained efforts at enforcement. But this is not surprising. Medieval governments in general found it easier to make laws than to implement them. But the effort to legislate was well intentioned and for the most part well received – especially now that the statutes passed in Parliament were printed (an innovation introduced by Richard III) and would therefore circulate among the ruling élites in the localities. At least it showed that the authorities cared, and perhaps that was all that could be expected. Then, as now, legislation was frequently symbolic, more a matter of making the right impression than making a real impact.

The Tudor era saw a marked intensification in the cruelty of English law. Among other things, this can be seen in the harsher exaction of the death penalty against medieval England's homegrown heretics, the Lollards. The law stipulating death by burning for recalcitrant or relapsed heretics had been passed in 1401, but under the Lancastrians and Yorkists, only around a couple of dozen people suffered under this law. Henry's reign saw over a dozen further executions, while that of Henry VIII added another three dozen (besides his later Protestant and Catholic victims). While this repression has sometimes been seen as a logical if morally questionable response to a simple resurgence of Lollardy, there is little reason to think that Lollards were in fact becoming more numerous. There may also have been an element of legitimisation in this policy. The defence of the liberties of the Church – which traditionally included freedom from competition – was one of the paramount obligations of Christian kingship. The suppression of heretics was therefore an obvious way for a king to affirm in action the legitimacy of his rule. This was doubly true for a king who had sought papal sanction for his title. Moreover, the traditional wisdom of English (and indeed of European) politics held that heresy and sedition were two sides of a single coin, partly because heretics were expected to be socially and politically subversive in themselves, and partly because sedition and rebellion, particularly at the popular level, were seen as almost natural disasters and, like other 'acts of God', might be sent down on earth by Almighty God to punish regimes or societies for their sins – such as not adequately defending his Church against heresy. A king like Henry VII, who was more than usually sensitive to the danger of sedition, would necessarily be more than usually concerned with the threat of heresy. He would therefore expect all his officials, and especially his churchmen, to show especial care in rooting it out.

Henry's policy in Ireland perfectly captures that combination of suspicion and lack of vision which helped make his reign, albeit unintentionally, a turning point in the history of these islands. For Ireland had tended towards the Yorkist camp since the 1450s, and its sympathies remained apparent through Henry's early years. Lambert Simnel and Perkin Warbeck were both proclaimed first in Ireland, and recruited some real military support there. The dominant Anglo-Irish family, the Geraldines or Fitzgeralds of Kildare, co-existed uneasily with the Tudor dynasty. Henry himself was too shrewd even to contemplate the sort of punitive raid against Ireland which he planned against Scotland after Scottish support for Warbeck in 1495–96. Perhaps he recognised that Ireland alone could never pose him a serious threat, or perhaps he simply knew too little about what was going on there. In any case, there was no attempt at invasion or military conquest. On the other hand, Henry was reluctant simply to leave the Fitzgeralds in uncontested control of his lordship.

His solution was to try and hamstring the Kildare affinity by curtailing its freedom of action. The famous Poynings Law, named after Sir Edward Poynings, a trusted companion who had landed with Henry at Milford Haven in 1485, and whom Henry made his direct representative in the Pale, prohibited the Irish Parliament from passing any legislation without prior approval from the English Parliament. This was something of a constitutional revolution, yet its origins were entirely short-term and political. The Irish Parliament had sanctioned the claim of the first pretender to the throne, Lambert Simnel. The notorious Poynings Law was therefore in conception nothing more than a guarantee against this form of legitimisation of potential rivals. However, its effect was, almost certainly unwittingly, to restrict the potential of the Irish Parliament to function as a focus for an emergent national identity in the way that, for example, the States General of the Netherlands was able to function in the later sixteenth century during the Dutch Revolt against the rule of Habsburg Spain. Likewise, Henry was too shrewd to attempt the wholesale destruction of the Kildares, yet he eroded their influence by periodically dismissing them from high royal office, even if he equally frequently found himself obliged to restore them to that office because, excluded, they rendered the Pale ungovernable. If nothing else, this erratic policy emphasised that high political office was a gift of the Crown, rather than a baronial birthright, and paved the way for later and more aggressive Tudor policies towards Ireland.

Foreign policy involved, in a word, securing general European recognition of the legitimacy of his dynasty. Henry had no intention of jeopardising this process by engaging in needless wars. In the late 1480s he took some steps to save ducal Brittany from absorption into France. But he committed only token forces, numbered in hundreds, in an exercise which probably had more to do with preventing France from interfering in England than with any real concern for the fate of the duchy which had saved his life. Once King Charles VIII of France had persuaded the heiress of Brittany to accept his hand in marriage (the other hand holding a metaphorical dagger to her throat), this particular method of stampeding his neighbour's cattle was no longer open to Henry. He turned instead to more direct methods, ostentatiously preparing for an invasion of France in 1492. In fact, this was not a serious military exercise: Henry feinted towards Boulogne from his base in Calais in October, and can hardly have been intending to lay a siege which would have had to be maintained through winter. Henry was banking on a repeat of the outcome of Edward IV's invasion of France in 1475. On that occasion, the embarrassingly hopeless showing of the English troops made Edward only too willing to accept a French offer to buy him off. Henry calculated on striking a similar bargain. As usual, he calculated well. This time the king of France, Charles VIII, whose ambitious eyes were already focused beyond the Alps on the kingdom of Naples, was only too willing to buy him off. The putative raid into Scotland, planned to punish the Scottish king for his support of Perkin Warbeck, had to be transformed into a campaign of defence against rebels whose rising was sparked off by the taxes raised to pay for the army! Henry's essentially pacific foreign policy meant that he did not need to call Parliament frequently to meet the costs of war, and that his country could flourish in peace.

Our vision of Henry VII has in fact been profoundly shaped by a comparison with Louis XI, the Spider King, of France, first drawn out in detail by Francis Bacon in his life of Henry VII. Louis was indeed the 'bourgeois king', with little time for the traditional noble pursuit of hunting, determinedly restrained and economical in his dress, assiduous and slightly demanding in his piety. He kept France anxiously out of war as far as he could, and treated the monarchy rather like an exalted family business, for profit rather than for glory. His preferred servants were drawn from the officeholders, the clergy and even the merchants, rather than from the military nobility. He built little. He took an unusually close personal interest in the minutiae of political and financial administration. He was suspicious of the ancient nobility – and rightly so, for they launched three 'wars of the commonweal' against him in the name of a justice which he served much more devotedly than they. Henry had some things in common with Louis. Henry, too, treated the monarchy like a family business, and was as acquisitive as Louis, and with the same love of the law as a fiscal expedient. Henry's servants, too, were more likely to be gentry or clergy than higher nobility, but this was very much the way the world was moving. He was as reluctant as Louis to engage in foreign war, and as suspicious of the nobility, having, like Louis, himself once been a troublesome nobleman. Yet despite his rapacity, Henry was no miser. He was capable of spending on a princely scale, but his expenditure was always calculated. Thus he spent lavishly on the ceremonial life of the court, but such expenditure certainly yielded interest in terms of establishing his princely status with both his own subjects and foreign ambassadors and visitors. Unlike Louis, Henry loved hunting. He also built, though his reputation as a builder has suffered not only from the poor survival of what he built but also by contrast with the megalomaniac construction activity of his son. Nevertheless, the palaces at Richmond and Greenwich were resplendent edifices, and these too were evidence of his royal standing.

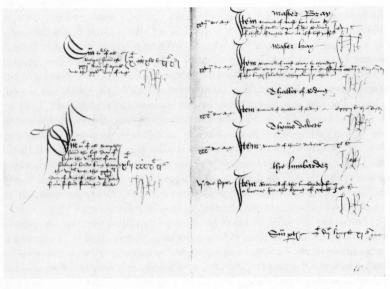

Receipt book of Sir Thomas Lovell, treasurer of the king's chamber to Henry VII. The king's sign-manual attests each entry – a remarkable tribute to the care Henry exercised in keeping accounts, or perhaps to the habitual distrust and suspicion with which he could look upon even his closest associates.

The last decade of Henry's reign was from a certain point of view relatively uneventful. Parliament met only once, as the king had more than enough money for his needs, had no intention of fighting foreign wars and felt no desire to embark upon ambitious legislative programmes. However, in a monarchy the boundary between private and public life is barely meaningful for the royal family, and within that family context there were events enough – some of them tragic. The grooming of the king's eldest son, Arthur, for his royal future began in earnest with the new century, when he was sent to Ludlow, in the Welsh Marches, to preside over the Council of the Marches as Prince of Wales (a title he had held since 1489) and to gain political and judicial experience through seeing government in action. His progress towards maturity was further marked by his marriage to Catherine of Aragon, which had been arranged in 1499 by a treaty with the 'Catholic Kings', Ferdinand and Isabella of Spain. The wedding took place in November 1501 at St Paul's in London, and much was to hang in the next reign on the vexed question of whether or not the marriage was actually consummated. Catherine always protested that she had remained a virgin, and Henry VIII, her second husband, never personally contradicted her. The young couple returned to Ludlow, but Arthur fell ill early the next year and died on 2 April 1502. He was buried shortly afterwards in Worcester Cathedral.

Henry's spirits, depressed by this heavy blow, were revived when his wife became pregnant shortly afterwards. But hope turned to tragedy in February 1503, when first the baby, a girl, died, and then her mother, Queen Elizabeth, followed her to the grave within a week. This double blow may have adversely affected the king's health, as for the rest of his life he was frequently and seriously ill. The following year he was described as 'but a weak man and sickly, not likely to be no longlived man'. Henry seems to have considered remarriage – his sights were at times set upon Juana of Castile, the widowed (and allegedly insane) daughter of Ferdinand and Isabella. But the Spaniards were never going to allow the succession to their throne to be complicated in this way, and his hopes came to nothing.

Later in 1503 Henry saw his elder daughter, Margaret, depart for Scotland to marry James IV. At home his attention was now focused upon his surviving son, Prince Henry, who was hastily groomed to take his elder brother's place, not only in line for the throne but also as a vital link in the alliance with Spain. In summer 1503 he was engaged to Catherine of Aragon (an arrangement which, if nothing else, saved the king from having to repay her generous dowry), for which a papal dispensation was required on account of the close relationship established by her first marriage. Having secured an option on the marriage, however, the king was reluctant to exercise it, not even when, in 1505, Prince Henry reached the age of fourteen, which both canon law and the Anglo-Spanish treaty saw as mature enough for marriage. Diplomatic concerns undoubtedly played some part in this, as Henry was by no means on the best of terms with Ferdinand of Aragon (Isabella of Castile had died in 1504). But it probably had as much to do with the king's fears for the health of his son. Premature sexual activity was thought liable to undermine health, and Henry may have felt that this had contributed to Arthur's death (Arthur had just turned

Margaret Tudor, daughter to Henry VII (and Henry VIII's sister). She was married off to James IV of Scotland in 1503. The marriage of the thirty-year-old Scottish king to the fourteen-year-old Margaret was intended to set the seal on the Anglo-Scottish 'Treaty of Perpetual Peace'.
Ten years later, at the battle of Flodden, Henry VIII's army crushed Scotland and killed James IV.

fifteen when he married Catherine). Henry showed himself, understandably, over-anxious about the health of his rather robust second son in these years of his own decline, and postponing the marriage may have been part of this protectiveness.

HENRY VII'S RELIGION

Henry's religiosity is best known from the elaborate provision which he made for the good of his soul after his death. His will, notoriously, requested 10,000 Masses for his soul. However, there was more to his relationship with the Church than this prodigious expenditure on somewhat mechanical and quantitative devotion. Henry was interested in the Church, as in so much else, primarily as a source of revenue. The 'translation' of bishops (that is, the transfer of a bishop from one diocese to another) was probably more widespread under this king than under any of his predecessors. The reason for this was not that he had strong and shifting views as to which churchman should serve which diocese, but that the royal prerogative included 'regalian rights' over Church property: during episcopal vacancies, the revenues of the diocese went to the king and incoming bishops were also mulcted for entry fines.

Besides that, the Church served as a source of reward for favoured servants and councillors. Episcopal appointments themselves were for the most part of trusted servants or their relatives. Stanleys and Audleys did pretty well on the basis of the political influence of their families, but without notably raising the intellectual or moral standards of the bench. James Stanley was made bishop of Ely for no better reason than that he was the stepson of the king's mother, Lady Margaret Beaufort.

Plan of the palaces of Westminster and Whitehall, from a later version of the 1578 map known as Ralph Agas's map (but not in fact by him). The Thames was in effect the main highway connecting London, Westminster, Lambeth, Southwark and Greenwich.

A hard-riding nobleman of the old school, he divided his time between the episcopal palace at Somersham, with his mistress and two children, and the family estates in Lancashire. His professional qualities are best summed up in the fact that we have no bishop's register for his working career. Stanley, though, was something of an exception. Most of Henry's bishops were hardworking, effective administrators, irrespective of whether their primary commitments were to Church or to Crown. John Morton, William Warham, Richard Fox, Thomas Ruthal, Oliver King, Richard Sherborne and the rest of the royal servants who were rewarded with bishoprics did not disgrace their calling, and one or two (such as Sherborne and Fox) proved, after their retirement from service at court, zealous and reform-minded pastors.

Henry's rather cynical churchmanship should not be allowed to obscure his obviously genuine and entirely traditional piety. He showed consistent favour to the Observant Franciscans (that wing of the Franciscan friars which sought to revive strict observance of the original rule of St Francis), whom he may well first have come across during his years of exile in Brittany and France, where they were spreading rapidly in the later fifteenth century. In the first year of his reign he confirmed the recent foundation (1482) of an Observant house at Greenwich, and in 1500 founded another at Richmond, both of them beside his palaces – and the terms of his will show that he regarded both these houses as his own foundations. He also encouraged existing Franciscan houses to adopt the Observant lifestyle. In 1499, the Observants of England became a province of the order in their own right, numbering five houses by the time Henry died. Even after his death, his generosity continued, with substantial cash bequests made on behalf of the Observants in his will.

The piety of Henry VII was displayed in gestures which were made on a truly royal scale, but which were perfectly in tune with the devotional practices of his people. This entirely traditional piety was apparent in his attachment to the cult of the saints. After his victory at Stoke in 1487, Henry had donated a splendid votive statue of himself to the shrine of Our Lady at Walsingham, to which he had been on pilgrimage shortly before embarking on the military campaign of that year. Throughout his life he remained a devout and regular pilgrim. The shrine of St Thomas Becket at Canterbury was a particular favourite, to which he returned frequently. In his will, he requested a statue identical to that which he had given to Walsingham to be made for the Canterbury shrine. Among Henry's other favourite saints was the patron of England, St George. Louis XII of France, who conquered the Duchy of Milan around the turn of the century, found a relic of St George – a leg – among the booty of war. In due course this was sent to Henry as a present, and he was so pleased that on St George's Day (23 April) 1505 he arranged and took part in a solemn procession which culminated in the public veneration of the relic, displayed for the purpose in St Paul's Cathedral. In his will, Henry bequeathed the leg to the chapel royal of St George at Windsor.

Another of Henry's works of devotion was the foundation in Westminster Abbey of a magnificent chantry chapel, the Lady Chapel, whose construction began in 1503. He intended it to house the shrine of his uncle, Henry VI (whose relics he planned

A view of Westminster, drawn by Anthony Van Wyngaerde, about 1550, from a collection in the Ashmolean Museum, Oxford. Charing Cross, at the west end of the Strand, is among the landmarks clearly visible.

to transfer from Windsor to Westminster), as well as his own tomb. A third votive statue of the king was ordered in his will, to be donated to the shrine of St Edward the Confessor, which was also housed there. The chapel itself was glazed with splendid windows – sadly, long since destroyed – depicting scenes from the Bible. These windows were to serve as models for those which still survive in King's College, Cambridge, and which, in their turn, give us a fair idea of what the glass in Henry's chapel was like. The chapel at the back of the abbey church was to become, in effect, the Tudor mausoleum. All the Tudor monarchs apart from Henry VIII were to be laid to rest there.

Besides his foundation at Westminster, Henry founded the Savoy Hospital for the benefit of the London poor. His religious foundations sat squarely in the tradition of fifteenth-century English kingship. There was no sign in Henry of any humanist distaste for popular superstition and mechanical religion, still less of Reformation anxiety about the effectiveness of the Church's intercession. But then Henry did not share his son's passion for theology: his interest in religion was entirely practical – designed to get him into heaven, if only by the skin of his teeth. His reign saw the high tide of traditional piety in England, at least as far as it can be measured in material terms. Partly, no doubt, because his largely peaceful foreign policy minimised the fiscal burden on the population at large, expenditure on parish worship and on prayers for the dead reached record levels around 1500 (the costs of war followed by the onset of the English Reformation depressed the figures in his son's reign). Henry played a full part in this movement, spending lavishly on the Church and on his own soul.

Henry's piety, like that of many worldly Christians, was susceptible to dramatic intensification under tribulation or the threat of death. When he himself fell dangerously ill in 1504, one year after the death of his wife and two years after the death of his eldest son, he experienced a spiritual awakening. Repenting his ruthless fiscal exploitation of the Church, he vowed henceforth to appoint only worthy and devout men as bishops, making a fine start with his choice of John Fisher (spiritual director to Henry's mother, Lady Margaret Beaufort) as bishop of Rochester. As he put it in his letter to his mother, seeking her blessing for the promotion:

I have in my days promoted many a man unadvisedly, and I would now make some recompense to promote some good and virtuous men, which I doubt not should please God.

Upon his recovery, however, the vow was forgotten, and as far as the episcopate was concerned it was business as usual. Church reform, like the crusade (to which Henry also paid lip service from time to time, especially in his declining years, when there was little prospect of his health permitting him to go on one), was something which everybody thought it would be a good idea for someone else to try. Five years later, on his deathbed, Henry recalled, or rather reiterated, his vow, promising that 'the promotions of the church that were of his disposition should from henceforth be disposed to able men such as were virtuous and well learned'.

At a time when many of his subjects, especially the educated clergy, were keen to increase the quantity and quality of preaching available in the Church, Henry enjoyed a good sermon. Fisher was just one of many learned clerics from both Oxford and Cambridge who were summoned to court to edify their sovereign. And Henry's chantry foundation in Westminster Abbey called for regular preaching by the learned monks both to their brethren and to the people. Not that he always took the spiritual admonitions of the Church too much to heart. Erasmus relates how a zealous friar preached censoriously before Henry VII on the vices of kings. Asked afterwards what he had made of it, Henry commented that putting that friar in the pulpit was rather like handing a naked blade to a madman. Nevertheless, it is plain from Henry's immense provision for his soul after death that he was worried about what lay ahead, although not too much should be read into this. His provision for his soul represented a prodigious expenditure, but it was not disproportionate to the sort of amounts which the nobility and gentry were accustomed to devote to such purposes.

Henry's increasingly frequent bouts of illness worsened early in 1509, and by March it was apparent that he was dying. He made his will on 31 March and died on 21 April in the palace he had built at Richmond. His agonies of conscience were reportedly intense, and his bodily agony more so. His only discernible achievement was to bequeath his throne to his son, and even that bequest looked distinctly shaky just five years before his death. Yet perhaps this was achievement enough. His three immediate predecessors had failed in this, the prime responsibility of the royal father, whatever other successes they might have enjoyed. And the throne that Henry bequeathed to his second son was more secure than it had been for a century at least. Luck there still was aplenty. King Arthur might have found his younger brother Henry rather a handful, and not even Henry VII's notorious disinclination to dissipate the Crown lands and establish magnates had prevented him from equipping Prince Henry with a substantial apanage in Arthur's lifetime. When Arthur died, Prince Henry's lands as Duke of York were as yet worth less than £1,000 a year, but it is hard to believe that his father would not in due course at least have elevated him above the wealthiest nobleman in the country (the Duke of Buckingham). Henry of York might well have turned out as dangerous as Richard of York before him.

John Fisher, the most accomplished preacher among the bishops, was the obvious choice to preach the sermon at Henry's funeral. There were the inevitable passages of eulogy. Fisher summarised Henry's kingly virtues even while dismissing them as 'vain transitory things':

> His politic wisdom in governance it was singular, his wit always quick and ready, his reason pithy and substantial, his memory fresh and holding, his experience notable, his counsels fortunate and taken by wise deliberation, his speech gracious in diverse languages, his person goodly and amiable, his natural complexion of the purest mixture, his issue fair and in good number, leagues and confederacies he had with all Christian princes, his mighty power was dread everywhere, not only within his realm, but without also.

There is little to quarrel with in this assessment. Yet his sermon was not just the usual encomium. Fisher also emphasised Henry's repentance as death approached, recalling his promise to undertake 'a true reformation of all them that were officers and ministers of his laws to the intent that justice from henceforward truly and indifferently might be executed in all causes', and his forlorn vow that 'if it pleased God to send him life they should see him a new changed man'. There is a passion about his call to his audience to assist their late sovereign with their prayers which leaves the unmistakable sense that Fisher really felt they were needed. A few months later he was called upon to preach in memory of the king's mother, Lady Margaret Beaufort, and the difference between the two sermons is striking. Whereas that on Lady Margaret is practically a case for canonisation, that on Henry is a meditation on the mysterious and wonderful mercy of God. Fisher is confident that Henry's soul is safe, yet it is clearly the salvation of a repentant thief rather than a royal road to heaven that he presents to his listeners and readers. Fisher's Lady Margaret is a model of sanctity; his Henry VII an object lesson in penitence. For all his own admiration for and gratitude to the king, Fisher knew how few there were who were really sorry to see him go:

> Ah, King Henry, King Henry, if thou were alive again, many one that is here present now would pretend a full great pity and tenderness upon thee!

2

HENRY VIII

Of all the kings of England, Henry VIII has left the deepest impression on the imagination of posterity. The arrogant and colossal pose of the great Holbein portrait, which survives in so many contemporary and subsequent copies, conveys the awesome personality of a man who would still stand out even in the well-nourished society of early twenty-first-century England. Although this was just an image, created by the genius of Holbein, it was successful because it did not belie reality. Henry's sheer physical presence was remarked by his contemporaries, and goes a long way to explaining just how some of the political changes of his reign were possible. This was a man who could dominate the council table or even, on occasion, the Houses of Parliament: a man to whom it was difficult to say no.

After the portrait, it is perhaps those six wives of his who have helped him catch the popular imagination, which, as so often, has latched onto something of real importance. The six wives are not in fact the emblem of sexual prowess which popular fancy has made them – many kings have been far more extravagant in their amours than Henry, who had an acutely religious if almost athletically flexible conscience – but they do testify to his ability to move mountains in order to get his own way. Henry was a man who would overthrow a Church to obtain a divorce, a man willing to sacrifice ministers and friends, even wives and children, on the altar of dynastic interest.

This is not to say that Henry's reign is all image and reputation, or for that matter all blood and brutality. For good or ill, intentionally or not, his reign proved a turning point in English history. To his reign can be traced the roots of the Church of England, the seeds of the Irish Question, the birth of the English Bible, the founding of the Privy Council, and the principle of the omnicompetence of parliamentary statute. His reign saw the destruction of English monasticism, which had helped shape the society and landscape of England for nearly a millennium. As a result, it also witnessed the greatest shift in landholding since the Norman Conquest, and saw the landed wealth of the Crown itself reach its highest level ever. His reign, in short, saw something little less than a revolution.

Only one of the Tudor monarchs was born to the throne, and it was not Henry VIII. Born in 1491, his earliest years were spent as second in line for the succession, after his brother Arthur. We know relatively little about those years, and myths have inevitably filled the gaps – most notably the idea that his father originally intended Henry for the Church. No English prince had been ordained since the Norman Conquest, and the idea that Henry VII was contemplating an unprecedented ecclesiastical career for his second son is adequately contradicted by Prince Henry's installation as Duke of York at the venerable age of three (1 November 1494). Moreover, this well-built youth was brought up on a regime of martial exercises, becoming an expert horseman, which does not suggest a priestly destiny.

We do not know much about his academic education, although his tutor was the leading English poet of that generation, John Skelton. Henry was evidently a talented and willing pupil, and his scholarly attainments won him the praise of Erasmus. He grew up an accomplished man, speaking four or five languages, and able to sing, dance and play. He wrote poems, and is one of the few English monarchs to have written a book – and in Latin at that. He dabbled in musical composition, writing songs and even, apparently, a setting of the Mass. Sadly, 'Greensleeves' was not by him, but 'Pastime with good company' certainly was. He was not above flattery on his musical talents. When Rowland Phillips, the Vicar of Croydon, earned himself a dressing-down from the king on account of a sermon which failed to please, the king's secretary wryly observed that he might have done better to imitate the example of the king's almoner, who that same day had preached to the royal household, by working in a few references to 'Pastime'.

ACCESSION

Only with Arthur's death in 1502 did Henry become the heir apparent. And even then it was still possible, a year or two later, for the question of the succession to be discussed in terms which took little account of his chances. Yet by the time Henry VII died in 1509, there were no longer any doubts. Even so, Henry came to the throne at an uncertain age. Not yet eighteen, he was clearly an adult, yet had not reached that age of twenty-one at which, under English law, a man became formally capable of managing his lands and his affairs in his own right. For the first few weeks his formidable grandmother, Lady Margaret Beaufort, the Tudor matriarch, looked like being the guiding force. But she soon followed her son to the grave, and could do no more than advise her grandson to pay heed to those mostly clerical royal councillors for whom she had the regard of a pious woman vowed to the widow's life: Archbishop William Warham of Canterbury, Bishop Richard Fox of Winchester, and her own spiritual director, Bishop John Fisher of Rochester.

The delicacy of the political situation and the inevitable cautiousness of churchmen were hardly a recipe for dramatic developments. The chronicle of the first years of the reign is therefore, not surprisingly, a tale of the arts of peace, taken up

Henry by the Grace of God King of England &c

Henry VIII processes to the opening of parliament, 4 February 1512.

with the joys and festivities of court life. Common law may not have reckoned Henry old enough to manage his own affairs, but the law of the Church reckoned him old enough to marry, and his first move was to fulfil his long engagement to his brother's widow, Catherine of Aragon. About two weeks later, fountains of wine ran for the people of London on 24 June to celebrate the coronation, as the king and queen were crowned together, like a couple in a romance of chivalry. Liberated from his father's smothering care, Henry threw himself by day into a career of hunting, enlivened at intervals by chivalric displays of jousting. By night, revels and dances were the rule. Edward Hall's chronicle of the reign tells us how Henry VIII and his companions dressed up as Robin Hood and his Merry Men for some Christmas frolics in 1509. This happy phase of Henry's long reign came to a climax on New Year's Day 1511 with the birth of a baby to the royal couple. Better still, it was a boy, Prince Henry. King Henry was so delighted that he made a pilgrimage to Walsingham to give thanks. Tragically, the baby prince was dead within two months and was buried in Westminster Abbey. Catherine's subsequent pregnancies were less successful. Several miscarried. Only one baby would survive: Mary, born in 1516. This early tragedy thus sowed the seeds of much of the later bitterness and injustice of the reign, focused as it was on the uncertainty of the succession, from the execution of the Duke of Buckingham in 1521 to the king's numerous divorces and their fatal, at times momentous, consequences.

WAR AND PEACE

In 1511 the king's mind began turning towards graver concerns of policy and war. The direction of his thoughts was fixed by his emerging conception of who and what he was. A convincing case has been made for regarding Henry as a practitioner of what has been called 'Renaissance self-fashioning': that is, the self-conscious construction of a public identity, or image as we would say. In the case of Henry VIII, that image was modelled on a royal predecessor, Henry V, as mediated for example through a biography translated from Latin and dedicated to Henry VIII in 1513. Henry V was one of the great exemplars of English, indeed of Christian, kingship, and Henry VIII had a lot in common with him. Each inherited the throne in the flush of youth from a middle-aged and unpopular usurper. Indeed, each inherited from a father who had outlived his usefulness through prolonged ill health. Thus each felt the need to establish his legitimacy and to secure his dynasty. Henry V pursued these ends through the zealous support of religious orthodoxy at home, and through a pro-papal ecclesiastical policy and a traditionally anti-French foreign policy abroad. Henry VIII did much the same. At home, he presided over renewed repression of the Lollards. Abroad, he looked to revive the glory days of the Hundred Years' War through an invasion of France.

As a fit, strong youth, his head filled with dreams of glory and the great days of Agincourt, Henry was almost bound to enter upon war with France. Through the chronicles, and perhaps most of all through the 'Agincourt Song', Agincourt was still a living tradition, the ultimate testimony to the prestige of English arms. The myth of Agincourt was still potent when Shakespeare wrote his *Henry V* at the end of the Tudor century. When Henry VIII came to the throne, the battle was less than a hundred years past – as much part of the folk memory then as the Somme is now, if not more.

At first Henry faced an uphill struggle. His father had no taste for foreign adventures, having seen quite enough of France during his years of exile, and the conservative and clerical council which he and his mother had bequeathed to the young king was not the sort of grouping to fling itself headlong into continental conquest. Now twenty-one, Henry was not to be gainsaid, and one of the ablest of the clerics broke ranks with his colleagues. Thomas Wolsey had arrived on the scene as a junior diplomat in Henry VII's latter years, on the coat-tails of Richard Fox, the Bishop of Winchester. He had a prodigious appetite for work, and seems in effect to have put his talents at the disposal of his new king, who in the company of his youthful jousting companions, men like Charles Brandon, William Compton and Edward Howard, looked forward to reviving the Plantagenet claims on French soil. Wolsey was the man who actually laid on the invasion, seeing to the tiresome details of supply and ordnance which were not the kind of thing gentleman-soldiers bothered themselves with. The emergence of Wolsey really marks Henry VIII's arrival at political maturity. The old guard of inherited councillors was edged out. Richard Fox (Lord Privy Seal) and William Warham (Lord Chancellor) soon betook themselves into graceful retirement from politics.

If the driving force of the war with France was Henry's ambition, the pretext on which the invasion was launched was not naked dynastic aggrandisement but the good of the Roman Catholic Church. Henry was able to combine self-interest with self-righteousness, making his invasion little less than a crusade. Louis XII of France, in pursuit of his own ambitions in northern Italy, had clashed with Pope Julius II, an enterprising reformer who believed that the renewal of the Catholic Church would be best served by a papal conquest of the Italian peninsula. In a quaint reversal of roles, while the Pope gathered armies to overcome the king, the king convened a council of the Church to depose the Pope. The Council of Pisa (1511) was something of wash-out – it was only attended by a handful of French bishops – but it gave Julius the chance to present his conflict with Louis as a religious war. His call for aid against France was a heaven-sent opportunity for Henry, and put his more peaceable clerical advisers in an impossible position. John Colet was a sufficiently representative figure of this party (though not at that time himself a member of Henry's council). When he took it into his head to preach to Henry's face on the subject of peace, the king took him aside and argued the case through with him, eventually persuading him to concede that the proposed conflict was indeed a just war. True or not, the story illustrates the problem for anyone who wished to oppose the war. It must have been very difficult for loyal churchmen to argue the moral or the pragmatic case against a war which had been authorised by the Pope.

The problems faced in early modern monarchies by well-intentioned councillors such as Colet were deftly sketched out by his friend Thomas More in the first book of his masterpiece, *Utopia*, which is of course not only a description of a fictitious transatlantic commonwealth but also a satirical commentary on European, and especially English, politics. The book's protagonist, Raphael Hythloday, is invited by Thomas More to justify his refusal to join a royal council and thus place at the disposal of a prince his immense political wisdom, accumulated through years of study and travel. Hythloday explains that the sort of policies advocated by humanist philosophers such as him would be entirely unwanted in the councils of kings. While he would advocate peace and justice, a pastoral concern on the part of the prince for the common good or 'commonweal' of his people, the hearts of kings were set upon conquest and glory. The flatterers who surround kings would encourage them in their unrealistic ambitions, disregarding the fact that it was hard enough for a king to administer justice and promote virtue in one realm without adding another to his burdens. He illustrates his point with an imaginary account of a debate at a royal council table – tactfully making France rather than England his example. We should not mistake Hythloday's cautionary tale for an account of debates at Henry VIII's council table in 1512. Still less should we read them as an outright condemnation of the king and his policy. After all, Thomas More accepted a place on Henry's council soon afterwards, putting into practice the principle which, in *Utopia*, he maintained against Hythloday: namely that those in a position to do so should accept service with a prince so that, even if they could not attain the best outcome, they could at any rate work for the 'least worst'. But *Utopia* does offer us a fair reflection and assessment of the motives and interests which drove policies like Henry's. In turn, the war in France vindicates the critique put forward in *Utopia*.

War with France was a traditional policy with a good pedigree. The nobility and gentry flocked to serve with their king, doubtless sharing his confidence that it would all be as easy as it had been for Henry V. Archers and knights were the key to Henry V's success – along with the weakness of the French monarchy, where the king was a lunatic, and rival princely factions struggled for power. But the long French campaigns of reconquest against the forces of Henry VI offered a better lesson in warfare than the almost miraculous achievements of Henry V. The French reconquest had been a matter of long sieges, with artillery the decisive weapon. English troops began to cross the Channel in the early summer of 1513, and Henry VIII joined them in Calais at the end of June. Moving out into the Low Countries in July, they soon found that conquest meant the long hard slog of siege, not the short, sharp shock of battle. The 'Battle of the Spurs' (16 August) outside Thérouanne, in which Henry 'won his spurs' in a glorious rout of French cavalry, was no contemptible feat of arms. But it was little more than a skirmish, repelling a force sent to relieve a besieged city. Thérouanne was in due course taken and sacked, and nearby Tournai surrendered to avoid a similar fate. But at that rate the conquest of France was utterly impossible. It was only because the French king had ambitions of his own in Italy that the English made any impact at all. The sort of forces which Louis XII took into Lombardy in 1512, or which Francis I took over the Alps in 1515, would have made mincemeat of the English invaders. Nevertheless, Henry's war was successful, and nobody criticises success in war.

Letter from Catherine of Aragon to the king's almoner (Thomas Wolsey), 2 September 1513. Dated at Richmond, and signed 'Katherine the Qwene' the letter recommends that Louis d'Orleans, Duke of Longueville, who had been taken prisoner at the Battle of the Spurs fought on the 17 August, be conveyed to the Tower 'as sone as he commethe' for 'it shuld be a grete combraunce to me to have this prisoner here.' At this time Henry VIII was in France and Catherine of Aragon was ruling England as Regent in his absence. The Battle of Flodden was not fought until a week later.

If conflict between England and France was traditional, so too was amity between France and Scotland. The 'auld alliance' rested on the principle that your enemy's enemy is your friend. Henry VIII's chief domestic concern once he had crossed the Channel was the prospect of a stab in the back from Scotland. To provide against this threat, he left Catherine of Aragon as regent in his absence, with Thomas Howard, Earl of Surrey, to provide whatever leadership in the field might prove necessary. Surrey, who had been one of the leading hawks on Henry's council, had been devastated to be left behind. He need not have worried, as he seized his chance for glory. No sooner had serious campaigning commenced in the Low Countries than the expected Scottish invasion materialised. James IV led over the border one of the largest Scottish armies ever gathered. Surrey marched to intercept him, and on the slopes and ridges between Flodden and Branxton, the Scottish king's tactical errors betrayed his forces to the greatest defeat the Scots ever met on English soil. James himself fell at Flodden Field (9 September), along with twelve earls and dozens of lairds and gentlemen. If we are to trust English estimates (which may in fact be inflated), then at 12,000 dead, Scottish losses were ten times those of England. Surrey's reward was restoration to his father's duchy of Norfolk the following year. The official English view of the Scottish king's fate was that it represented God's punishment upon him for taking arms against the cause of the Pope (and thus incurring excommunication). John Fisher was called upon to preach a sermon to this effect, lamenting James IV's 'ill death and perjury', and it was not until absolution from the Pope was secured that he was granted Christian burial.

Letter from Henry VIII to Cardinal Wolsey, March 1518. The letter, which is a holograph, shows the affable side of Henry's character. The king addresses Wolsey as 'Myne Awne good cardinall', and continues on the same friendly note to thank Wolsey for 'the grette payne and labour' that he takes with regard to the king's affairs. Henry sends the queen's good wishes ('most harty recommendations'), and concludes: 'Wryttyn with the hand off your lovyng master, Henry R'.

Despite his victories for the honour of his crown and the defence of the Church, Henry found that he was unable to follow up his success owing to the collapse of the anti-French alliance in Europe which had made his invasion possible. His chief ally (and father-in-law), King Ferdinand of Aragon, was manoeuvring for peace with France. The death of Queen Anne of France, though, gave Henry the chance for revenge, as he was able to offer his younger sister, Mary, to Louis XII as a far more attractive replacement. Ably assisted by Wolsey, who showed himself a consummate diplomat as well as a brilliant administrator, Henry certainly won the peace, though the value of his victory was reduced by the fact that the exertions of marriage to a demanding young bride brought the French king to the grave in a matter of weeks. On the whole, things had gone well enough, and Wolsey's reward came in the form of a stream of ecclesiastical preferments. In 1514 he received in quick succession the bishoprics of Lincoln and Tournai, and then the archbishopric of York. The following year saw him add to this the Lord Chancellorship of England and a cardinal's hat (at Henry's request) from Pope Leo X. Wolsey was in the midst of the kaleidoscopic diplomacy of the next few years, alternately angling for war or peace at the lowest cost or the maximum profit for his king. The stunning victory of the new king of France, Francis I, at Marignano in 1515, which gave him control of northern Italy, threw Henry's victories of 1513 into the shade and made peace the only realistic option. But at least the Treaty of London which Wolsey successfully negotiated in 1518, bringing together almost all the major international players, allowed Henry to pose as the peacemaker of Europe. Gestures like the recruitment of John Colet and Thomas More to his council enhanced this benevolent image, enabling him to present himself as an open-minded king prepared to give serious attention to the views of fashionable and at times critical intellectuals.

Not that peace was Henry's real intention. He paid lip service to the treaty's proposal for a European crusade against the Ottoman Turks, who were steadily extending their hold over the Balkans and the eastern Mediterranean. And peace between Christian nations was the theme of one of history's most famous summit meetings, the Field of Cloth of Gold, near Calais, where Henry VIII met Francis I in person in June 1520. Yet beneath the genial gallantry and conspicuous consumption which filled three weeks of that summer so pleasurably, the real political tensions were building up. Henry's mortification at being cleverly thrown by Francis in a wrestling bout said more about their relationship than all the outward show. Even as he was going through the motions of international peace and harmony at the Field of Cloth of Gold, he was secretly negotiating with the new Holy Roman Emperor, Charles V, for a renewal of hostilities. War recommenced for England with a raid from Calais into Normandy during the autumn of 1522, followed by a more substantial but no more successful campaign in Picardy in 1523. By now, the expenses of war were pressing heavily on the English people, and objections to taxation were voiced in the Parliament of 1523. Henry's ally, Charles V, shouldered the burden of the war in 1524, but his stunning victory at Pavia in February 1525, which reversed the results of Marignano ten years before, aroused Henry's martial spirit once more. Unfortunately for him, his people had reached the end of their

Henry VIII in the House of Lords, 1523 or 1529 (a later copy of a contemporary drawing). The Duke of Buckingham would have been seated above the Dukes of Norfolk and Suffolk, had he not been executed in 1521. The cardinal's hat surmounts Wolsey's coat of arms on the king's right.

fiscal tether. Wolsey knew full well that Parliament would grant no further revenue, so he endeavoured to finance yet another army with a forced loan, the so-called 'amicable grant'. The resulting tax-strikes and riots in Kent and East Anglia burst the bubble. The people were not as friendly as had been thought. Henry's ambitions had outstripped his purse. But even as this phase of his reign drew to a close, Henry's attention was shifting towards the problem of the succession. His attempts to solve it, and the consequences of those attempts, would keep him out of continental war for nearly twenty years.

DEFENDER OF THE FAITH

Henry's piety and interest in religion had always been a matter for comment. Of course, medieval and early modern kings were expected to be decently religious. Nobody ever suggested that Henry's father was anything other than a loyal son of Holy Mother Church. Yet there were degrees of commitment even among kings. Henri III of France, who later in the century participated in public processions of penitential flagellants, was widely seen as taking his religion to extremes. Henry VIII was pious and conscientious without being extravagant. It is tempting to write his piety off as so much hypocrisy. But if it was perhaps hypocritical, it was far from cynical. Henry may have been at times obnoxiously self-righteous, spotting splinters in other people's eyes despite the heaps of timber blocking his own lights, but nobody could say he was not sincere.

More remarkably, but still acceptably in an age when, if it was understood that philosophers would hardly become kings, it was felt that kings might profitably endeavour to be philosophers, he had an educated interest in the faith he professed. In 1515 Henry took a personal interest in the furore over the death in an episcopal gaol of Richard Hunne, alleged by the clergy to be a heretic but regarded by the citizens of London as a man victimised by the clergy for taking legal action against them in the king's courts. While the clergy maintained that Hunne had hanged himself, the coroner's jury returned a verdict of murder by his captors. Attempts to bring them to justice turned the episode into a full-scale dispute over 'benefit of clergy', the jurisdictional privileges of churchmen with respect to the law of the land. It was Henry who presided over a thorough airing of the issues involved and managed to cobble together a compromise solution. Henry loved theological arguments, and topics such as the value of mental prayer and the merits of Erasmus's radical edition of the New Testament in Greek were debated in his presence at court. Many books were dedicated to this intellectual among monarchs, and, if he did not always have time to read them himself, he would pass religious books to a couple of his chaplains for review and sit in judgement while they argued to and fro.

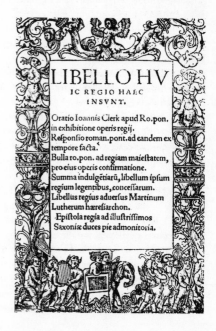

Title page of a later edition (1523) of Henry VIII's *Assertio Septem Sacramentorum*. Henry's book against Martin Luther, written and first printed in 1521, was at first only circulated to the Pope and other selected recipients. This title page advertises the supplementary materials now added, including the papal bull naming Henry 'Defender of the Faith', and an open letter from the king to the Dukes of Saxony (originally sent 20 January 1523), urging them to take firm action against Luther. Note the description of the king as 'his royal majesty' ('regiam maiestatem'), a usage rare before Henry's break with Rome.

Henry's theological interests went beyond this dilettante dabbling. Famously, he composed a book against Martin Luther in 1521, when the radicalism of Luther's teachings had finally become apparent and had earned the German friar papal condemnation and excommunication. It was generally rumoured at the time, and has been generally accepted ever since, that the *Assertion of the Seven Sacraments* (as his book was called) was by no means his own unaided effort. There were at the worst of times troops of learned priests within hailing distance of the royal study, and it also looks as though Henry summoned professional theologians from Oxford and Cambridge to vet its orthodoxy and check its references. Besides which Thomas More was called in to apply some stylistic polish. Yet there is no disputing that Henry laboured upon it himself, for hours at a time in the first flush of enthusiasm. We can see his hand in the fact that the bulk of the book defends Catholic doctrines of the Mass against Luther. The Mass was a central and lifelong preoccupation of the king's.

Now, Henry had long been anxious to add a religious dimension to the English royal title in emulation of the 'Catholic' kings of Spain and the 'Most Christian' kings of France. This book earned him the papal accolade of *Fidei Defensor* (defender of the faith) which still adorns the coin of the realm. The Pope was no doubt especially pleased with Henry's comments on papal authority:

> I have no intention of insulting the pope by discussing his prerogative as though it were a matter of doubt... Luther can hardly deny that all the churches accept and revere the holy Roman see as mother and ruler of the faithful...

Yet it should not be thought that Henry's aversion to Luther was anything other than heartfelt. In addition to the *Assertion*, Henry wrote a couple of other pieces against Luther. First of all there was an open letter to the Dukes of Saxony, urging them to suppress this troublesome friar before he did any more damage. A few years later he wrote a rather longer open letter to Luther himself – this, unlike the *Assertion*, was translated into English for the benefit of his own people.

The Catholic world was duly impressed by the English king's efforts. Catholic writers agonised over which to praise more highly, his learning or his virtue. That was the sort of reaction Henry had been expecting. The 'philosopher king' was one of his favourite roles. What he was not expecting was the thundering riposte which Luther launched. The man who had braved papal anathema and Imperial outlawry was not to be intimated by the royal pen. Luther was quite possibly the only person who ever dared address Henry in such roundly offensive terms (even from such a safe distance). Henry found himself in the unwelcome situation of being impotent against defiance, and never forgave the affront. Luther's intemperate reaction ensured that, even after Henry himself had broken with the Roman Church, the Lutheran brand of Reformation would not find many friends in England. In the meantime, the task of dealing with Luther was delegated to Thomas More. Luther had lowered the discussion to the level of the dungheap, and More cheerfully kept it there, out-Luthering Luther in one of the most sustainedly and inventively vituperative tirades ever to be published under the guise of theology. The urbane author of *Utopia* was understandably anxious for this *tour de force* to appear under a *nom de plume*.

THE KING'S 'GREAT MATTER'

Henry's theological credentials stood him in good stead when he found that he needed a way out of his sonless and therefore burdensome first marriage, to Catherine of Aragon. Precisely when their relationship broke down irretrievably is unclear. In the years after 1510, Henry and Catherine were young and in love, but by the 1520s the age-gap was showing and the relationship weakening. The birth of Mary Tudor back in 1516 had given cause for hope that a son might yet follow, after the dreadful disappointment of 1511 and the intervening record of miscarriages. Catherine was again pregnant in summer 1518, and one of her maids of honour caught the king's eye. Elizabeth Blount played a prominent part in revels laid on to entertain some French ambassadors around Michaelmas 1518, and about nine months later bore Henry a son, whom the king acknowledged as his own. Meanwhile, Catherine's pregnancy proved both unfortunate and her last. By the 1520s her child-bearing years were clearly past, and her looks were fading. Henry was looking for pleasure in the arms of other women, and although the numbers of illegitimate children whom contemporary and later rumours fathered upon the king are hard to credit, there is no smoke without fire in these matters. His affair with Mary Boleyn, wife of William Carey, probably belongs to these years. After his experience with Bessie Blount, he may have decided that affairs with married women were more convenient. Henry Carey, reputedly Henry's son, arrived in 1526.

Henry's decision to seek a formal way out of his first and failing marriage depended upon both a change of circumstances and a change of heart. The change of circumstances was the fortunate death in battle of the only potential rival for the English throne who was not within Henry's reach. Richard de la Pole, 'White Rose', the last surviving son of Edward IV's sister, having spent his adult life in the service of the king of France, met his death at the great battle of Pavia in February 1525, when control of northern Italy was wrested from Francis I's grip by the armies of Charles V. The Imperial victory was in itself good news for Henry, who hoped to make it the occasion for yet another invasion of France (Francis I had been taken prisoner in the battle, and France seemed ripe for the picking). But it was the death of White Rose which accounts for his instructions that bells be rung and thanksgiving processions be held throughout the land. Only now could alternative solutions to the succession crisis be entertained. The first such possibility was the public recognition of his bastard son, Henry Fitzroy, who was made Duke of Richmond and Somerset (denoting his Tudor and Beaufort ancestry respectively). Perhaps Henry was considering putting him into line for the succession.

It was not long, though, before a more promising alternative presented itself: a divorce from Catherine of Aragon would free him for a second marriage. ('Divorce' meant not, as now, the termination of a valid marriage, but what is now called an 'annulment', a judgement that a marriage had not in fact been validly contracted.) By the close of the Middle Ages annulment was a familiar solution for the matrimonial problems of royal houses, and granting annulments was in effect a prerogative of the Pope in his capacity as Christ's vicar on earth. Many unhappy royal marriages had been terminated in this way – most recently and notoriously that of Louis XII of France to his first wife, Jeanne, after what amounted to a travesty of judicial proceedings sanctioned by the Pope. Pretexts for divorce could almost always be found. Complex family relationships within a relatively narrow élite obsessed with genealogy provided plenty of grist to the mill of Catholic canon law, with its intricate and extensive system of legislation and jurisprudence about marriage.

But Henry did not want a divorce on these terms. His case was far simpler, based on the text of the Bible and theological principle. It rested on biblical texts (Leviticus 18:16 and 20:21) forbidding marriage to a brother's wife, which seemed to cover his case exactly. He maintained that his marriage to Catherine was flatly prohibited by the law of God, that not even the Pope had any right to dispense anyone from their duty to obey that law, and that therefore his marriage, although originally sanctioned by a papal bull, was invalid.

Letter from Anne Boleyn to Cardinal Wolsey. Writing before her marriage to the king, she thanks Wolsey for his great services in her cause, and promises that if, after the attainment of her hopes, there is anything in the world she can do for him, 'you shall fynd me the gladdyst woman in the woreld to do yt'.

Although initial discussions of the divorce were held behind closed doors, news soon leaked out. By May 1527, rumours were rife in London that the king's confessor (John Longland, Bishop of Lincoln) and other learned clerics had told Henry that his marriage was invalid. Henry ordered the Lord Mayor to quash the rumours. It was not long before wagging tongues were also talking of a daughter of Sir Thomas Boleyn, saying that if the king were once more free to marry, she would be his bride. Her name was Anne, sister of the king's former lover. This was the first that the public knew of Henry's change of heart, the other driving force of the whole process. As David Starkey has recently demonstrated, Henry's infatuation with Anne compelled him to seek a divorce, because she refused to tread her sister's path, and held out for marriage. It was to be a long wait. Henry himself always insisted that his doubts about his first marriage originated in scruples of conscience – but he was hardly going to say that he had gone off one wife and fancied another. He always preferred the moral high ground, and certainly convinced himself that he was acting from the purest of motives. His knack for combining conscience with convenience, self-righteousness with self-interest, made his wish for a divorce an irresistible political force.

Among the experts consulted about the divorce was, inevitably, John Fisher, whom Henry had once described as the most learned theologian he had ever known, and who was now renowned throughout Europe thanks to the powerfully argued books which, following Henry's lead, he had published against Luther. It was Fisher who threw the first spanner into the works, pointing out that the scriptural argument against the marriage was by no means clear. For the book of Deuteronomy contained a divine precept commanding a man to marry his deceased brother's wife when that brother had died without children (Deut. 25:5). This special case exactly described the case of Henry, his brother Arthur, and Catherine of Aragon. From that point on, the debate over Henry's marriage, which sucked in scholars from all over Europe for nearly ten years, concentrated on the problem of relating the prohibition in Leviticus to the injunction in Deuteronomy. Ultimately, it would be politics rather than theology which decided the issue. But Henry not only liked to win, he liked to be in the right. So enormous efforts went into trying to put him there.

The text of Deuteronomy which Fisher put into play made it far harder for Henry to keep the theological high ground, and might have become an embarrassment had not an ambitious young Cambridge don come up with some answers. Robert Wakefield – ironically a former protégé of Fisher's – was Tudor England's leading expert in Hebrew. On first being asked for an opinion in 1527, he wisely replied that he would not offer one until he had Henry's clear instructions to do so. His request for formal authorisation was shrewd enough: under the Tudors, academic discussions about the royal succession could easily be construed as treason. More to the point, he wanted to know what answer the king wanted. Wakefield's skill in Hebrew enabled him to deliver the goods. The prohibition in Leviticus had a curse attached to it, warning anyone who married his brother's wife that he would be 'without children'. As Henry had a child, Mary, this had not seemed very helpful until Wakefield observed, rightly, that in context this had to mean without sons to carry on the family name.

Letter from Anne Boleyn to 'Master Stephyns' (i.e. Stephen Gardiner, the king's secretary), 4 April 1529. Dated at Greenwich and signed 'Anne Boleyn', the letter expresses the hope 'that the ende of this jorney shall be more pleasant' to her than the first. Gardiner was in Italy for the second time trying to procure papal assent to a divorce between Henry VIII and Catherine of Aragon.

Moreover, he argued, while Leviticus was speaking of full brothers, Deuteronomy was using the word 'brother' in the wider sense of male relatives in general. He therefore proposed that Leviticus was prohibiting one special case of the general obligation imposed in Deuteronomy. This was not watertight, but it would do. And now Henry saw himself as the victim of a providential punishment in the miscarriages or deaths of his lost sons, he was more than ever convinced that his understanding of Leviticus was correct, no matter what Deuteronomy might say.

While the theological aspects of the divorce were being investigated, there were other paths to be pursued. The divorce would require political support, and this would have to come from France. So Cardinal Wolsey himself set off on a rare personal mission abroad, to consolidate new contacts with the French king, who was to be a reliable and helpful ally for the next ten years.

Dissolving marriages was the pope's business, and Henry naturally expected the Pope to co-operate. From his point of view, that was what the Pope was for. Henry had lent his considerable prestige to buttress papal authority by writing in person against Luther. Now it was time to call in the debt. Characteristically, Henry was oblivious to the obstacles in his path. First, the Imperial victory at Pavia which had given Henry the incentive to seek a divorce denied him the means to get one. For it left Charles V in control of Italy. Imperial armies went on to sack Rome in 1527, making the Pope a virtual prisoner in his own fortress of Castel Sant'Angelo. Clement VII was in no position to offend the Emperor by granting Henry a divorce which would proclaim that Charles V's aunt had been living in incest for nearly twenty years. (Sixteenth-century Europe was a man's world, in which sexual disgrace attached itself far more readily to

A carving in wood, from Canterbury Cathedral. Perhaps from a series of carvings caricaturing Henry's enemies, this shows Catherine of Aragon flanked by Cardinal Wolsey and Cardinal Campeggio. All three had incurred his wrath at the public hearing of his divorce case at Blackfriars in summer 1529: Catherine by appealing to the pope, Campeggio by accepting her appeal, and Wolsey by failing to secure Henry the outcome he wanted.

women than to men.) The second obstacle was Catherine's own acute sense of honour and dignity. While these royal matrimonial problems could be sorted out amicably if the woman was prepared to accept a kind of respectable retirement, Catherine would not give an inch, and she was every inch a Spanish princess. Finally, as his first marriage had itself required a papal dispensation from canon law (which, like Leviticus, forbade marriage to a sister-in-law), Henry was asking the Pope to reverse a decision by a recent predecessor. While this was not beyond the bounds of possibility, it would have been very bad timing in the 1520s. The Protestant Reformation then gaining ground in Germany and Switzerland was not only challenging papal authority in principle (denying that Christ had granted St Peter or his successors any special authority in the Church) but also impugning it in practice, arguing that its judicial proceedings were corrupted by wealth and power. Not exactly the moment to overturn an earlier papal bull in order to do a favour to a friendly king.

The Pope's only option was to play for time in the hope that death would solve his problem. Almost anybody's death would have done: Charles, Henry, Catherine, or Anne Boleyn. In the meantime, he strung Henry along, for if he could not risk offending Charles V by granting the divorce, no more could he afford to alienate Henry by ruling it out. So when royal envoys suggested having the case tried at a special court in London, he played along, and sent Cardinal Campeggio to preside with Cardinal Wolsey. Campeggio knew the rules of the game, and it was six months after his arrival before the court finally convened in June 1529. As soon as it did, Catherine pulled the plug. She maintained, reasonably enough, that she could hardly expect a fair hearing in her estranged husband's capital city, and therefore appealed to the Pope to have the case revoked to Rome. As Henry was also present, Catherine's behaviour was a mortal insult, a blow to that image of fair-mindedness which he had cultivated so assiduously. After a desultory airing of the arguments over the marriage itself by representatives of the king and queen, Campeggio suspended the court and referred the case back to Rome. Catherine's appeal was his pretext, but his decision was more to do with Italian politics than anything else. For a year or more the French had been trying to prise Italy from Imperial hands. The last throw of the dice came in June 1529 at Landriano in the Po Valley. A French army marching south to relieve other French forces under siege near Naples was cut to pieces by Imperial troops, and papal diplomacy was left in tatters.

TURNING AGAINST THE CLERGY

The revocation of the case to Rome infuriated Henry, who responded, as so often when baulked of his heart's desire, by lashing out. In this case the target was Cardinal Wolsey. His career had been built on giving the king what he wanted, and his precipitous fall was the price of failure. Fifteen years at the top had left Wolsey with enemies galore, and the predators who led the attack at court and then in the Parliament which Henry summoned that autumn were followed by the carrion birds who flocked in for the pickings. The lands and offices which Henry was able to redistribute that autumn doubtless helped convince many English gentlemen of the righteousness of his cause. Not that he took Wolsey's head straightaway. The cardinal was rusticated to the diocese of York, which he had held since 1514 but never visited. It was only his mistaken belief that he could remain a player in European politics despite having lost the king's favour that finally destroyed him. His private contacts with representatives of Charles V were almost calculated to offend Henry, who certainly did not think foreign affairs a proper arena for the meddling of unauthorised subjects. Summoned to London in 1530 to face charges of treason, Wolsey was lucky enough to die en route, thus cheating the headsman.

The fall of Wolsey in 1529 was accompanied by a clutch of statutes nibbling away at the privileges and interests of the clergy. Catherine of Aragon enjoyed a good deal of support among the clergy, and the constant pressure put upon them over the next few years was designed not only to intimidate the Pope but also to bring the clergy at home into line. When three English bishops (and supporters of hers) appealed to Rome against these statutes, they were promptly imprisoned. To crown it all, the whole body of the English clergy was fined an astronomical £100,000 for having breached the ancient statute of 'praemunire' through being accomplices, so to speak, in Wolsey's exercise of his powers as papal legate in England over the previous ten or fifteen years. The Defender of the Faith was beginning to attack the Church. A year or so later, a discontented friar described him as the 'Destroyer of the Faith'.

Letter from Cardinal Wolsey to Henry VIII desiring forgiveness, 8 October 1529. Signed 'Your Graces moste prostrat poore chapleyn, creature, and bedisman.' In terms reminiscent of a prayer to Almighty God, the letter states that he, the king's 'poore, hevy, and wrechyd prest' daily calls upon the royal majesty 'for grace, mercy, remyssyon, and pardon'.

Letter from Cardinal Wolsey to Stephen Gardiner (the king's secretary), February or March 1530. Wolsey never abandoned his hopes for recall to the king's service. Here, he writes after his fall with reference to arrangements respecting appointments in the province of York, and trusts 'yt wole now please hys maiste to shewe hys pety… without sufferryng me any leynger to lye langwyshyng and consumyng awey'.

53

Meanwhile, Henry's scholars were on overtime. Some were detailed to work on Thomas More, whom Henry had appointed Lord Chancellor in succession to Wolsey. In the complex matter of the divorce there was no one whose approval Henry would rather have had than that of More, the one councillor who could be guaranteed to stay on the right side of the line which divides the statesman from the yes-man. Henry took a close personal interest in the research into his divorce (the document which had presented his case to the papal tribunal in 1529 was called 'the king's book'), and with his own conscience now impregnably fortified by the arguments of Wakefield and others, he could not fathom how anyone of goodwill could possibly disagree with him. But to the king's growing frustration, More could not be persuaded, although he compromised his personal feelings far enough to present Henry's case formally to Parliament in 1531 in his official capacity as Lord Chancellor. Other royal scholars, following a suggestion made by Thomas Cranmer, whose career in Henry's service was now taking off, were touring the universities of Europe canvassing opinions from sympathetic theologians and lawyers. Others still were combing chronicles and archives for useful precedents and ideas, on the impossibility of summoning an English king before a tribunal outside his kingdom, on the right of a local or national Church to resolve its problems on a local basis (rather than at Rome), and on the circumstances in which papal sanctions could legitimately be ignored. It was out of these research materials that the doctrine of the 'royal supremacy' would be born – though it was far from obvious as yet that such would be the fruit.

This major research effort underpinned Henry's decision to 'go public' on the divorce. There was, not surprisingly, a great deal of public sympathy with Catherine, who looked like the traditional 'wronged woman'. When royal agents sought the opinion of Oxford University in 1530, they were pelted with rotten vegetables by the women of the city. Henry's infatuation with Anne Boleyn was also common knowledge by then, and she was typecast as the home-breaker. 'Burnt arse whore' was the phrase that sprang to people's lips. Henry wanted everyone to know that his situation was not so much an instance of the eternal triangle as a personal tragedy which could engulf his entire kingdom in disaster. So the opinions of foreign universities on his cause were presented to Parliament on 30 March 1531. Published first in Latin, and later in an English translation by Thomas Cranmer, the *Determinations of the Universities* offered a full statement of the royal case. Having thus prepared his people's minds, Henry now publicly separated from his wife (though for some years their relationship had been nothing but a façade). During the summer progress, he left her at Windsor on 14 July, and never saw her again.

Catherine's friends were not slow to respond to the king's publicity blitz. However, while Henry was still anxious to be seen as the Utopian prince, taking advice from all sides and eschewing flattery – after all, Thomas More was still his Lord Chancellor – nothing written on Catherine's behalf could be printed in England. John Fisher's views had been published in 1530 – at Alcalá in Spain, in Latin, having been smuggled

Whitehall Palace. Acquired by Henry VIII on the fall of Thomas Wolsey in 1529, it became a principal royal residence for the remainder of the Tudor period

out of the country by Charles V's ambassador. One of the queen's chaplains, Thomas Abel, published an English treatise in her favour, the first of a handful of such books which would be printed clandestinely in the Netherlands (another of Charles V's territories). Abel's book, a masterly presentation of the queen's case, was sufficiently notorious to earn a mention in Edward Hall's chronicle, and was deeply resented by the king. Henry's vengeful arm was long. Abel, steadfastly loyal to his queen, would be thrown into the Tower of London in 1534, emerging only to be hanged, drawn and quartered in 1540.

All the propaganda in the world, however, did not bring a solution any nearer. There were plenty of ideas around, but no policy. Early in 1531, still goading the clergy, whom he rightly suspected were by no means solidly behind him, Henry required Convocation to recognise him as 'Supreme Head of the Church of England'. After much anxious consultation, they granted his demand, 'as far as the law of Christ allows' – a useful proviso which could mean anything or nothing. With a view to influencing the Pope, Henry reiterated his absolute refusal to have the case settled outside his dominions, and, in 1532, threatened to cut off English revenues to Rome. Meanwhile, his ministers, led by the emerging figure of Thomas Cromwell, stirred up time-honoured lay grievances against the clergy over excommunication, the powers of Church courts, and the extensive immunities of clergymen from royal courts. Even the affair of the unfortunate Richard Hunne was dragged up again. Early in 1532, Thomas Cromwell had compiled the 'Supplication against the Ordinaries', a bill of complaints against the clergy which was launched in Parliament as a 'spontaneous' petition to Henry to curtail clerical privilege and arrogance. By way of a response, Henry called upon Convocation to abandon its traditional claim to legislative autonomy and to agree that in future all its legislation should be subject to royal assent or veto. This in effect overthrew the 'liberty of the church' guaranteed by the first article of Magna Carta. When Convocation gave way and agreed on 15 May, it was too much for the Lord Chancellor. Although More's resignation next day was tactfully framed in terms of ill health, the timing made its true significance unmistakable. Thomas More could no longer reconcile service to the king with his conscience.

The late 1520s and the early 1530s, in the political context furnished by the divorce, saw a reconfiguration of religious interest groups which jeopardised the dominance of the Catholic faith in England. Essentially, while many devotees of the traditional religion and its practices tended to sympathise with Catherine of Aragon and therefore to oppose the king, those who were attracted to the 'new learning' (as it was called) of Protestantism sensed their chance to win the king's favour and sympathy. Although William Tyndale, now a refugee abroad and rather out of touch, opposed the divorce, regarding it as a machination of Cardinal Wolsey's, other Protestant theologians such as Robert Barnes, Hugh Latimer and Thomas Cranmer took Henry's side.

On the other hand, none of the three Englishmen who had published books against Luther in Henry's wake (Thomas More, John Fisher and an Oxford theologian named Edward Powell) felt able to support the divorce. The Observant Franciscans, who owed so much to the patronage of the king's father, were closer to Catherine than to Henry, and were very active in mobilising support for her and preaching in her favour. On Easter Sunday 1532, the head of the order in England, William Peto, went so far as to preach a sermon before the king in person at Greenwich, impugning his motives in seeking a divorce and suggesting that he was being misled by evil councillors. Henry found that Peto remained defiant in a subsequent private interview, so he had one of his own chaplains preach a reply the following Sunday. Still more disturbingly, one of the most influential English religious figures of the day, a nun named Elizabeth Barton, known as the 'Holy Maid of Kent', was throwing her enormous personal charisma behind the queen's cause. Having been cured of epilepsy by the intervention of the Blessed Virgin Mary in dramatic circumstances, Elizabeth Barton was credited with miraculous and prophetic powers and became the leader of a sort of Catholic revivalist movement. The poor and middling sort flocked in thousands to see and hear her, while the rich and powerful sought her advice and intercession. Her public message, mediated through a group of scholarly monks and friars (especially Observant Franciscans) based at religious houses in Canterbury, combined calls for moral renewal with apocalyptic warnings against the spread of Lutheran heresy, against Henry's obvious plan to get rid of his wife, and against his encroachment on the privileges of the Church. The Holy Maid commanded a great deal of popular support. She also earned the hatred of the king.

The Holy Maid's chief impact upon the political situation in England was to stiffen the resolve of the Archbishop of Canterbury, William Warham, not to take any action prejudicial to the position of the papacy. Elizabeth Barton was a Kentishwoman by origin, and had become a nun at the convent of St Sepulchre's in Canterbury itself. It was a commission under Warham's authority which had authenticated her miraculous cure and her spiritual experiences, and he subsequently had more than one personal interview with her. Henry's great principle was that the case had to be resolved in England – which meant, in effect, by the Archbishop of Canterbury. As long as Warham was Archbishop, there was no prospect of that.

DELIVERING THE DIVORCE

It was Warham's death that started the countdown. The obvious choice to replace him was Stephen Gardiner, who, after a glittering career at Cambridge University, had joined Cardinal Wolsey's service in the 1520s and had then been poached by the king in 1529 to serve as his principal secretary. He had been tireless in his efforts for the divorce, and in 1531 he had been rewarded with appointment as bishop of Winchester. However, since then he had blotted his copybook. For early in 1532 he drafted the clergy's reply to the 'Supplication against the Ordinaries', a misjudgement which for a while cost him Henry's trust and favour. Gardiner was therefore passed over, and the see of Canterbury was bestowed upon the still little-known Thomas Cranmer. Cranmer had now risen far enough in royal service to be posted as Henry's ambassador to the court of Charles V in Germany, but his summons to Canterbury was a surprise to everybody – not least to him. While in Germany, Cranmer had become attracted to the new 'evangelical' teachings of Luther and his followers, and had rather rashly (and, for a Catholic priest, strictly illegally) taken a wife: Margaret, the niece of a prominent German reformer, Andreas Osiander. Concealing this alliance from his sovereign, who set his face firmly against allowing priests to marry, was not the least of the challenges which Cranmer faced over the next fifteen years.

Before Cranmer had even made it back from Germany, Henry was preparing the diplomatic chessboard for the dramatic moves that he was planning. Another cross-Channel summit meeting with the king of France was arranged. It was not the Field of Cloth of Gold, and there were no wrestling matches this time – both men were a little old for such youthful high-jinks. But the meeting was far more momentous in terms of practical politics. Its most important aspect was that Henry took with him not Catherine – whom he certainly no longer considered in any sense his wife – but Anne Boleyn, who on 1 September 1532 was made a peeress in her own right, Marchioness of Pembroke, to let her rank second only to the king in his entourage. The trip itself lasted over a month (11 October–14 November), and secured French support for a divorce and second marriage which would detach Henry from the Imperial camp.

The Act of Appeals (1533), with its portentous opening claim 'that this Realme of Englond is an Impire [Empire]'. By this act, passed after Cranmer had obtained from Rome the necessary bulls for his appointment as Archbishop of Canterbury, Henry, through the English Parliament, made the first open breach with the Holy See. For the Act of Appeals not only declared England to be an empire governed by one supreme head and king: it stated that the king's jurisdiction was competent to adjudge finally all spiritual cases which might arise in his realm, and definitively forbade all appeals to the Pope and to 'any foreign princes or potentates'.

Even more importantly, it was probably on this trip that Anne finally surrendered to the king's advances. Counting backwards from her daughter's birth in early September 1533, we can see that she became pregnant shortly after the trip to France. According to one source, Henry actually married Anne secretly upon their return, on 14 November. Other sources, however, suggest a date in January.

Anne's pregnancy added urgency to proceedings. Whatever else happened, the child had to be born within lawful wedlock to be capable of inheritance under English law. If to modern eyes Henry's decision to remarry before securing his divorce looks like bigamy, we must remember that he had already convinced himself that his first marriage was contrary to God's law and that he was therefore not married at all. In the meantime, Thomas Cromwell, emerging now as the king's chief minister, was busy drafting the enabling legislation under which the incoming Archbishop of Canterbury would deliver the required verdict on Henry's marriage. The resultant Act of Appeals (forbidding judicial appeals to Rome) opened with a ringing declaration:

Where by divers sundry old histories and chronicles, it is manifestly declared and expressed, that this realm of England is an empire... governed by one supreme head and king... unto whom a body politic... ought to bear, next unto God, a natural and humble obedience...

This claim to 'imperial' status, tantamount to what we understand by 'sovereignty', was the basis on which the act maintained that no English person could lawfully be summoned to answer before any foreign jurisdiction, nor, for that matter, lawfully appeal any such jurisdiction. It did not need to spell out the fact that the papacy was the target of this law. There was no other foreign jurisdiction to which English people at that time addressed legal petitions or appeals.

Thomas Cranmer set foot once more upon English soil early in the new year, and was consecrated Archbishop of Canterbury on 30 March 1533. Almost his first task was to put in place the final groundworks for the divorce. The Convocation of the clergy was presented in April with two crucial questions: whether marriage to

A letter from Cranmer at Dunstable (17 May 1533), informing Henry VIII of the date when 'your graces grete matter' will be resolved, and apologising because the liturgical calendar for the week meant it could not happen earlier than Friday.

a deceased brother's widow was forbidden in the Bible, and whether the Pope had any power to suspend this prohibition in particular cases. Three years of anticlerical agitation and fiscal pressure had done their work. The required answers (respectively, yes and no) were given on 5 April, with only a handful of clergymen daring to defy the king. Their last-ditch resistance was led by John Fisher, who was arrested next day (Palm Sunday) to prevent him from preaching against the decisions, and was kept under house arrest until after Anne's coronation in June. This was an era when a well-judged sermon at a critical moment could provoke a riot or even a rebellion, and Cranmer now issued a general ban on preaching.

Armed with the conclusions of Convocation, and shielded by the Act of Appeals, Cranmer summoned Henry and Catherine before him at Dunstable on 10 May to defend the legitimacy of their marriage. The proceedings were relatively simple, as Henry offered no defence and Catherine refused to come. Cranmer annulled the marriage on 23 May and Catherine was consigned to internal exile under the title of 'Princess Dowager', which she refused to accept.

Henry had been unable to give Anne a splendid wedding, but he made up for this with her coronation, on Whit Sunday (1 June) 1533. Although the pamphlet published to record the event insisted on the joyous acclaim of the people, the Imperial ambassador's account suggests at best a sullen acquiescence. The show was spectacular, but it did not win people over. Nor was the coronation an overwhelming success among the aristocracy. Even some peers failed to attend, most notably George Talbot, Earl of Shrewsbury, one of the king's oldest and closest companions (who was represented, in his absence, by his son). Thomas More was deliberately provocative about it. Some of his clerical friends clubbed together and sent him £20 to buy some new clothes and make his peace with the king by turning up to the coronation. He refused their invitation but took their money anyway! A satisfying gesture, no doubt, but perhaps for once his taste for a sharp jest betrayed him. The joke was hardly calculated to soften Henry's heart towards him.

Catherine was not short of friends abroad, however, and her appeal was pressed at Rome, where, in September, the Pope adjudged her marriage to Henry valid, and began to take sanctions against Henry for divorcing her. As Anne had now borne Henry's child (disappointingly for him, another daughter, Elizabeth), it was essential to safeguard the claim to the throne of that child, and of any further offspring. In the meantime, there was also unfinished business with the Holy Maid of Kent. She had predicted, according to one version of her prophecies, that if Henry divorced Catherine, he would lose his throne within six months. Six months to the day since Cranmer had annulled that marriage, Elizabeth Barton was compelled to stand outside St Paul's Cathedral and publicly confess herself a fraud. Was there an element of caution as well as showmanship in the timing?

THE BREAK WITH ROME

Given the Pope's decision to act against Henry, it was essential to undermine and perhaps terminate papal authority in England. At a meeting of the king's council in December 1533, it was decided that henceforward the Pope would be known in England as 'the bishop of Rome', a change in style which obviously belittled papal claims. It is from about this time that imperial motifs become prevalent in Henry's public documents and official propaganda. The traditional English appellations of the king, as 'his highness' and 'his grace', start to be joined by the new formula 'his majesty': 'majesty' was the quality which Roman law attributed to the person and office of the emperor. Hitherto it had been rare in English, and almost unknown in official documents. Appearing for the first time in statutes and proclamations in 1534, 'his majesty' became first common and eventually normative.

The king's vengeance against the Holy Maid of Kent did not end with her humiliation. Early in 1534, an act of attainder was drawn up to condemn her and her supporters for treason. Acts of attainder were statutes hitherto used to confirm the guilt and punishments of notorious traitors – those who had borne arms against the king or who had been convicted of treason in a court of law. However, Thomas Cromwell used them to shortcut due process, simply declaring people guilty of treason and liable to its punishments without the trouble and expense of a trial. Henry was out to make a clean sweep of his opponents. While only a couple of Observant Franciscans were included in the act of attainder, the order as a whole found itself facing Henry's fury. In effect, the English Observant Franciscans were closed down. Their houses were handed either to the ordinary Franciscans or to the Austin Friars, and many of their members fled the country rather than accept their transfer to another rule.

Opposite: Henry VIII in the prime of life. After the celebrated cartoon by Hans Holbein.

Henry also sought to use the act of attainder against his two most prominent opponents. John Fisher, Bishop of Rochester, was included in the bill on the grounds that he had met the Maid and listened to her prophecies without reporting them to the king, an omission here interpreted as 'misprision' (that is, concealment) of treason. His defence, that her prophecies were public knowledge, was perfectly reasonable, but that was not enough to persuade the House of Lords to risk royal displeasure by exempting him from the act. Thomas More was luckier. Canny lawyer that he was, he had been careful to keep the Holy Maid at arm's length when she came to see him, refusing to hear anything about her prophecies. This really was a powerful defence, and the Lords accepted it, removing his name from the bill. Henry was furious, and wanted to go down to Parliament and browbeat the Lords into putting More's name back in, but his councillors, led by More's successor as Lord Chancellor, Thomas Audley, talked him out of it, convincing him that even a personal appearance would not secure More's condemnation, and that the consequent loss of face would be a political catastrophe.

Thomas More had escaped, but not for long. The net began to close with the next major piece of legislation, the Act of Succession, which enshrined in English law the recent alterations in the king's matrimonial arrangements, and required every adult English male to uphold them by swearing a personal oath to the contents of the act. In this extraordinary requirement we can for a moment see what is otherwise concealed from us by the fulsome words of flattering chroniclers and the pompous pleonasms of statutes – the very real nervousness of a king who, driven on by urgent personal and dynastic necessities, was pursuing a revolutionary and plainly unpopular policy. The oath, which included statements prejudicial to papal primacy, was at first administered to select groups: the peers, members of Parliament, courtiers and royal servants. On Friday 17 April it was offered to the clergy of London, and met with a handful of recalcitrants. John Fisher refused it, as did Thomas More, who was called in with the clergy. They were promptly thrown into the Tower. The following Monday, the oath was put before a wider public: the people of London. Nobody refused it. Unanimity may have been fostered by the spectacle of the Holy Maid and a handful of her closest associates being dragged that morning through the streets of the city to Tyburn (roughly where Marble Arch now stands), hanged, cut down and then cut up, before being displayed in crudely butchered pieces on the gates of the city and London Bridge. The man who did this ghastly work, 'a cunning butcher in quartering of men', was himself hanged a few years later for robbery.

Henry's general worries about his own people, whose sympathy for Catherine of Aragon was clear, were accompanied by more specific concerns about powerful noblemen in his domains and the power of the Emperor abroad. The spring of 1534 saw him summon to London the two men who might do most to threaten his position: the Earl of Kildare, the most powerful man in Ireland, and at this point the king's appointed lieutenant governing it; and Lord Dacre, the Warden of the Marches, exercising the king's authority in the far north of England and the man primarily responsible for protecting the kingdom against the Scots. At the same time, he despatched a new and vigorous agent to impose law and order on the traditionally violent and disorderly Welsh Marches, where English government merged into the less clearly defined jurisdictions and social systems of Wales. The general Tudor preoccupation with these three regions (Ireland, Wales and the north) derived chiefly from the fact that they tended to provide so much of the manpower in times of civil war. If there was going to be an internal threat to Henry's regime, it would have to involve one or more of these regions. The governmental interventions of early 1534 were pre-emptive strikes against potential centres of opposition.

Ironically, one of these interventions provoked the very crisis it was trying to pre-empt. The Earl of Kildare's son, Thomas Fitzgerald (known as 'Silken Thomas'), fearing, probably rightly, that his father's summons to London and imprisonment in the Tower heralded a general assault on their family's pre-eminent position in Ireland, raised his standard against Henry VIII. Appealing to the Emperor and the Pope for assistance, he put himself forward as a defender of the Church, beginning the process by which the Catholic faith and incipient Irish nationalism would combine to form a powerful ideology of opposition to English rule. It took Henry's forces two years to restore to Ireland the approximation to peace which generally prevailed there, and much of the rest of the reign was taken up with efforts to extend and strengthen direct royal authority in the island.

The other interventions were more successful. The reign of terror which was implemented in the Welsh Marches by Rowland Lee, Bishop of Coventry and Lichfield, went down in bardic literature as a legendary time of implacable and draconian justice, and paved the way for the full integration of Wales itself into the kingdom of England in 1536, when the English system of shires, justices of the peace, and representation in Parliament was extended to that whole region. Yet perhaps the biggest lesson of the developments in Wales was that they were implemented not by some great peer or magnate but by a bishop, whose political power was derived entirely from office under the Crown. The last major Welsh magnates, the Duke of Buckingham and Rhys ap Griffith, had both been destroyed in the 1520s. The new regime for Wales fostered the emergence there of a gentry class, as in so much of the English south-east, which would look directly to the king for protection and preferment, rather than to traditional baronial intermediaries.

Lord Dacre was put on trial for treason before his peers. The charges were piffling, and mostly revolved around the negotiations with the Scots which any Warden of the Marches had to keep up if a reasonable degree of stability was to be achieved in the frontier zone. He secured an acquittal, a very rare achievement in the annals of Tudor treason trials. The fact that his defence proved convincing shows how gingerly the king had to tread at this time. Not that vindication meant that Dacre kept his job. Henry replaced him anyway. Later Catholic lore handed down a tale that Henry brought him down for fear that he might lead opposition to royal policy in the House of Lords. And it was also rumoured that once Henry had broken with Rome and established the royal supremacy, he asked Dacre what he thought about it, only to receive this reply: 'Hereafter, then, when Your Majesty offendeth, you may absolve yourself.' It is of course unlikely that Lord Dacre dared address his sovereign in such an insolent fashion, but the story may well give us a sense of what a typical Catholic peer really thought of Henry's proceedings. But whatever Dacre thought, Henry had achieved his immediate objective. Although the north was to prove less amenable to Henrician reform than Wales, for now, in 1534, all was quiet.

The Act of Succession of 1534 was not the end of the road. When Parliament reconvened in autumn, it was presented with a still more radical bill to establish the 'royal supremacy' over the Church of England, removing England entirely from the jurisdiction of the Pope, whose authority had been under open attack in England for about a year. More than any of the previous acts, this was seen to be a point of no return. Stephen Gardiner, who voted as a bishop in the House of Lords when the bill was passed, was to recall twenty years later that Parliament 'was with most great cruelty constrained to abolish and put away the primacy from the bishop of Rome'. Henry's supreme headship, 'under Christ' but otherwise without any qualification or restriction, represented the apotheosis of Henry as royal theologian. He was now not only emperor in his own kingdom, but Pope as well. The act was carefully phrased to make it clear that Parliament was recognising a power which already belonged by right to the king, rather than claiming to confer a new power upon him. Various acts in 1534 and 1535 invested him with power to appoint bishops (rather than simply nominate them to the Pope), to reform canon law (although this was never achieved!) and to collect for himself the traditional taxes paid to the Pope (taxes he collected more effectively than any Pope had ever done). Indeed, by an act passed many years later – one which did little more than recognise what was by then political reality – Henry was personally granted the power to define the doctrine of his Church and to amend it as he saw fit. True, he never actually exercised this power, but in theory it gave him powers exceeding even that of papal infallibility. The armchair theologian of the 1520s now sat in the 'cathedra' of the Pope, and was happy, from time to time, to appear in public in this welcome guise.

So attached was Henry from the start to his new title that supporting legislation rapidly followed making it treason to deny his right to it. This, too, caused problems in Parliament, as it was generally seen as making mere words a matter of treason. The Commons managed to insert what they thought was a limiting clause restricting the penalties of treason to those who would 'maliciously' deny the king's supremacy. It was a hollow victory. In the summer of 1535, Thomas More, John Fisher and a handful of Carthusian monks were charged in a series of trials with denying the supremacy. The Carthusians had mostly volunteered their opinions. John Fisher had been induced, perhaps by some simple deception, to give his. Fisher's defence was that his denial of the supremacy was not malicious. The trial judges ruled that the adverb 'maliciously' was describing, rather than qualifying, the action: any denial of the supremacy, they concluded, was by definition malicious. Fisher was convicted easily. Thomas More had been much more careful, and defended himself adeptly in court. His conviction was secured on the testimony, probably perjured, of a single man, Richard Rich. It is of course possible, as so many historians currently seem to think, that Thomas More lied in denying what Rich affirmed. Yet More's defence remains compelling: if he thought so little of oaths as to perjure himself in court, why he should he have baulked at taking oaths to the succession and the supremacy when, even at this late hour, submission would have restored him to favour and fortune?

The victims went to their deaths at intervals from May to July. The Carthusians were treated to the full barbarity of hanging, drawing and quartering. Fisher and More enjoyed the dubious mercy of the king who had once been their friend, and were beheaded. Henry VIII is said to have attended More's execution in disguise. Thomas More's scaffold joke about his beard (he asked the headsman to be careful not to cut it) apparently led Henry to shave off the beard he had sported for years, and go clean-shaven.

The executions of dissidents were part of a twofold strategy of enforcement. The other main thrust was through propaganda, to some extent in print, but even more by the main mass medium of what was still a predominantly oral rather than literate culture – the sermon. The systematic way in which the new theory of royal supremacy over the Church was promulgated is, again, testimony to the clear-headedness of Henry and his ministers about what it was they were doing. The propaganda campaign was certainly unprecedented in English history, in volume and orchestration. Printed books also played their part. Stephen Gardiner, for example, penned the fullest theoretical case for Henry's position in his treatise *On True Obedience*. Published in Latin, however, it was written more for the benefit of a learned readership in Europe than for that of the English people. It was also designed to restore Gardiner to royal favour. In this regard its success was mixed. He was rewarded with appointment as ambassador to the court of the French king. This was prestigious (as well as onerous), but probably also represented an easy way for Thomas Cromwell to keep his main potential rival at a safe distance.

Excerpt from the Treasons Act (1534). This statute provides that 'everie offendour... hereafter laufully convicte of any maner of high treasons... shall lose & forfayte to the kynges highnes his heires and successours all suche landes tenementis and hereditamentis whiche any suche offendour... shall have of any estate of inheritaunce yn use or possessyon, by anye right title or menes, within this realme of Englonde.' The innovation of this act was that it extended its coverage to denial of the royal supremacy (as of any other part of the king's title), which many contemporaries saw as making treason of mere words.

GOD'S WORD AND HENRY'S REFORMATION

Those who shouted loudest in the chorus of denunciation of the Pope were those who had already begun to lean towards the 'evangelical' Protestant teachings coming into the country from Germany and Switzerland. As far as Protestants were concerned, the papacy had already revealed itself to be the Antichrist by its resolute condemnation of their key doctrine, 'justification by faith alone'. The fiery rhetoric ignited by this identification of the Pope as the sworn enemy of Christ and devotee of the devil was extremely useful to Henry, who privately inclined towards this view himself, even though he was as hostile as the Pope to justification by faith alone. He was more than happy to let his preachers off the leash with this idea, and Archbishop Cranmer himself set the trend on Sunday 6 February 1536 with a two-hour tirade denouncing the papal Antichrist. Henry's official publications never invoked the 'papal Antichrist', but the concept was heavily used in the sort of 'arm's length' propaganda issued by royal supporters such as Richard Morison.

Preachers galore jumped on the bandwagon. Heartfelt denunciation of the papacy became for a while the passport to success. From 1534 to 1536, the men whom Henry appointed as bishops in his Church were all drawn from the ranks of the evangelicals. This reflects the influence of his new wife, Anne, who had herself been interested in the persons and the writings of the Protestant reformers since the late 1520s. The best known of these new bishops, Hugh Latimer, Nicholas Shaxton and William Barlow, had in fact been chaplains in her service before their promotion. These bishops in particular, and the evangelical preachers in general, eagerly stretched their new freedom to its utmost, and did as much as they dared to advance their broader Protestant agenda under the cover of establishing the supremacy. Given that many of these men were preaching regularly in the presence of the king, it is hardly to be thought that he was oblivious to their little game. But he probably reckoned he could control the pace of change, and was prepared to pay the price for some talented and unequivocal pulpit support for the supremacy.

It was not only the Protestants who preached the supremacy, though. Conservative clergy, and especially bishops, were expected to show where their true loyalties lay. John Stokesley of London, Cuthbert Tunstall of Durham, John Longland of Lincoln and many lesser figures had to perform at court or at Paul's Cross, publicly committing themselves to the new orthodoxy. At every level of the Church, the message was controlled and pumped out. In June 1535 every parish priest in the country was instructed to preach the royal supremacy to his flock week in, week out; this obligation was reduced a year or so later to preaching on the subject at least twice every three months. The intensity of this preaching campaign reflected not only Henry's nervousness about the reception of the new doctrine, but also the nature of his commitment to it. He did not just like to be obeyed: he liked to be right. It was not enough for him that people accept the supremacy or even that they swear to it (an explicit oath was in fact required only of clergymen). He wanted them to believe it sincerely and without any reservation.

From this time on, the royal supremacy was at the heart of Henry's religious sensibility. As usual with him, the expedient became a matter of conscience, so much so that we should think of his adoption of the royal supremacy not as a cynical ruse, but as a religious conversion. He spoke of it in theological, almost mystical terms. For him, the supremacy was 'the Word of God'. His subjects swiftly adapted to the new habits of thought and speech he required of them, and learned what he liked to hear. Henry Parker, Lord Morley, an old-fashioned aristocrat who often bestowed upon his sovereign the fruits of his limited literary skills, offered him these thoughts in a pamphlet published in 1539:

> Blessed mayest thou be called, Most Christian King Henry the VIII, Supreme Head of the Church of England. Blessed art thou, whom God hath taught to spy out the perilous doctrine of the Bishop of Rome, whereby the people of England are brought from darkness to light, from error to the highway of right knowledge, from danger of death eternal to life that never endeth, to be short, even from Hell to Heaven.

Henry was 'evangelical' about it, and spoke of opening the eyes of his fellow princes to this truth. He fully expected to lead an international movement of princes against the Pope, and opened negotiations with the Schmalkaldic League with a view to this. Unfortunately, the committed Lutheranism of the German princes was, in the end, too much for him to swallow, although his own evangelical advisers, such as Cromwell and Cranmer, did their very best to sugar the pill and tickle it down his throat. When the negotiations finally broke down, in 1538, it was largely because Henry himself looked at what the League was saying about the Mass – the focus of his own attack on Luther back in 1521 – and refused to make any compromise with them. Compromise, for him, meant other people adjusting to his views. When it became apparent that the Schmalkaldic princes were not moving, he simply gave up on them. There was to be no future in England for what Henry regarded as 'the damnable heresy of the Lutheran sect'.

The Act of Supremacy (1534), declaring that 'the kynges maiestie iustely and ryghtfully is & oweth to be the supreme heed of the churche of England'. The act was carefully phrased to make it clear that Parliament was recognising the king's supremacy in the Church, and not conferring it upon him. By letters patent of 15 June 1535, Henry formally added the phrase 'in terra supremum caput Anglicane Ecclesie' to his full 'royal style' or title.

Henry's personal commitment to the royal supremacy explains why the expedient so triumphantly survived, in 1536, the rapid unravelling of the complex web of circumstances which had given rise to it. At the start of the year Catherine of Aragon died, doubtless of natural causes (albeit hastened by grief and ill treatment) rather than of the poison of which rumour was soon whispering. Soon afterwards, Anne Boleyn lost a child through a miscarriage, and her failure to bear the king a son after three years of marriage weakened her hold upon his affections. Within a few months, she would follow Catherine to disgrace and the grave.

The fall of Anne Boleyn was sudden and dramatic. While Henry VIII was sitting and watching May Day jousts at Greenwich, a message was brought to him which caused him to leave the festivities abruptly and grimly. That message purported to bring proof of accusations that Anne was guilty of adultery (a treasonable offence in a queen) which had first been brought to the king's attention a day or two before. Historians still disagree about the truth or falsehood of the allegations (though the consensus is that they were false). But Henry called for an investigation, and became rapidly convinced that they were true. Suspicion ran through the court like ripples in a pond, and some of the king's closest friends were implicated, most notably Sir Henry Norris, the Groom of the Stool and thus the head of Henry's Privy Chamber, responsible for attending on the king's person. Another victim was George Boleyn, Viscount Rochford, Anne's own brother – with whom she was accused of conducting an incestuous affair which not even historians unsympathetic to her claims of innocence tend to credit. Norris and Rochford had been the leading riders in the jousts which Henry left in rage. Anne was arrested the next day, and was tried and executed, like her alleged lovers, within three weeks.

Henry might have been less receptive to the charges against Anne had his eye not already fallen upon a pretty young girl at court, Jane Seymour. His infatuation with her was common knowledge around the court in March. Henry lost no time. On 20 May 1536, the day after Anne's execution, Henry and Jane were betrothed. The wedding took place ten days later. A new Act of Succession soon undid the provisions of its predecessor of 1534, conferring upon Henry, in the absence of heirs by Jane, the power to determine the succession by letters patent or even in his will.

The disappearance from the scene of both Catherine of Aragon and Anne Boleyn might have cleared the way for a reconciliation with Rome. This was certainly how Stephen Gardiner saw things from the distant vantage-point of the French court, where he was Henry's ambassador, and he even started putting out unofficial feelers towards papal diplomats there. Gardiner, however, had read the signals wrongly, and received no encouragement from home. He was fortunate that no word of his dealings came to Henry's ears, as such contacts could very easily have been construed as treason and employed to terminate his career.

But reconciliation of a different kind was afoot. Implicated in her mother's disgrace, Mary Tudor had remained loyal to her mother as long as she lived. Now, though, deprived of her mother's support and perhaps heartened by the sudden elimination of her mother's rival, Anne Boleyn, she was at last induced to conform to her father's will and make her peace with him. Following Thomas Cromwell's helpful advice, she subscribed to the royal supremacy, the repudiation of the papacy, and the 'incestuous and unlawful' nature of her parents' marriage. Even so, the price of his forgiveness was high. Her rehabilitation was completed only when Henry deigned to receive from her a letter couched in terms of repentance and humility befitting an address to the Deity:

> Most humbly prostrate before the feet of your most excellent Majesty, your most humble, faithful and obedient subject, which hath so extremely offended your most gracious Highness, that mine heavy and fearful heart dare not presume to call you father, nor Your Majesty hath any cause by my deserts, saving the benignity of your most blessed nature doth surmount all evils, offences, and trespasses, and is ever merciful and ready to accept the penitent calling for grace, in any convenient time...

Mary's self-abasement secured her return to court and favour – and may even have saved her life. Though the stigma of illegitimacy remained, she would in due course regain her place in the line of succession.

In the meantime, led by Cromwell and Cranmer, the 'evangelicals' continued to make all the running in the Church of England and sowed the seeds of religious change, partly by spreading Protestant ideas at the grass roots (though real Protestants remained in a distinct minority), but more importantly by persuading the king himself to take tentative steps towards a thorough reformation. Three major religious policies were sold to the king during the three years following the executions of Fisher and More: the dissolution of the monasteries, the abolition of pilgrimages and associated practices, and the publication of the Bible in English. Henry took some convincing over the first two, but had always had some sympathy for the third.

If almost anyone in England in 1535 had been told that within five years every monastery, convent and friary in the kingdom would have been closed down and their vast assets transferred to the king, they would never have believed it. Looking back at the process, and especially at its sheer speed, it is easy to conclude that it was the outcome of some master plan. Cardinal Pole later claimed that Thomas Cromwell had bought Henry VIII's favour by promising to make him richer than any previous king of England. Henry himself, looking back from the vantage point of the 1540s, credited himself with extraordinary sagacity and subtlety in implementing a grand plan to close down the monasteries. Yet the story looks very different when seen from the front rather than the back.

The valuation of all Church property which the government organised in 1535 was undertaken not with a view to expropriating the Church, but in order to tax it more effectively now that all Church taxes went to the Crown. The visitation of all the monasteries undertaken in late 1535 and early 1536 was designed to gather material to discredit monks and thus smooth the way for the statute which, in 1536, declared that, unless specifically spared by the king, all religious houses whose gross income was less than £200 a year would be taken into the king's hands, and their occupants either rehoused in other monasteries or else released from their vows to live as priests in the world. Despite the lurid tales which were paraded before members of Parliament, this act went out of its way to praise the moral standards of the larger and wealthier religious houses. This concession, combined with the fact that many poorer houses were in fact spared (usually at some considerable cost in fines and sweeteners) and that all who wished to remain in the religious life were allowed to do so, casts doubt on the idea that, at this point, Henry envisaged the complete abolition of the religious life. Even more decisive evidence to the contrary comes from the fact that Henry himself actually refounded two religious houses – one of monks, the other of nuns – out of the proceeds of this first plunder. Bisham Abbey and the nunnery of Stixwold were re-endowed, re-staffed, and renamed after Henry VIII himself. It might perhaps have been a blind. But it would be unlike Henry to play with large sums of money and to take his own name in vain. The declared aim of his new monasteries was to pray for the welfare in life and the eternal rest after death of himself, of his new wife, Queen Jane Seymour, and of their heirs and ancestors. There is no particular reason to disbelieve him.

The other religious policies first emerged clearly that same year, 1536, and were similarly tentative. Thomas Cromwell secured from the king a grant making him the king's 'vicegerent' (or deputy) in all spiritual and ecclesiastical matters. Armed with viceregal powers in the Church, Cromwell pursued a modestly evangelical agenda, hand in glove with Thomas Cranmer, and much to the dismay of the conservative majority of the clergy. Pulpit disputes became commonplace as theological rivals at every level dismissed each other as 'papists' or 'newfangled fellows'. Things came to a head at the meeting of Convocation (the representative body of the clergy) in the summer. The mainly conservative representatives of the various dioceses compiled a huge list of erroneous doctrines, the 'mala dogmata', which they wished to see condemned, while Cromwell and Cranmer, with a few allies such as Hugh Latimer among the bishops, sought to impose unwelcome religious changes upon them.

With the king's blessing, Cromwell and Cranmer backed a statement of faith, the Ten Articles, drafted by another ally, Bishop Edward Foxe of Hereford, in an attempt to resolve the divisions at Convocation, to foreclose on public disputes and debates over doctrine, and to do so in a way which smuggled in as much quasi-Protestant thinking and terminology as possible. This caused such dissension that it had to be referred to Henry VIII himself for final adjudication. Perhaps thanks to the influence of some powerful conservative clergymen close to the king, chief among them Richard Sampson, the Dean of the Chapel Royal, the Ten Articles as they finally appeared over the king's name were much less radical than they were to start with. While Lutheran buzzwords gave away the origins of the draft, subtle modifications or additions of words and phrases blunted any radical edge in the articles concerned with doctrine. Later articles, concerned with devotional practices such as pilgrimages and prayer to the saints, criticised them in terms of superstition, abuse and excess, but without laying an axe to the trunk of popular religion. The most important feature of the document, in fact, was precisely that it was not simply issued in the name of the king, but phrased as though delivered by him in person. It depended for its authority neither on Convocation, nor on Parliament, nor indeed on the Bible, but purely upon the royal supremacy. However many hands meddled in the drafting, the Ten Articles spoke with the king's voice.

Cromwell was able to put something of the radical edge back onto the Articles by means of his 'Injunctions' (i.e. Instructions) issued to all the clergy of England later that summer. In particular, the Injunctions actively discouraged pilgrimages, the veneration of relics, and the reporting of miracles performed by saints – a complex of beliefs and practices which, often summed up as 'the cult of the saints', was of central importance in the religion of the people. He also instructed parishes to buy a copy of the Bible in English – reversing a prohibition of more than a century's standing. In fact, as only one edition of the English Bible had been printed so far (and abroad at that), and he did not say who was to pay (parish priest or parishioners), this instruction was almost universally ignored. But the very issuing of the instruction was a blow to those conservative clergymen who saw 'English books' (from which most of the 'mala dogmata' had been drawn) as the source of all evil. More importantly still, it unmistakably aligned Cromwell, who issued the Injunctions in his own name, on the basis of the authority committed to him by the king, with the movement of religious innovation. Indeed, one of the foremost members of that movement, William Tyndale, who had translated the New Testament into English, was burned for heresy in the Netherlands that same summer. The message could not have been clearer. Cromwell was on Tyndale's side.

THE PILGRIMAGE OF GRACE

The religious policies of 1536 provoked the great crisis of Henry's reign, the Pilgrimage of Grace, the greatest rebellion ever faced by a Tudor monarch, and in the whole of English history second only to the Peasants' Revolt of 1381 as a popular uprising. The rising started in the context of the visitation of the churches of northern Lincolnshire by Church commissioners implementing Cromwell's Injunctions in September. This visitation, combined with a tour by other commissioners collecting a tax and with the beginning of the dissolution of the monasteries, fuelled apocalyptic rumours about government plans to strip parish churches bare and close down most of what people knew as their religious life. These fears of spiritual and material impoverishment were a potent mixture, and the spark was an inflammatory sermon denouncing the rumoured changes, which was preached on Sunday 1 October 1536 by the local vicar, Thomas Kendall, in the great parish church of Louth, the administrative centre of the region, where clergymen and local notables from miles around had gathered for the visitation. Within days Lincolnshire was up in arms. Henry VIII reacted vigorously and furiously. A proclamation denouncing the disobedience of the rebels was circulated, and troops were rapidly called up under the command of the Duke of Suffolk. As this royal army marched on Lincoln, the rebels quickly calmed down, and were dispersed with some easy promises of amnesty.

All seemed well, and the royal army itself started to disperse. But then it became apparent that, beyond the fog of events in Lincolnshire, still worse things were afoot in the north. While the government had focused its attention on Lincolnshire, revolt had spread like wildfire through the six counties of northern England. Popular and clerical risings recruited the support of the gentry and even of some peers, notably Lord Darcy. A rebel force, organised as though it was an army, concentrated around the royal castle of Pontefract, which became its headquarters. It was, in effect, the English army of the north, for the most part led by the same families, and often by the same individuals, who had commanded the English forces against the Scots at Flodden Field in 1513. Adopting as its badge the Five Wounds of Christ (the wounds he received at the crucifixion) and calling itself, in the solemn oath which bound together its adherents, the 'Pilgrimage of Grace for the Commonweal', it looked remarkably like a crusade (usually defined among historians as 'an armed pilgrimage'). With other large rebel groups gathered at Carlisle and elsewhere, almost all England north of the Trent was under the control of the Pilgrims through the autumn of 1536. Their grievances were voiced at a representative assembly, and were consolidated into a list of demands which began with a call for reconciliation with Rome, went on with the reversal of recent religious changes and the restoration of suppressed monasteries, included a number of material demands relating to taxation and land law and, most threateningly, emphasised the need to eliminate the king's 'low-born' councillors, who were tactfully blamed for everything the Pilgrims hated. Foremost among these villains was of course Thomas Cromwell, but Cranmer and Latimer were not far behind in the rebel demonology.

We learn a great deal about Henry from the way he dealt with this broad-based challenge to his entire regime. The idea of resorting to concessions or compromise was inconceivable for him. His young wife, Jane, made her only venture into politics at this moment, begging Henry on bended knee to reverse his policy towards the monasteries. Henry pulled her roughly to her feet and warned her not to meddle in things which were not her concern, reminding her of the fate of her predecessor. Instead of holding out the prospect of concessions, Henry launched against the northern rebels a proclamation still sterner than that issued for Lincolnshire, and his instructions to the Duke of Norfolk were for direct military action and dire vengeance. The Pilgrims actually reopened some of the monasteries suppressed earlier that year, and Henry took this as a particular affront. He ordered Norfolk to hang some of the offending monks from the steeple of their own church. What irritated Henry more than anything was the presumption of the Pilgrims in telling him whom he should or should not have on his Privy Council. He told them in no uncertain terms that nobility was what he wanted it to be, that if he chose someone for his council that was a greater honour than any inherited rank, and that in any case his council had an ample supply of the well-born nobles whom the rebels claimed it lacked: and with

Opposite: Henry VIII in council. The king sits enthroned beneath a 'cloth of estate' expressing his royal rank.

King Henry the eyght.

men like Norfolk, Suffolk and Shrewsbury among his councillors, he had a point – although of course everybody, including the rebels, knew that Cromwell mattered more on the council than all the others put together.

Had it not been for the tactful diplomacy of the Duke of Norfolk on the ground in Yorkshire, Henry's personal intransigence might have cost him his throne. For if Norfolk had followed early royal instructions and given battle to the rebels with his inferior force, he might have been cut to pieces, in which case the road south would have lain open to a force which had tasted blood, gone too far to consider retreat, and learned that the king would not listen. In the event, Norfolk persuaded the king that negotiation was the only realistic policy, although even the non-committal concessions which he offered were probably more than Henry would have liked him to make. He guaranteed them a full and free pardon if they dispersed, and promised that the king would listen to their grievances. The fact that they believed him helps us to understand the success of the English Reformation in particular, and of the Tudor regime in general. The Pilgrims were convinced that Henry was essentially one of them, conservative in religion and politics alike, and they were thoroughly indoctrinated with the ideology of monarchy, which had long been ingrained into the English mind by the common law and the Church, and which the Tudors, trading heavily on the memory of the uncertainties of the Wars of the Roses, had made indispensable to the general sense of the viability of the social order. The fact was that Henry himself was irreversibly committed to the revolutionary policies of the 1530s, and the only way to reverse them was to remove him from the throne. This solution was simply beyond the mental horizon of the Pilgrims.

Henry reluctantly accepted Norfolk's *fait accompli*. But when an unstable northern knight, Sir Francis Bigod (ironically, one of the few northerners sympathetic to religious change and really enthusiastic for the royal supremacy), attempted for reasons of his own to raise the standard of rebellion anew early in 1537, Henry was quick to seize the chance for revenge. The embers of revolt were stamped out in fact by many of the local gentry who had themselves risen the previous autumn. But Henry reckoned this betrayal released him from the promises Norfolk had made in his name. He ordered exemplary executions across the north, and had the ringleaders of the original Pilgrimage brought to London for trial and execution. It was not justice, but it was a brutal display of power. Henry would see no further rebellions in England.

The politics of 1536 were certainly the most complex of any year of Henry's reign, and the year itself has as good a claim as any to be considered 'the' crucial year of the reign – more because of what did not happen than because of what did. Most importantly, it did not see Anne Boleyn bear a son, a failure which played a large part in her downfall. Her fall, in turn, might have meant the end for the men who had done so much to put her on the throne, Cromwell and Cranmer – but they survived and even came out of the debacle ahead. With Catherine of Aragon and Anne Boleyn both dead, many conservatives, such as Stephen Gardiner in his virtual exile at the French court, hoped for a rapprochement with Rome. Their hopes were in vain. Cranmer and Cromwell, having survived, might in their turn have hoped for a more decisive lurch towards the religious policies of the Reformation, but Henry himself drew back and curbed them. Finally, the great rebellion of autumn 1536, the Pilgrimage of Grace, might have reversed his policy by main force, indeed, might have cost him his throne. It did neither, and Henry emerged stronger than ever. 1536 was one of the most indecisively decisive years in English history. What it showed about Henry was his reluctance to go back.

REFORMATION AND REACTION

Instead of reversing Henry's policies, the Pilgrims had if anything only managed to entrench them. There was no way Henry could even consider going back without looking as though he was bowing to pressure. Cromwell and Cranmer therefore managed to advance the cause of religious change. Smaller monasteries continued to be closed down, and royal fury at monastic involvement in the Pilgrimage accelerated the process. Some were taken into the king's hands by forfeiture on the grounds that their abbots had been guilty of treason. Others voluntarily surrendered into the king's hands for fear of the same charge. Henry had been infuriated by the involvement of monks and friars in the Pilgrimage, and from this time showed no love for the 'religious life'. 1537 saw the compilation of a new, full statement of the doctrine of the Church of England, the product of lengthy and often fraught discussions between representatives of the conservative and the evangelical factions among the higher clergy. Under normal circumstances, this was the sort of project into which Henry would have thrown himself with enthusiasm. However, he had more pressing concerns even than religion. His new queen was expecting their first child, and Henry was too excited to worry about catechisms. Jane bore him a son on 12 October, and the new book, the *Institution of a Christian Man*, was handed to him for approval around the same time. Preoccupied with the delights of fatherhood, he simply nodded it through. However, rather than issue it in his own name, he had it set forth in the name of the bishops (it was commonly known as the Bishops' Book), and only for a trial period of three years. When, later, he found time to examine the book in detail, he found much to cavil at.

The christening of Edward on 15 October – the last christening of an English prince to be conducted amid the full ceremonies of the Catholic liturgy – was one of the high moments of Henry's life. God seemed to be smiling on him, and not even the tragic death of Jane Seymour from complications following a difficult birth could cast a shadow over his joy. Reconciliation within the royal family was symbolised by the role of his elder daughter, Mary, as Edward's godmother. Archbishop Cranmer was one godfather, and the Dukes of Norfolk and Suffolk also enjoyed this distinction.

Cromwell and Cranmer continued to press on with religious change, and in 1538 Henry was persuaded to go a little further down the road of replacing the saint-based piety of late medieval Christianity with the Bible-based religion of Protestantism.

Page from *The Institution of a Christian Man* showing corrections made by Henry VIII in his own hand. Henry relishes his opportunity to add relentless detail and exhaustive clarity to the repudiation of papal pretensions.

Customs such as going on pilgrimage to shrines which held the wonder-working relics or images of saints, or of lighting votive candles before images, were abruptly redefined as idolatry. This radical shift was facilitated by the fact that the Bishops' Book had re-edited and re-numbered the traditional Ten Commandments to bring them into line with the version favoured by some Protestant reformers and thus to give more prominence to the divine prohibition against the making and worshipping of 'graven images'. To drive the point home, the great shrines of England were closed down in a nationwide campaign that summer. The relic of Christ's blood at Hailes in Gloucestershire was brought to London and publicly burned, as was the great statue of Our Lady which had been venerated for centuries at Walsingham in Norfolk.

The campaign culminated at the end of September with the destruction of perhaps England's most famous shrine, that of St Thomas at Canterbury. It had been a hard job to convince Henry VIII to sanction the iconoclasm of 1538. Hugh Latimer later commented on how difficult it had been to persuade the king to take down the Holy Blood of Hailes. But the destruction of the shrine of St Thomas showed that the king had identified himself wholeheartedly with the iconoclastic policy. Henry came to preside in person at the ceremonies on 8 September, which included the burning of Thomas's bones and the staging of a play by John Bale, a former friar turned zealous reformer, which turned on its head the traditional tale of Thomas's death. The burning was followed up by a proclamation which denied St Thomas's claims to sanctity and martyrdom, denounced him as a traitor, and decreed that his feast days (there were three) were to be deleted from the calendar of the Church of England. Henceforth, St Thomas of Canterbury, martyr, was to be known as Thomas Becket, traitor.

Henry's growing disenchantment with the religious orders was symbolised by the burning of Friar John Forest. Forest was an Observant Franciscan, a member of the order which had resisted Henry in the early 1530s more steadfastly than any other group, and he had for a while served as confessor to Catherine of Aragon. Now he was condemned for both treason and heresy (he was the only Roman Catholic ever to be formally condemned for heresy by the Church of England) and was executed in a spectacularly gruesome fashion, hanging in chains over a pyre fuelled by a sacred wooden image fetched all the way from Wales. The combination of hanging and burning, first designed for Lollard rebels in the reign of Henry V, drew attention to the dual character of his offence. Other public gestures that year demonstrated Henry's new-found hatred for monasticism. The bishop of London was charged in the King's Bench with the offence of 'praemunire' (a variety of treason, essentially that of seeking to implement a foreign jurisdiction within the king's domains) on the grounds that he had conducted the liturgical ceremony at which a monk made his final vows. The bishop was let off with a token fine, but the point was clear: no more monks and nuns were to be recruited in England. The 'voluntary' surrender of religious houses seen in the wake of the Pilgrimage of Grace was extended to monasteries which had not in any way offended against the law, and Henry's own two recent foundations, at Bisham and Stixwold, both surrendered into the king's hands. As if to confirm that he had in fact decided to close down all religious houses, in spring 1538 Henry issued a public denial of the widespread rumours to that effect. The process of suppression would not be complete until 1540, but its progress was inexorable.

The high tide of evangelical influence in Henry's Church of England was reached with the publication under royal patronage of the English Bible. Despite the traditional association of vernacular scripture with Lollardy, and its recent association with Lutheranism, Henry had always had some sympathy for it in principle. He had said as much in the early 1520s, in the open letter in which he urged the Dukes of Saxony to silence Luther. It was, after all, an idea which had been made fashionable by Erasmus before Luther appeared on the public stage. However, Henry and his bishops had laboured to suppress Tyndale's translation of the New Testament in the later 1520s, and it was only after the break with Rome, when so many conventional ecclesiastical attitudes were called into question, that the English Bible became practical politics. Both Cromwell and Cranmer were strongly in favour. Henry himself seems to have been convinced partly by the logic of the royal supremacy and partly by its rhetoric. Logically, in breaking with Rome, the Bible was the only alternative source of Christian authority to which appeal could credibly be made. This made the case for vernacular scripture difficult to resist. And in practice Henry

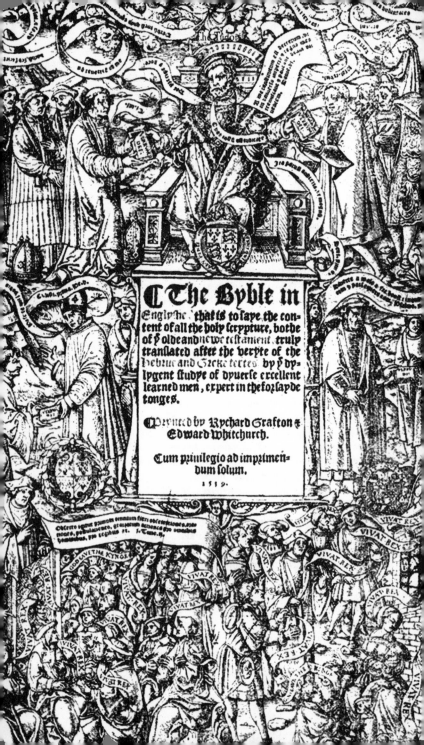

¶ The Byble in
Englyſhe: that is to ſaye the con=
tent of all the holy ſcrypture, bothe
of ÿ olde and newe teſtament, truly
tranſlated after the veryte of the
hebrue and Greke textes by ÿ dy=
lygent ſtudye of dyuerſe excellent
learned men, expert in the forſayde
tonges.

¶ Prynted by Rychard Grafton ꝫ
Edward Whitchurch.

Cum priuilegio ad impꝛimen=
dum ſolum.

1539.

VIII's preachers and propagandists appealed endlessly to the Bible, especially the Old Testament, to establish the authority of kings in general, and their authority over priests in particular. The 'Word of God' was invoked against the 'human traditions' of the Bishop of Rome. Indeed, it was in the 1530s that the description of the Bible as the 'Word of God' became current in English, largely because of its adoption in royal propaganda. The Word of God was regarded as a lesson in obedience: Henry's favourite virtue (in others). As John Bale put it in *King John*, a play celebrating Henry's triumph over the clergy:

> If Your Grace would cause God's Word to be taught sincerely,
> And subdue those priests that will not preach it truly,
> The people should know to their prince their lawful duty.

Parish churches were instructed to obtain English Bibles in the injunctions of 1536 and again in those of 1538. But although copies had been printed abroad in 1535 and 1537, it was not until 1539 that they became easily available. For that year saw the appearance of the 'Great Bible', financed by Cromwell, edited by Miles Coverdale, and published by Richard Grafton and Edward Whitchurch. Several editions followed over the next few years, with a lengthy preface by Cranmer added in 1540. Royal approval for the 'Great Bible' was vividly symbolised by the frontispiece (sometimes mistakenly attributed to Holbein), which showed Henry VIII handing out the 'Word of God' to Cromwell and Cranmer for distribution to his grateful priests and people.

Even as the tide of religious change reached its height, circumstances were shifting at home and abroad. At home, the relaxation of pressure against heresy in the 1530s had fostered the emergence of one heresy Henry could not abide: 'sacramentarianism', denial of the real presence of Christ in the sacrament of the eucharist. Abroad, the destruction of the shrine of St Thomas had shocked Catholic Europe, and an outbreak of peace between France and Spain gave the Pope the chance to excommunicate Henry anew, with fair hope of seeing the sentence executed by the newly reconciled continental powers. Henry's response was twofold. First, he invested heavily in defence, especially coastal forts, many of which were built or rebuilt out of materials recycled from suppressed monasteries. Men were mustered for possible military service throughout the land. In summer 1539, Henry lorded it over a magnificent march-past of the mustered men of London, equipped in new uniforms of fine white cloth (at their own expense! – those who could not afford the uniform were not allowed to take part).

In addition, the king put the brake on religious change, most notably by presiding, in another dramatic personal intervention, at the show trial of a sacramentarian, John

Opposite: Title page of the first edition of the 'Great Bible', 1539. Enthroned as God's vicar, Henry symbolically hands out the Word of God to the spiritual and temporal hierarchies of his realm, headed respectively by Cranmer on his right and by Cromwell on his left. The preacher (bottom left) proclaims what was for Henry the Bible's chief message: 'Obey the prince...', and his grateful subjects, duly enlightened, chorus 'Long live the king'.

Lambert, on 16 November 1538. Vested symbolically in white, Henry presided while his bishops disputed with Lambert in an effort to change his mind. Finally, Henry himself argued with him and urged him to recant, all to no avail. He personally ordered Cromwell to sentence Lambert to the stake, and that same day he issued a proclamation upholding traditional doctrines of the eucharist and of baptism against recent innovations. Even his more reformist bishops loathed the 'Anabaptists' (upholders of adult rather than infant baptism). But it was Henry himself who added the word 'sacramentaries' to the draft proclamation, thus potentially sweeping in many of the reformist bishops' friends. Some Dutch Anabaptists were burned a week after Lambert, to show that the proclamation meant business.

Among the bishops who assisted at Lambert's trial were two whose stars had been waning since the break with Rome, but who were now returning to favour. Stephen Gardiner had, at long last, been recalled from his three-year mission to France, and the bishop of Durham, Cuthbert Tunstall, also made himself useful as the king cast around for willing helpers in the suppression of heresy. Gardiner and Tunstall appealed to the more conservative side of the king's character, and were prominent in manoeuvres which led, in spring 1539, to the passage of the Act of Six Articles against sacramentarianism and one or two other religious bugbears of the king's, notably the marriage of priests. Henry's hand can be seen in the draconian sweep of this act, which enjoined burning as the penalty for a first offence (traditional heresy law in England had allowed for escape by recantation for first offenders). Under these fierce new powers, a vigorous campaign against heresy was launched in London in the king's name. At the same time, Henry made a show of observing traditional Church ceremonies in 1539, making sure that foreign ambassadors came along to see. They duly reported home that Henry was Catholic about everything except the Pope and the plunder of the clergy. As most kings might find themselves in conflict with the Pope from time to time, and were often obliged to tap the wealth of the Church, Henry now seemed much less alien than before.

While the Pope was proceeding against Henry VIII on account of his pillaging of shrines and monasteries, Henry initiated proceedings of his own against the English relatives of Cardinal Reginald Pole, who was entrusted with the task of implementing papal sanctions against the king. Evidence against those involved in the so-called 'Exeter conspiracy' was elicited from Sir Geoffrey Pole, the rather suggestible younger brother of the cardinal, in exchange for his life. The victims executed in December included the Marquis of Exeter (Pole's cousin), Henry, Lord Montague (Pole's brother) and Sir Edward Neville (brother to Lord Abergavenny and a prominent courtier). They were belatedly followed in February 1539 by Sir Nicholas Carew, the Master of the King's Horse. Terror rather than justice was the object. Unable to get at Cardinal Pole, Henry had to make do with destroying his family – and thus thinning the ranks of possible non-Tudor claimants to the throne. The element of sheer vengeance in all this is seen in the treatment of the cardinal's mother, the aged Margaret, Countess of Salisbury (a niece of Edward IV). Condemned in 1539 in an act of attainder which wrapped up condemnations of a host of Henry's enemies (both living and dead) she was kept in the Tower until 1541, when she was executed on 27 May. Executions such as these made it clear that no one, however nobly born, was above the law, and no one, however powerful, was secure from the wrath of the prince. No English king ever shed more noble blood than Henry VIII. Where his father had taken their money, Henry took their lives, and often on equally flimsy pretexts. As much as his father, he deserved the fully-fledged baronial revolt that he never faced. The fact that neither of them faced it is an index of how English politics was changing.

THE FALL OF CROMWELL

The increasing influence of conservative churchmen around Henry was an implicit threat to the dominance of Thomas Cromwell, who strove to counter it by pursuing his own favourite policy: alliance with the Protestant princes of Germany. A somewhat flattering portrait by Hans Holbein helped him convince Henry to take a new bride from one of those princely dynasties, that of the Duke of Cleves. The marriage which might have saved Cromwell's career actually ended it. Although Henry's marriage to Anne of Cleves was celebrated on 6 January 1540, it was never consummated. Henry found his new wife unattractive, and the embarrassment of impotence in her company led him to reject with equal ferocity the marriage and its architect. Worked on by the Duke of Norfolk and Bishop Stephen Gardiner, who at some point waved before his eyes the shapely person of the duke's teenage niece, Catherine Howard, Henry set in motion the wheels of divorce. Vengeful as ever, the full force of his wrath fell upon Cromwell, who as recently as April 1540 had been rewarded with elevation to the earldom of Essex.

Anne of Cleves, wife number four. Henry VIII aggrievedly observed that she was not as attractive as he had been led to believe, leaving him unable to consummate the marriage.

The decade of revolution in Henry's reign was brought to a close by Thomas Cromwell's dramatic arrest in the Council Chamber on 10 June 1540. The pace of religious change had already slowed almost to a halt, and the debacle of the Cleves marriage temporarily reduced Cromwell's credibility to zero. That window of opportunity was all his enemies needed to persuade the king that he had been fomenting heresy and meditating treason. The latter charge was of course absurd, but there was enough substance in the former, and the reliable Richard Rich was as willing as ever to see to the legal niceties. Cromwell was convicted by attainder without trial – a crime which was ironically suited to the punishment he had so often meted out to others – and went to his death on 28 July 1540 protesting his loyalty and his orthodoxy (although his confession of belief in fact included nothing which a convinced Lutheran could not have said in perfect good faith).

The fall of Cromwell precipitated one of the defining achievements of the reign of Henry VIII, the formal establishment of the Privy Council as a department of government. Although in some ways a traditional institution (kings had always had their councils), and although in others a creation of Thomas Cromwell's (the name 'Privy Council' first appears in the 1530s, notably when Henry VIII was refuting the Pilgrims' charge that he was surrounded with baseborn, evil councillors), the Privy Council only came into its own with Cromwell's fall. Henry never again allowed one man to dominate policy as Wolsey and Cromwell had done in their day. The Privy Council was to become the primary instrument for the formulation and execution of the sovereign's will for the next century or so. In the immediate term, its significance perhaps lay more in the new rules of courtly precedence which were associated with it. Although men of noble birth were frequently recruited to the council and held high office under the Crown, and although gentlemen who worked their way up to the council in royal service were often rewarded with peerages, Henry VIII laid down rules by which the highest officers of royal government and household as such took precedence over nobles, whatever their rank. This was in effect to underline the point he had made to the Pilgrims in 1536, that nobility derived from and depended upon the Crown, and that its ultimate criterion was not so much birth as service to the king.

On 8 August 1540, less than a fortnight after Cromwell's execution, Henry VIII married Catherine Howard. Unfortunately for Norfolk and Gardiner, the weapon which they had deployed against Cromwell was, though powerful, unstable, and in the end blew up in their faces. Catherine may have inflamed the passion of the middle-aged king, but his feelings were not entirely reciprocated. During their summer progress in 1541, which for the first and only time in the reign took the royal household to the north (reaching York by way of Lincoln, Gainsborough and Pontefract), she began to hanker for the company of one of her old friends and suitors, Thomas Culpeper, a Gentleman of the Privy Chamber. Their nocturnal assignations were relatively discreet, and although it would only have been a matter of time, they had not in fact become lovers when the court returned to the south in autumn. They were not to get the chance. It was shortly after Henry VIII's return to Hampton Court that Archbishop Cranmer shared with his sovereign, by means of a

Catherine Howard, the fifth wife, who was not entirely satisfied by the attentions of her aging husband.

Catherine Parr, Henry's last wife. Thanks to Queen Catherine's comfortable relationship with Henry, her quiet sympathy for the cause of 'evangelical' (i.e. Protestant) religion helped retain for it some breathing space in the otherwise hostile religious atmosphere of Henry's declining years.

tactful letter, some extremely disturbing news: namely, that Catherine had enjoyed intimate sexual relationships with two young men before her marriage to Henry. Her frank confession of the youthful indiscretions which a delicate but thorough investigation soon brought to light might just have saved her. But once the hounds caught the scent of her summer dalliance with Culpeper, her fate was sealed. They had not become lovers, but her record made it impossible to credit the innocence of their intentions (which they made no attempt to maintain). Catherine was condemned for treason by act of attainder, and was beheaded on 13 February 1542. The act included a declaration that it was treason for a woman to marry the king if she had had premarital sex. As the Imperial ambassador caustically observed, this rather narrowed the field.

It was a year and a half later, on 12 June 1543, that Henry took his sixth and last wife, Catherine Parr, a mature but still relatively young widow (it was premarital sex, not previous marriage, that constituted treason), the sister of one of his Privy Councillors, William Parr. It is worth remarking that, for all Henry's claims of excellent sexual health at the time of his marriage to Anne of Cleves in 1540, neither of his last two wives became pregnant by him. Yet Catherine Parr, who was to marry Thomas Seymour with almost indecent haste after the king's death, was soon with child by her third husband. Henry's health was generally worsening throughout the 1540s. He was persistently troubled by a festering sore in his leg, and was massively overweight. It was in this context that, in 1544, Henry put through his final Act of Succession, which established the succession, in order, on Edward, Mary and Elizabeth, tacitly passed over the Scottish line of the Stuarts, descended from his elder sister, Margaret, and provided that, in the event of his own line failing, the succession should pass to the heirs of his younger sister, Mary, who had married the Duke of Suffolk.

THE LATTER YEARS

To speak of a foreign policy holiday through the 1530s would be an exaggeration, as English ambassadors criss-crossed Europe seeking alliances, trying to forestall papal countermeasures, and spreading Henry's new gospel of royal supremacy. But Henry's policies had put him into virtual isolation, and for years he was all but irrelevant to the rivalry between the Habsburg and Valois monarchies, which was the central axis of European affairs. In 1538, when he ceased to be an irrelevance, it was only so as to become a potential target. But some well-timed displays of religious conservatism had helped avert that danger. Now, in the 1540s, his dynastic problems had been resolved, and the pace of religious change had been slowed almost to a standstill. In addition, the consequent tensions in English politics had been relaxed thanks to the destruction of Cromwell, and the plunder of the Church had made him richer than any previous English king. Henry was once more in a position to contemplate a return to his overriding political ambition: that of conquests in France. The monarchy was very different after the turmoil of the 1530s. But the monarch was very much the same, even if he had added some new ideas to the old ones.

The military campaigns of the 1540s were in some ways a replay of those of the 1510s. However, this time Henry decided to deal with the threat of Scottish intervention by a pre-emptive strike. Diplomatic pressure and border incidents of increasing ferocity culminated in English military action which was as politically decisive in the long term as it was tactically futile at the time. The Duke of Norfolk was entrusted with the task of chastising the Scots in October 1542, but his raid was a fiasco, and probably cost the raiders more than their victims. Norfolk's stock sank: the hero of 1536 now looked something of a clown, and Henry would look elsewhere for military leadership in future. However, the Scottish riposte was the customary catastrophe. A huge force of Scots underwent a crushing defeat at Solway Moss (November 1542). Where James IV had died in battle, James V died from the shock on hearing of the scale of the defeat. Now, inspired by the imperial rhetoric of the royal supremacy and by the knowledge of traditional English claims to sovereignty over Scotland which had been unearthed in the course of researching that supremacy, Henry went fully onto the offensive against Scotland. He demanded the new queen of Scots, the infant Mary, as a bride for Prince Edward, to unite the crowns in perpetuity. Initially, the Scots conceded the demands in the Treaty of Greenwich (1 July 1543), but the kaleidoscopic rotations of Scottish politics soon saw the treaty repudiated. As Henry prepared for war with France, a second, punitive strike against Scotland was planned. It was not to Norfolk that Henry turned this time, however, but to Edward Seymour, Earl of Hertford and uncle to Prince Edward, whose honour had thus been injured. In May 1544 he attacked Edinburgh by land and sea, devastating the Lowlands. Returning laden with plunder, Seymour's stock rose as Norfolk's had fallen.

With the Scots knocked out of the war, Henry trained his sights on France. Several years of assiduous diplomacy had restored the traditional Anglo-Imperial axis, and in the previous year Henry had already provided troops to fight for Charles V in the Netherlands. Now, despite his declining health – the problems in his legs alone would have immobilised a lesser man – Henry VIII crossed the Channel for the fourth and last time in July 1544, once more bent on conquest. He was no longer in a position to lead his men in battle, so he established a central command in Calais while two armies sallied forth against the French. The first, under the Duke of Norfolk, laid siege in vain to Montreuil. The second, under the Duke of Suffolk, successfully laid siege to Boulogne, taking it in September. Norfolk's stock continued its fall. The campaign of 1544 expired when, as before in the 1510s, Henry was suddenly let down by his ally, who made a separate peace at Crépy just days after the fall of Boulogne. At least Henry came away with something.

A more welcome lesson learned in the 1540s was the absolute importance to English security of a strong navy. Henry himself was perhaps more interested in his ships as an offensive force, or at least as a display of might. But even if glory and display were his aims, Henry's concern with and expenditure on the navy were vindicated in 1545. Having made peace with Charles V, Francis I attempted to turn the tables on Henry by invading across the Channel. But his fleet was beaten back from the Isle of Wight in a naval action second only to the defeat of the Spanish Armada in the annals of Tudor seamanship, but now, somewhat unfairly, remembered chiefly for the foundering of the *Mary Rose* before she had even left the harbour approaches. (The over-gunning of the *Mary Rose*, which contributed to its foundering, is somehow typical of Henry, both in the boundless and groundless faith in his own ingenuity which caused him to interfere in the design and refitting of the ship, and in the naïve faith that more is always better which flawed the design itself.) This setback to the French was the first of many which would frustrate enemies over the next 400 years, as increasing naval strength rendered England increasingly secure from invasion. Politically and militarily, the campaigns of 1545 blooded the new generation of Tudor statesmen and commanders. Around 100,000 men were mobilised at home against the threat of invasion. John Russell (Lord Russell) commanded by land, and the rising star John Dudley (Lord Lisle) by sea. Seymour, at first entrusted with the defence of Boulogne, was later in 1545 once more unleashed against the Scots.

The fall of Cromwell was to some extent a result of the halting of religious changes in the later 1530s, and it seemed to open the way to a reversal of those changes. In the event, Henry was characteristically reluctant to retreat. The tone for the remainder of his reign was set by the black humour of 30 July 1540, two days after Cromwell's execution, when Henry sent six dissidents to their deaths. Three of them (Edward Powell, Thomas Abel and Richard Featherstonehaugh) were Catholic priests who had spent years in the Tower after supporting Catherine of Aragon and refusing the oaths of succession and supremacy. The other three were Protestant preachers (Robert Barnes, William Jerome and Thomas Garrett) who had enjoyed royal patronage in the 1530s and had been zealous in promoting the supremacy. None had been tried in a court of law: an act of attainder spared the expense of a trial. They were drawn to their deaths in pairs, a Catholic and a Protestant side by side on a hurdle, the Catholics to be hanged and butchered, the Protestants to be burned at the stake. The point was unmistakable. The fact that Henry was not prepared to tolerate heresy did not for one moment mean that he was going to compromise on the royal supremacy.

It was around this time that Henry turned his attention to the official doctrinal position of his Church, giving close personal scrutiny to the Bishops' Book which he had approved on a temporary basis in 1537. He was far from happy with the tone of much of it, and engaged in a vigorous debate with Cranmer and others about how it should be amended. Eventually, it was handed over to a select committee of bishops and theologians for revision. Their revisions were almost all of a markedly conservative character, in accordance with the clear wishes of the king. For example, they reiterated traditional teachings on the eucharist, and left rather more room than the Bishops' Book had done for the intercession of the saints and prayer for the dead. The outcome of their labours was published in 1543 as *A Necessary Doctrine and*

Erudition for any Christian Man (and was given statutory backing by the Act for the Advancement of True Religion later that year). It was commonly known as the 'King's Book', because it was described on the title page as 'set forth by the king's majesty', and had a preface written by him. Henry was as happy as ever to play the theologian, preening himself on his efforts 'to purge and cleanse our realm' from 'hypocrisy and superstition', and reproving his subjects for their 'inclination to sinister understanding of scripture, presumption, arrogancy, carnal liberty and contention'.

Henry's ecclesiastical policy in the 1540s combined the repression of heresy, especially sacramentarian heresy, with some mild measures of reform and continued plunder of the Church. Having disposed of the monasteries, he turned his attention to the collegiate churches, first picking them off piecemeal by 'surrender' and later passing a statute (1545) permitting him to dissolve ecclesiastical institutions at will. In addition, he carried on cherry-picking houses and estates from his bishops by means of exchanges which were distinctly to his advantage. Thanks to methods such as these, by the end of the reign he had more houses than he knew what to do with. Such reform as transpired was mainly the work of his archbishop, Thomas Cranmer, who was continually proposing alterations designed to edge the Church of England a little closer towards the Protestantism of Europe without alarming Henry about heresy. Thus he was able to persuade Henry to sanction an English version of the Litany (prayers of general intercession) in 1544, and next year to follow this with a complete English prayer book, or 'primer', for private use. The way in which he sold this policy to the king can be seen from the prayer book's preface, written in Henry's name. Here, the king proclaimed his confidence that this new book would help his subjects learn their 'duties to God, their king, and their neighbour'. Placing himself between God and neighbour, he showed not only his sense of his own special place in the order of creation, but also his complacent assumption of the viability of his peculiar ecclesiastical compromise. If there was any kind of direction in the development of English religion in these years it was not so much towards Protestantism as, precisely, towards a more English religion.

The religious fissures which had opened among English élites during the 1530s assumed considerable importance in politics after Cromwell. Court faction, which at its extreme became a matter of life and death for the leading players, took religion as its badge. The combination of political rivalry with theological division was a powerful mixture under a suspicious and religious king. The evangelicals regained some ground thanks to the indiscretions of Catherine Howard, and benefited further from Henry's last marriage, as Catherine Parr herself developed evangelical sympathies. In 1543 Bishop Gardiner sought to destroy his great rival, the evangelical Archbishop Cranmer, by gathering evidence that he was fostering heresy in Kent. But Henry refused the bait, and Cranmer survived. A counter-coup in 1544 sought to implicate Gardiner in treason, but he likewise survived – although his nephew and secretary, Germain Gardiner, went to the block. Henry himself sought to stand above this endemic factional strife by adopting a pose of Olympian loftiness. He attached more and more importance to the rhetoric of the 'middle way', and in his public pronouncements, most notably in an address to Parliament in December 1545, he presented himself as the honest broker, as the wise Solomon protecting his Church from the squabbles of its own bishops and preachers, of whom, he said, invoking a recent scholarly proverb, 'some be too stiff in their old Mumpsimus, others be too busy and curious in their new Sumpsimus'.

In 1546 Henry's declining health signalled that his reign was drawing to a close. Factional struggle intensified. Summer saw the conservatives in the ascendant. Anne Askew, a gentlewoman with connections to Catherine Parr and the court, was convicted of the sacramentarian heresy which Henry abominated, and the Lord Chancellor, Thomas Wriothesley, personally set his hand to the rack in his desperation to extract information which would compromise evangelical rivals at court. But Anne gave him nothing of value. She was burned, along with a number of other heretics, in the presence of the Lord Chancellor and the Duke of Norfolk. Meanwhile, the bishop of London, Edmund Bonner, was striking fear into the heart of London's small but growing minority of Protestants, and heretical books were being burned as late as the end of September.

THE LAST DAYS

By autumn, the pendulum was swinging the other way. The Duke of Norfolk's son, Henry Howard (Earl of Surrey), was foolish enough to flaunt his Plantagenet ancestry by quartering the royal arms into his own heraldic bearings – an act easily portrayed as treason in the charged atmosphere of the dying king's court. The Howards' rivals pounced, and the duke and the earl were both charged with treason, the earl for the act itself, and his father for not informing against him. The case rested, interestingly enough, on the powers of visitation and enquiry into heraldic bearings with which Henry VIII had invested the College of Arms (the corporation of royal heralds) in the 1520s. The new authority of the heralds was just one sign of how the relationship between Crown and nobility was changing, for it showed that the very concept of nobility was now dependent upon the king's will and pleasure. One of the 'Kings of Arms', thus established by their sovereign as arbiters of heraldic propriety, had warned Surrey against his heraldic pretensions – which were intended not as a claim to the throne but, more realistically, as a claim on his family's behalf, as the premier family in England, to exercise the regency for the young king who would soon succeed his father. Henry Howard defended himself with such vigour that the jury hesitated long over their verdict. (His earldom was a courtesy title, not a peerage as such, so he was indicted before commoners at the Guildhall rather than before peers at Westminster.) However, William Paget rushed to court to seek the advice of his sovereign. On his return, he was allowed to interview the jurors, who promptly returned a guilty verdict. Even from his deathbed the ailing king could still overawe his subjects. Howard was beheaded on 19 January 1547, Henry's final victim. Rather than proceed by such means with the even flimsier case against the Duke of Norfolk,

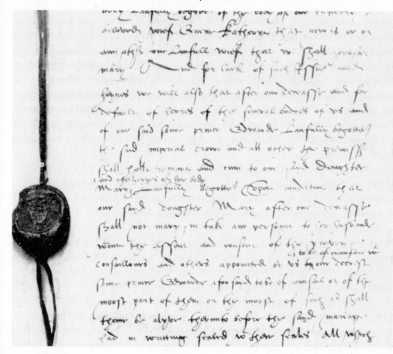

Section of the will of Henry VIII, 30 December 1546, bequeathing the 'imperial crown' of England to Mary in the event of Edward's death without issue. Note that while Edward is described as Henry's 'deerest sonne prince Edward', Mary is simply his 'daughter'.

he was condemned by act of attainder a few days after his son's death. Destined for the scaffold on 28 January, he was saved only by the king's own death in the early hours of that morning.

As the end came, it was therefore the evangelicals who surrounded the dying king. In his will he endeavoured to provide collective government for his young son, nominating sixteen men to form Edward's Privy Council. But with the disgraced Howards excluded, along with their episcopal ally, 'wily Winchester', the shrewd Bishop Stephen Gardiner, the prospects of balance and stability among this group were slim. Asked why he had omitted Gardiner, the king explained that while he, Henry, could manage the bishop, nobody else could. The bishop, Henry reckoned, would end up running rings around the rest of them and taking sole charge. Henry's anxieties about the future were accurate in everything except their focus. The exclusion of Gardiner delivered Edward VI into the hands of his predatory uncle, Edward Seymour.

Henry VIII died shortly after midnight, in the early hours of the morning of Friday 28 January. Had he died six months earlier, England would have remained a Catholic country. His own will encapsulated the ambiguities of his idiosyncratic religious compromise. Endowing a chantry for his soul at St George's Chapel, Windsor, where his splendid Renaissance tomb, cannibalised from Wolsey's, was still unfinished, and never to be finished, requesting thousands of Masses and seeking the intercession of the saints – Henry's imperious frame of mind is wonderfully expressed in the unselfconscious comment, 'we do instantly require the Blessed Virgin Mary... to pray for us' – it could be the will of any late medieval king. Yet alongside this entirely traditional provision for his soul we can see the hand of Cranmer (or perhaps of Catherine Parr) guiding the royal pen into expressing confidence in evangelical terms:

> that every Christian creature living here in this transitory and wretched world under God, dying in steadfast and perfect faith... is ordained by Christ's Passion to be saved and to attain eternal life, of which number we verily trust by his grace to be one...

It was the conservative bishops Gardiner, Tunstall and Bonner who presided over the exequies of the king. Gardiner celebrated the requiem Mass on Sunday 13 February, and two days later presided over the arrival of Henry's coffin at St George's, Windsor. Later Catholic historians reported that it burst open under the pressure of the rapid decomposition of his corpse, so that it could be licked by dogs. Some added that Mary Tudor had him exhumed and burned. These stories are but myths of vengeance against one for whom they thought the very fires of hell barely adequate. To Gardiner also it fell to preach the sermon at the burial on 16 February. Sadly, no text survives: it would have been illuminating to hear the final judgement on his master of a loyal servant who was at times so close to him. Henry was buried beside Jane Seymour, beloved among all his wives because she had given him a son.

3

EDWARD VI

Of all the Tudors, Edward VI is the least known. Coming to the throne aged nine, reigning barely half a dozen years, dying before his prime, overshadowed by the memory of his father and by the two dukes who successively ruled England on his behalf, Edward was in no position to make his own mark upon English history. His reign is the history of what was done in his name: first by the Duke of Somerset, his uncle Edward Seymour, and then by the Duke of Northumberland, John Dudley, who became the father-in-law of Edward's nominated heir. Yet what was done in those half-dozen years made them among the most significant in English history. For those years saw nothing less than a religious revolution, the transformation of England into a Protestant country. Under the guidance of the Archbishop of Canterbury, Thomas Cranmer, the broad outlines of the Protestant Church of England were laid down. The creative and adaptive genius of Cranmer added the stately and emotive phrases of the *Book of Common Prayer* to the plainer and more direct words of William Tyndale's New Testament, defining what would for the next 400 years be the voice of English religion. Even if the moving target of those years only ended up by chance as the fixed point of the 'Elizabethan Settlement', even though the reign of Mary Tudor showed how shallow and vulnerable the achievement was, Edward's reign was the cradle of English Protestantism.

As the son of Jane Seymour, who had been a young noblewoman of impeccably conservative religious inclinations (when the Pilgrimage of Grace broke out, she begged Henry on bended knee to reverse the dissolution of the monasteries), Edward VI might have seemed heir to an essentially Catholic religious tradition. Yet Jane had died within days of giving birth, and circumstances had given a rather different shape to the boy's upbringing. His uncle, Edward Seymour, like many upwardly mobile young gentlemen in the king's service, was sympathetic to the still fresh ideas of the Protestants, which were rendered doubly attractive by the sanction that they gave to asset-stripping the Church. His godfather was none other than Thomas Cranmer (his two other godfathers, the Dukes of Norfolk and Suffolk, were hardly in a position to influence his religious life). Most importantly of all, his formal education was in the hands of moderate Protestants.

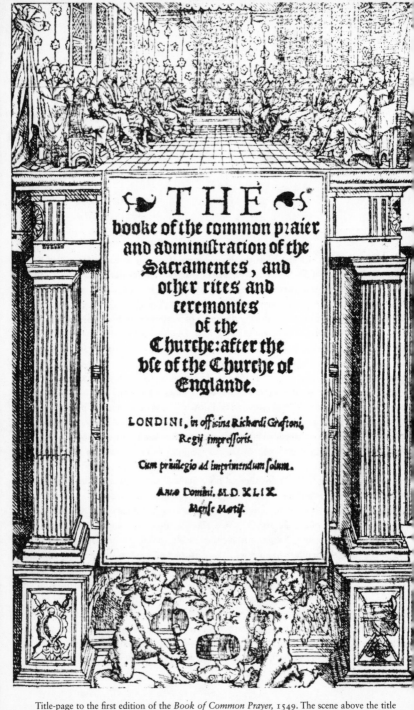

THE

booke of the common praier
and administration of the
Sacramentes, and
other rites and
ceremonies
of the
Churche: after the
use of the Churche of
Englande.

LONDINI, in officina Richardi Graftoni,
Regij impressoris.

Cum priuilegio ad imprimendum solum.

Anno Domini. M.D.XLIX.
Mense Martij.

Title-page to the first edition of the *Book of Common Prayer*, 1549. The scene above the title
shows Edward VI sitting in council.

EDUCATION

Much significance has rightly been attached by historians to the role of Edward's tutors, first Richard Cox (who was later the boy king's almoner) and then from 1544 John Cheke, because their religious inclinations were, and were known to be, towards the evangelical side in contemporary terms. Some have seen in the choice of these men evidence that Henry intended the Reformation to proceed further under his son than it could under his own control. But this is certainly to overinterpret the case and to ascribe both too broad a mind and too narrow an ambition to the ageing tyrant. Had Henry wished to push through further religious reform, then, as Cranmer later remarked, there was no one who would have dared gainsay him. The king, who was in a state of almost perpetual astonishment at the temerity of those who departed in the slightest degree from his idiosyncratic middle way, would certainly not have expected the hired help to pursue its own religious agenda while educating his only son. Cheke was chosen because he was the brightest star in a constellation of talent emerging at Cambridge University, and associated above all with St John's College – a college whose academic excellence had been fostered by Bishop John Fisher as a bulwark of Catholic orthodoxy but which after his execution in 1535 was rapidly becoming a bridgehead of the English Reformation. The king's son had to have the best education that England could offer, and Cheke was the man to provide it, with his fine italic handwriting and his utter mastery of Latin and Greek.

In fact, there was more to the appointment of Cheke than meets the eye, more than the mere selection of a first-class humanist scholar. It was also a slap in the face for the conservative bishop of Winchester, Stephen Gardiner. In his capacity as chancellor of Cambridge University, he had intervened in a scholarly controversy over the pronunciation of Greek. Cheke was the protagonist, and Gardiner had soundly rebuked him for his temerity in challenging traditional practices, enjoining him to refrain from further efforts in that direction. There was little love lost between them. In the matter of finding a schoolmaster for young Edward, the choice did not have to fall upon Cheke – there were other possibilities. Gardiner would doubtless have preferred some of the other humanist talents available from St John's College: John Seton, the author of Tudor England's best-selling textbook of logic, or Thomas Watson, author of a Greek tragedy based on the biblical story of Jephtha. Both men were soon to join Gardiner's household as chaplains.

Their orthodoxy was beyond doubt (Watson went on to become the last Roman Catholic bishop of Lincoln in the reign of Queen Mary), but Gardiner's political influence was temporarily waning when the crucial decisions about Edward's education were being taken. His own attempt to bring down Archbishop Cranmer on charges of heresy having failed, a counter-coup against him had resulted in the execution for treason of his nephew, Germain Gardiner, in 1544. It seems likely that Cheke's merits were thrust upon Henry's attention by other evangelical sympathisers, such as Sir Anthony Denny and Dr William Butts, who held influential positions in the king's personal service. Denny was by this stage the head of the king's Privy

Hugh Latimer preaching before Edward VI from the 'preaching place', the new pulpit Henry VIII had built in the palace garden at Whitehall.

Chamber, which attended upon his daily needs and provided him with company and amusement. Butts was one of the most highly regarded of the king's physicians. Both men were thus intimate with the king in the day-to-day context in which decisions such as that regarding the education of the prince were bound to be taken. Nevertheless, had Gardiner's star been in the ascendant, he might well have blocked Cheke's appointment. Gardiner's failure to gain control over the education of the young prince was to spell disaster for him and his cause in the next reign.

THE RISE OF THE DUKE OF SOMERSET

Henry certainly neither expected nor envisaged that his servants, especially not the complacent Cranmer, would dare to alter the religious settlement he had bequeathed them, at least while his son was but a boy. Indeed, the Duke of Somerset admitted soon after Henry's death that the late king 'had very expressly commanded both him and all others of his Council to keep not only the laws but all else in the state of the realm in such condition as he had left them, without changing anything'. And Henry was a man of unparalleled vanity, quite incapable of appreciating that shrewd and ambitious men might duck and dive around his deathbed, or that his posthumous memory might exert a less powerful influence upon them than his dying yet still awesome frame. Still less would he have expected Cox, Cheke and the others to have undermined his son's attachment to the Henrician compromise during his own lifetime. Cox, after all, had been one of the compilers of Henry VIII's definitive statement of English orthodoxy, the King's Book of 1543, and Cheke was simply a tutor. But the reforming wing had always been the most zealous in maintaining his new-found royal supremacy, and that, above all, was the legacy which Henry wished to preserve and pass on to his son. While a certain latitude was allowed to theological speculation in the 1540s, he would have expected his son's tutors to stay safely within the limits he had himself laid down.

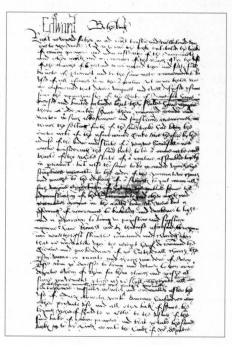

The first page of a letter from Edward VI to his bishops, quashing the popular rumour that the fall of the Duke of Somerset heralded the withdrawal of the Book of Common Prayer and the restoration of the old Latin liturgy. Edward reiterates his own commitment to the new book, and goes on to instruct his bishops to call in all old Latin service books for immediate destruction. These letters, signed at the head by Edward and at the foot by members of the Privy Council, went out in January 1550.

Neither did Henry intend or imagine the sort of political arrangements which rapidly emerged to cope with his son's minority, with Edward Seymour securing viceregal powers under the titles of Lord Protector of the Realm and Governor of the King's Person. Henry's will established a council of sixteen men to govern his realms during his son's minority. If Henry had meant one of those men to take charge, then he would have nominated one of them himself and lent him the authority and prestige of his will. He was hardly the man to leave his intentions obscure. On the contrary, in precisely defining a regency council to govern in his son's name, he was doing everything he could to prevent a dominant male asserting personal control over the pride of aristocrats which would surround the young king. This was his express justification for the otherwise inexplicable exclusion from that council of perhaps his ablest surviving servant, Bishop Stephen Gardiner. Henry was concerned that 'wily Winchester' would run rings round his other executors and end up dominating them – and probably undoing much of his Reformation to boot. Edward Seymour, though a competent enough commander in the field and the king's uncle, was not of the blood royal and cannot be said thus far to have shown spectacular abilities or overweening ambition. It was far from obvious that he would grasp at supreme power, still less that he would secure it.

However, the manoeuvres around Henry's deathbed not only excluded most of the major conservative figures from real power but also left scope for the subversion of the collective regime he had so carefully tried to bequeath. Whatever Henry's intentions, Seymour had enormous advantages in the events which followed the king's death. He was the king's senior male relative. He was a successful military man: in defeating the Scots at Solway Moss, he had crippled Scottish politics for a generation. He had been on the Privy Council since its formal creation in 1540. The fall of the Howards late in 1546 left him, as Earl of Hertford, the highest-ranking peer on it. And the exclusion of Bishop Gardiner left him with no obvious rival.

Henry VIII died in the night of 27–28 January 1547. The first thing those attending upon him did was to keep his death secret. Parliament was allowed to meet the next day as though nothing had happened, though in principle it was dissolved by the very fact of the king's death. Access to the king's bedchamber was controlled even more tightly than usual, and meals continued to be delivered to the door. Meanwhile, the young Prince Edward and his sister Elizabeth were hastily fetched to court. Not until Monday 31 January was the new king proclaimed, although for official purposes, of course, the regnal year was dated from 28 January. With the Duke of Norfolk safely in the Tower of London and Stephen Gardiner safely away from court, Seymour and his allies could do what they liked. Over the next few days, apparently concluding that Henry's will had not been sufficiently generous to them, they parcelled out lands and titles among themselves (above all to Seymour himself, who emerged as Duke of Somerset), subsequently reporting this as being in accordance with the spoken instructions of the dying king. It may have been so, but it seems most unlike him.

The key moment in the early politics of Edward's reign was the exclusion from the government of the powerful Lord Chancellor (and newly created Earl of

Above: 1. Portrait miniature of Henry VII, from the Bosworth Jewel. The portrait miniature was not part of the limited artistic vocabulary of the late medieval English Court, but was introduced into England around the middle of the sixteenth century, as pictures of royalty assumed greater cultural importance. This example was one of a series of royal miniatures produced by Nicholas Hilliard to illustrate the Tudor heritage of Queen Elizabeth.

Above right: 2. Lady Margaret Beaufort above the gate at Christ's College, Cambridge. Mother of Henry VII and Grandmother of Henry VIII. Based on the Tudor images of Lady Margaret, this later statue honours her role as a patroness of religion and education.

Right and following page, top left: 3 & 4. This pair of portraits of Henry VII and his queen, Elizabeth of York, depicts the royal couple holding the red rose of Lancaster and the white rose of York to symbolise the union of the two warring houses in their marriage and their children. The Tudor resolution of the 'Wars of the Roses' was a constant feature of Tudor propaganda through the sixteenth century.

Above right: 5. Edward IV, father of Henry VII's queen, Elizabeth of York. This typical late medieval portrait emphasises the wealth and status of its subject, who wears cloth of gold with plenty of showy jewels. Henry VIII was noted for his resemblance to Edward, his maternal grandfather.

Left: 6. Richard III. This upper body portrait is typical of late medieval English portraiture.

7. The family of Henry VII with St George and the dragon. This depiction of the entire royal family (including deceased children) is another typically medieval piece, symbolising the devotion of the dynasty to one of its heavenly patrons, St George. It may have been painted to celebrate the gift to Henry of a notable relic, a leg of St George presented to him by the King of France. Note the liberal use of Tudor roses and portcullises, as well as the imperial crowns worn by Henry and his queen.

8. Arthur, Prince of Wales, Henry VII's eldest son, who died in 1502. Although commonly identifie as Henry's unfortunate elder brother, Arthur, there is a case for identifying this as a portrait of Henr himself. Certainly the resemblance is marked.

9. Margaret Tudor, Henry VIII's elder sister and Queen of Scotland. This much later representation of Henry's elder sister, who was married off to James IV of Scotland as part of Henry VII's dynastic consolidation, was painted in the early seventeenth century, once Margaret's descendants had added the crown of England to that of Scotland.

12. Richmond Palace as built by Henry VII. Built on the site of a palace that had burned down in 1497, and renamed Richmond after the family earldom (Richmond in Yorkshire), this was the grandest of Henry's palaces, soaring to three floors, with fantastical turrets and chimneys. A house of Observant Franciscans stood nearby. Richmond became Henry's favourite residence in his declining years, and he died here on 21 April 1509.

Above left: 11. Laughing child, possibly Henry VIII, c.1498. Although this bust is today commonly said to represent Henry VIII as a young boy, there is in fact nothing beyond its probable date and its presence in the royal collection to support this identification.
Above right: 14. Catherine of Aragon.
Opposite: 10. Henry VIII c.1535. The origins of this portrait, which is ascribed to the Dutch painter Joos van Cleve (d. 1541), are obscure, but the scroll in the king's hands, which cites Mark 16:15 ('Go ye into all the world and preach the gospel to every creature'), suggests that it was painted to encourage the king to publish the Bible in English.

ERINA PRIMA VXOR HENRICI OCTAV

Above left: 15. The grave of Catherine of Aragon in Peterborough Abbey (which Henry converted into a cathedral in 1541). There was no royal tomb: Henry took undisguised and vindictive delight in the news of Catherine's death, and spent as little as possible on disposing of her earthly remains. He would not have been pleased at the label 'Queen of England' added on the much later ironwork.

Above right: 16. Henry Fitzroy, Duke of Richmond and Somerset, c.1534. One of England's earliest portrait miniatures, this shows Henry Fitzroy (1519-36), Henry VIII's illegitimate son by Elizabeth Blount, and was probably made to mark his marriage to a daughter of the Duke of Norfolk in 1533, when he was in his fifteenth year, his age in this picture.

Above: 17. The tomb of Henry Fitzroy, Duke of Richmond, Henry VIII's bastard son, at St Michael's church, Framlingham, Suffolk. Henry's burial was arranged by the Duke of Norfolk, his father-in-law, and he was originally laid to rest in Thetford Priory church, in effect a mausoleum of the ducal house. At the dissolution of the monasteries his remains were transferred to the church at Framlingham, which was also under ducal patronage, and where this fine tomb was later erected by the family in his memory.

Opposite: 13. Catherine of Aragon, Henry VIII's first wife. She never accepted Henry's claim that their marriage was invalid and incestuous, and paid the price in isolation, ill health and premature death. This image of Catherine of Aragon was certainly not contemporary. Probably a companion piece to the picture of Anne Boleyn reproduced later in this section, it dates from long after their deaths, when copies of royal portraits were almost mass produced to decorate the galleries of aristocratic homes, and the political sensitivities surrounding these two queens had long since settled.

Above: 18. The Battle of the Spurs, 16 August 1513. This large canvas gives an idealised depiction of Henry VIII's youthful victory over the French, and was probably commissioned by the king himself.

Below: 19. The Embarkation of Henry VIII. This depiction of Henry VIII setting off with his fleet was probably also painted to mark the events of his war with France in 1512-13.

ANNA BOLLINA VXOR · HENRICI · OCTAVI

21. Anne Boleyn's determination not to follow her sister Mary into Henry's bed as his mere mistress was fraught with consequences for English history. Probably a companion piece to the picture earlier in this section of Catherine of Aragon, this too is a later image from a time when the politics of Henry's marriages were a distant memory.

Above: 20. 'The Field of the Cloth of Gold, 1520'. The Field of Cloth of Gold, the summit meeting between Henry VIII and Francis I a few miles from Calais in June 1520, was probably the most spectacular royal show of the entire sixteenth century. A tent city of the finest materials was erected to house the huge royal entourages during two weeks or more of splendid entertainments.

Above left: 22. Sir Thomas Wyatt. Among Holbein's subjects was Sir Thomas Wyatt, the poet, courtier and friend of Anne Boleyn who was arrested along with her many alleged lovers in 1536, and who was widely considered lucky to have escaped with his life. His son, also named Thomas, would rebel against Mary I in 1554.

Above right: 23. The Tower of London. The Norman White Tower at the Tower of London, which remained in Henry's days one of the most potent and terrible symbols of the authority of the English Crown, the place where so many political and religious dissidents were housed before execution.

24. A view of Pontefract Castle. This early seventeenth-century view of the lost castle of Pontefract shows why the leaders of the Pilgrimage of Grace made it their headquarters in the autumn of 1536. But it also shows why Henry VIII could not believe in the protestations of Lord Darcy, who had surrendered it to the Pilgrims because, he claimed, he could not have held it against them. The castle was razed to the ground after the English Civil Wars.

Opposite: 25. Jane Seymour by Hans Holbein. This Holbein pencil drawing of Jane Seymour is one of many such sketches he made of prominent persons at Henry's court, usually in preparation for panel paintings. Jane's success in bearing Henry a son made her his favourite wife, and they are buried together at Windsor.

Above, left: 26. Catherine Parr.

Above, right: 27. Detail from the window of King Solomon and the Queen of Sheba in King's College Chapel, Cambridge. It is believed that the image of the Queen of Sheba is modelled on Catherine Howard. This stained glass was created during Henry VIII's reign and paid for by Henry himself.

Right: 28. Jane Seymour. Another of the miniatures that formed part of the 'Bosworth Jewel' commemorating the Tudor accession.

Above: 29. Detail from the title-page to the Hagiographa in the Great Bible (1539). Henry VIII hands copies of the Bible to Cranmer on his right and to Cromwell on his left. Thomas Cranmer stands bare-headed in the presence of his king, his mitre at his feet. This beautifully and expensively coloured copy is from the library of St John's College, Cambridge, where a college tradition says that it was the property of Thomas Cromwell himself. *Master and Fellows of St John's College, Cambridge.*

Opposite: 30. Henry VIII. Holbein's classic pose has made Henry VIII the most readily recognised of all England's kings.

31. The Family of Henry VIII c.1545. There is a clear dynastic message in this group image from Henry's declining years. Jane Seymour and his son Edward, first in the succession, flank the king, while his daughters, both then classified as illegitimate, literally wait in the wings, in case the legitimate line expires.

Above left: 32. Henry VIII's nephew, James V of Scotland. The court of Scotland lagged some way behind England in terms of cultural production, owing to its relative poverty. Nevertheless, this image of James V shows his ambition to be seen as a Renaissance Prince.
Above right: 33. A sketch of Henry VIII by Thomas Smith (1513-77), in the margin of one of his books. *President and Fellows of Queens' College, Cambridge.*

Above left: 34. Sir Thomas More by Hans Holbein. There is a steely quality to the gaze of this intelligent and sensitive face, alerting us to the conscience that would always do its duty – whether in sentencing others to death or in accepting death before dishonesty.

Above right: 35. Drawing of Archbishop William Warham by Hans Holbein. It is easy to believe Catherine of Aragon's claim that this lugubrious clergyman's mantra was 'the wrath of the prince is death'.

Right: 36. Hans Holbein's drawing of Bishop John Fisher, neither the first nor the last of the king's friends to find himself face down on the block.

Above left: 37. Henry Howard, Earl of Surrey by Hans Holbein. Eldest son of Thomas Howard (third Duke of Norfolk), he was one of Henry VIII's courtiers, accompanying Henry to France in 1532 and served in Scotland, France and Flanders. Tried for treason in the last weeks of Henry VIII's reign, he was convicted only after a personal message from the king was conveyed to the hesitant jury.

Above right: 38. Thomas Howard, Third Duke of Norfolk, Anne Boleyn's uncle. Arrayed in his ducal finery, and with the chain of the Order of the Garter round his shoulders, the duke leaves the viewer with no doubts as to his loyalty, which probably saved Henry's throne when he successfully defused the Pilgrimage of Grace in autumn 1536.

41. Desiderius Erasmus. This fine portrait shows Erasmus in a pose commonly used in Renaissance art to depict St Jerome. Jerome was the inspiration and model for Erasmus's own scholarly career. His Latin name, Hieronymus, is written on the largest book on the shelves, which probably represents a volume from the critical edition of Jerome that Erasmus had published in 1516. Erasmus himself is here shown, like Jerome, engaged in scholarly reflection on the Bible.

39. A Protestant Allegory c.1538-44. Girolamo de Treviso's panel represented a new departure in English religious painting: a visual polemic with a clear propaganda message. There could be no more potent expression of Henry VIII's claim that the Word of God – represented by the stones (labelled Matthew, Mark, Luke, and John, after the writers of the four gospels) overthrew papal authority – represented by the fallen figure of the pope, surrounded by such symbols of Catholic piety and power as a rosary, a cardinal's hat, and papal bulls (the lead seals on the document). Stoning was the biblical punishment for, among other things, blasphemy and false prophecy.

40. The meeting of Henry VIII and the Emperor Maximillian I c.1545. Another in the series of paintings commemorating Henry's triumphant campaign against France early in his reign, this shows his meeting with his chief ally, the Holy Roman Emperor Maximilian I.

42. Hampton Court Palace c.1665-7. Hugely extended and embellished by Cardinal Wolsey in the 1520s, Hampton Court was a palace fit for a king. Henry VIII frequently stayed there before he took it over from the cardinal in 1528 and began his own programme of alterations there. Edward VI was born here in 1537. This painting shows it much as Henry VIII had left it, before the substantial alterations made by William III.

Above and below: 43 & 44 Two views of the Tudor palace at Greenwich, massively and expensively rebuilt by Henry VII. Until the 1530s, a house of Observant Franciscans formed part of the palace complex. Within easy reach of London and Westminster by water, it was a favourite residence of all the Tudors. Henry VIII was born here (1491), as were his daughters Mary (1516) and Elizabeth (1533). It was here, at the end of April 1536, that the infant Elizabeth saw her mother, Anne Boleyn, for the last time before she was rowed away to the Tower and her death.

Above left: 45. The keep of Windsor Castle, another unmistakeable statement of royal authority. A fortress rather than a favoured residence, but Henry VIII chose to be buried there, in the St George's Chapel *below*: 46.

Above right: 48. A portrait miniature of Edward VI, from the Bosworth Jewel. This miniature completes the set in the 'Bosworth Jewel', commemorating the Tudor succession. It shows Edward in the fourteenth year of his age, but it was painted c.1600.

Opposite: 47. Edward VI. This portrait of Edward as Prince of Wales dates from late in Henry VIII's reign, and depicts the little boy in the somewhat incongruous pose of Holbein's massive Henry.

49. A view of old St Paul's, with the spire that was lost in 1561. The highlight of Edward VI's Coronation procession from the Tower of London to Westminster was a spectacular descent by a performer, who, hands and feet outstretched 'not tochynge the roppe', slid down a cable which was run from the tip of the steeple to an anchor in the square below. The interior saw many changes in the Reformation. The wonder-working cross, 'the rood of grace', was taken down in 1538, and the great rood or cross in 1547. The altars were stripped out in 1550, replaced in 1553, and removed again in 1559.

Above left: 50. Edward VI. This depiction of Edward VI, though based on a contemporary image, is typical of the sort of thing widely copied to hang in wealthy households in the seventeenth century.
Above right: 51. Mary Tudor. Mary I was renowned, as queen, for her expensive tastes in clothing. This portrait fulfils one of the typical purposes of Tudor portraiture, to impress the viewer with the wealth and power of the sitter. Mary is shown here bedecked with jewels and wearing a dress shot through with gold and silver thread.

Above left: 52. Mary Tudor. Based on the same original as the painting opposite, this shows how the portraiture of past monarchs later became part of household décor.
Above right: 53. Mary I's husband, King Philip. The Spanish Court often affected a somewhat plainer and more restrained aesthetic than the English Court, as can be seen in this later copy of a Titian of Philip II of Spain.
Right: 54. Mary Tudor's husband, Philip II.

Left: 55. Bust of Philip II, 1554. This fine bust show Philip as King of England and Mary's husband, before he inherited the throne of Spain as Philip II.

Above right: 56. London Bridge. Unable to force London Bridge on 3 February 1554, the rebel Thomas Wyatt and his Kentish followers had to go upstream to Kingston in order to cross the Tham (6 February).

57. Hatfield House, Hertfordshire. The childhood home of Elizabeth I. It was at Hatfield th Elizabeth received the news of Mary's death, which made her queen.

58. Elizabeth I when Princess. The 'Lady Elizabeth' of Henry VIII's later years, illegitimate but acknowledged as third in line for the throne, is shown here in simple but fine portrait that emphasises status through its expensive colour and her fine dress, and piety in the books open and held.

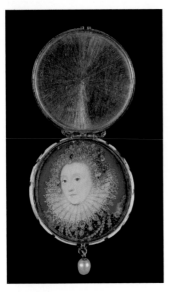

Left: 59. Elizabeth I. Miniatures of Queen Elizabeth were a must-have accessory of her nobility, allowing her courtiers and others to display their loyalty and devotion.
Above: 61. The Traitors' Gate at the Tower of London, through which Elizabeth passed on her way to prison in 1554.

60. Elizabeth I and the Three Goddesses, 1569. Tudor tapestries had often showed classical subjects, but the Renaissance taste for classical painting here makes its first appearance at the Tudor Court. Elizabeth's arrival shows her outdoing the goddesses of love, wisdom, and queenship – though as Juno, apparently beckoning her, was also goddess of marriage, the painting may have played its part in the incessant attempts to persuade Elizabeth to take a husband.

62 & 63. Elizabeth I. In Mary's reign, Elizabeth had affected plain costume in contrast to her sister's extravagant dress sense, but once queen, she reverted to royal type.

Above left: 64. Mary, Queen of Scots. The detail of the ring for the fourth finger suggests that this miniature of the young Mary was made to mark her first marriage to the Dauphin Francis (later, briefly, Francis II of France).

Above right: 65. Mary, Queen of Scots. The Hilliard miniature of the Scottish Queen emphasises her traditional Catholic piety with the prominent crucifix.

Left: 66. Henry Stewart, Lord Darnley, and his brother Charles Stewart. Henry's considerable height at first made him seem a suitable husband for Mary Queen of Scots, who was notably tall. But their compatibility went little further, and their marriage had thoroughly broken down by the time of his murder in 1567.

Southampton), Thomas Wriothesley. If Gardiner was the ecclesiastical leader of English Catholicism, Wriothesley was, after the fall of the Howards, its political heir apparent. His religious and political commitments were undisguised. He had personally assisted in racking the Protestant gentlewoman Anne Askew in 1546, hoping to extract from her information which would compromise prominent evangelicals at the court, perhaps including even Henry's last queen, Catherine Parr, herself. In the jockeying for position which followed Henry's death, it was Wriothesley who stood in Edward Seymour's way. Seymour's elevation to the rank of Lord Protector of the Realm could not take legal effect without being formally expressed in 'letters patent' issued under the Great Seal of England – the ultimate tool of authentication, which Wriothesley, as Lord Chancellor, personally controlled. The Great Seal was not only the badge of the Lord Chancellor's office but its very essence. As long as Wriothesley remained in possession of it, he steadfastly refused to apply it to any document investing Seymour with supreme authority. His motives seem to have been a mixture of religious antipathy with a canny assessment of his opponent's ambitions and limitations and an unshakeable loyalty to the memory of his late master.

Wriothesley had been in government longer than Seymour, and was a far more able administrator. He had worked his passage first with Stephen Gardiner, under whom he had studied at Cambridge, and then with Thomas Cromwell, whose private office he ran in the later 1530s, before coming to the king's attention after Cromwell's fall in 1540. Like Cromwell, he was one of the new breed of aristocrat which emerged in the Tudor era, an officeholding class or 'service nobility' which rose from modest or even humble beginnings through proven talent in administration and political management. In the jargon of the time, they were men 'of the pen' rather than 'of the sword'. Thomas Wriothesley, even when dignified with the office of Lord Chancellor and the title of Earl of Southampton, could not disguise the fact that he was an *arriviste*. His administrative skills and inbred caution were no match for Seymour's audacious schemes and superficial affability. Nor could he offer anything to match Seymour's military prestige and royal connections.

Somerset moved swiftly against the man who blocked his way. In a dubious legal process, Wriothesley was accused of abusing his powers, and, in order to escape a worse fate, he was induced on 5 March to resign from the Privy Council and, by surrendering the Great Seal, from the Lord Chancellorship. At least Somerset was not a vindictive man. Wriothesley was encouraged to retire to the ample family estates which he had built up in Hampshire thanks to a successful career and a key role in the dissolution of the monasteries. Custody of the Great Seal was in the meantime entrusted to William Paulet (recently created Lord St John), but it was in effect under Somerset's control, and within a week it had been used to issue the letters patent he needed to sanction his own appointment as Protector. Later in the year, once Somerset had established a firm grip on power, the pliable and reliable Richard Rich was made Lord Chancellor.

Under Somerset's direction, the Privy Council which Henry had so laboriously constructed in his will rapidly became a paper tiger. The centre of power shifted to

Somerset's own household, where men like William Cecil (later to become Elizabeth I's chief minister) and Michael Stanhope staffed his secretariat. His household was, in short, much like that of a king. But Somerset was not a king. He might be the king's uncle and rejoice in the title of Lord Protector, but that was no substitute for the blood royal and for the anointing with holy oil that was at the heart of the coronation. His arrogant usurpation of the governmental machinery stirred up resentment among his erstwhile colleagues, and this would, in the end, cost him dear.

In the meantime, the only challenge to Somerset's pre-eminence came from his younger brother, Thomas, who shared some of his advantages and all of his temperamental flaws. Thomas Seymour envied his brother's success and set out to rival him. He married Henry VIII's widow with indecent haste to cement his own ties with royalty, and took full advantage of the fact that the late king's younger daughter, Elizabeth, continued to live in Catherine Parr's household, treating her with a familiarity which today would probably have been categorised as child abuse. After his wife's death in childbirth in September 1548, he set his sights on Elizabeth as his next bride. He also exerted his considerable charm on the boy king, who was increasingly ignored and sidelined by his arrogant Protector. His aim was to instil in Edward a sense of the scope of royal authority, and use this to displace his elder brother. But Seymour's ambitions were too much for Somerset, who in 1549 cut through his web of intrigue and destroyed him on charges of treason so flimsy that they would never have stood up in a court and were therefore simply stated in an act of attainder. Somerset's ruthlessness towards his flesh and blood did little to enhance his own chances of survival when the tide of events turned against him later that year.

Somerset was loyal to Henry's memory in one respect, his continuation of the late king's policy towards Scotland, which aimed to bring about a marriage between Edward and Mary, Queen of Scots, thus uniting the two kingdoms under one dynasty – and defusing for ever the 'auld alliance' between Scotland and France which was so troubling to England in times of war. As the Scots still remained strangely reluctant to commit their queen and their country to English embraces, Somerset prepared a punitive expedition which he led across the border in September. His victory was so overwhelming that, although the campaign had been envisaged only as a raid, he was able to seize and garrison a number of strongholds throughout the Lowlands. However, his entire policy had the bottom knocked out of it the following year, when the Scots managed to smuggle Mary out of the kingdom to the safety of France, where in due course she was married to the Dauphin Francis. All that was left of Somerset's triumph was yet another drain upon limited military and fiscal resources.

The fiscal straits of Edward's reign were certainly not helped by the acquisitive appetites of the aristocracy, which had been inflamed by the bonanza of monastic land that had become available in the previous reign, and which now ran riot with the removal of a strong king's restraining hand. This certainly did nothing to hold up the progress of the Reformation. There was still much landed wealth locked up in the Church of England, and an affiliation to Protestantism made it not merely a pleasure but a duty to release it. Edward's first Parliament, later that year, swept into the king's hands the property of the chantries, guilds and colleges (except those of Oxford and Cambridge). Henry's policy of securing 'voluntary' surrenders or exchanges of Church lands was also continued throughout this reign. Such booty tended to find its way swiftly out of the king's hands again, and into those of his faithful servants.

THE PROTESTANT REFORMATION

The religious tone of the reign was set at the coronation on 20 February 1547, when Cranmer accorded Edward the papal title of 'Christ's vicar' within his dominions, and urged him to emulate the Old Testament King Josiah in ensuring that God was 'truly worshipped, and idolatry destroyed, the tyranny of the bishops of Rome banished from your subjects, and images removed'. Gone was the careful balancing act which had marked Henry's final years, with representatives of the 'new learning' (Protestantism) invariably shadowed by those of the 'old learning' in preaching at court or in royal appointments to ecclesiastical office. Instead the 'new learning' was given free rein. The preachers invited to perform before the king at court were the likes of Nicholas Ridley, William Barlow and Hugh Latimer – convinced Protestants to a man.

The clearest possible message was sent out to the clergy, the printers and the general public when England's premier theologian, Dr Richard Smyth, a firm defender of traditional Catholic doctrines about the Mass, was compelled to make humiliating public recantations of his views in London (15 May) and Oxford. Smyth, the Regius Professor of Divinity at Oxford, was a man of the 'old learning', personally selected for the professorship by Henry VIII when he founded it in 1540. In 1546, Smyth had dedicated to Henry his *Assertion of the Sacrament of the Altar*, a lengthy justification of the Catholic doctrine of the Mass, a subject dear to the late king's heart. Now, less than a year later, Smyth's public humiliation was accompanied in London by a bonfire of his books – an open enough warning to the printing trade about the financial risks of publishing the wrong kind of material. At the same time, restraints on the publishing of Protestant literature were relaxed. Modern historians have spoken of Somerset's policy towards the press as 'permissive', but, like most forms of permissiveness, Somerset's was highly selective. Both Somerset and, later, Northumberland did their best to prevent Catholic literature being published in England or imported from abroad. The humiliation of Richard Smyth, then, although at first sight a mere sidelight on history, in fact sheds a good deal of light on government policy. At the time it was deemed important enough to be mentioned in several chronicles. The young king himself reported it in the political journal in which he recorded some of the outstanding events of his reign. Edward's own engagement with the Protestant Reformation, at first no doubt largely under the influence of his tutors, was a fact of political life right from the start.

The signals broadcast at and after the coronation did not lie, and religious change was soon under way. In July 1547 Cranmer published his official book of homilies or sermons for use throughout the Church of England. These were uncompromising in their repudiation of the 'traditional religion' of the English people, Catholicism, as a mish-mash of 'papistical superstitions'. Their presentation of evangelical Protestantism was more muted, but the drift was perfectly clear to theologically literate observers, such as Stephen Gardiner. He was wryly sceptical about the value of intensive preaching, observing of the majority of people that 'when they have heard words spoken in the pulpit they report they were good and very good and wondrous good... but what they were... they cannot tell'. More tellingly, in a series of letters to Cranmer he spelled out remorselessly how the archbishop's homily on justification contradicted the King's Book of 1543, and impugned Cranmer's good faith, daring him to justify his decision to jettison the doctrine to which he had subscribed for the last four years of Henry's reign.

The Homilies were imposed upon the clergy by a fresh set of royal injunctions for the Church of England issued on 31 July 1547. Based on the injunctions of 1538, these went much further in their efforts to root out traditional Catholic customs. All images were to be removed from churches, and parishioners were to be urged to dispose of their private devotional images as well. The rosary was no longer to be recited. Parish priests were to exhort their flocks not to leave money for Masses for their souls. Parish funds maintained for the support of church worship and decoration were to be diverted to the relief of the poor. All candles were to be extinguished except for a minimal pair on the altar. Parish processions were no longer to be held before high Mass on Sundays and feast days. The use of holy water was to be abandoned. Little wonder that ordinary Christians the length and breadth of the land remembered Edward's reign, rather than Henry's, as the time of schism.

The injunctions themselves were rigorously implemented over the autumn and winter of 1547–48 by a team of royal 'visitors' or commissioners who personally supervised the transformation of parish churches throughout the land. In vain did a few Catholics protest. Edward Bonner, Bishop of London, found himself imprisoned for his pains. Stephen Gardiner fought a desperate rearguard action from his diocese of Winchester. He made a nice point in the summer of 1547, forcefully reminding Somerset that the Homilies and Injunctions were strictly illegal under the Act for the Advancement of True Religion which Henry VIII had passed in 1543. Taking his stand on this legislation, Gardiner refused to accept the royal injunctions, but his protests to the Privy Council resulted only in his own committal to the Fleet prison, and the distinction in due course of a mention in the king's political journal. Cranmer and Somerset carried on regardless, taking care to repeal Henry's legislation that autumn in the first Parliament of the reign.

It was the almost immediate introduction of disturbing religious changes at a time when Edward himself was barely ten years old that brought on the second political crisis of the reign, a public controversy over the nature and exercise of kingship during a royal minority. Royal minorities were not unprecedented. There was a tacit consensus in such situations that the government pursued an uncontentious policy until the king was of age to take decisions for himself. 'Steady as she goes' was the motto. Somerset's determined furtherance of the Protestant Reformation breached that consensus. The constitutional mythology of monarchy was of course that kingship was continuous: 'The king is dead, long live the king!' Every judicial and executive function of the government continued to be carried out in the name of the king. But when the king was an immature young boy, this indispensable legal fiction was all too obviously fictitious. Hence the need to avoid straining credulity, and perhaps even loyalty, by undertaking in his name divisive and contentious policies. It was not long before Catholics, aggrieved at the dismantling of their religion, began to complain that a faction was pursuing its own ends in the name of a king who was too young to be giving their policies a real and informed consent. They did not have to look far for arguments with which to challenge their opponents. 'Woe to thee, O land, when thy king is a child', they quoted from their opponents' favourite book, the Bible (Eccles. 10:16). Moreover, they had constitutional grounds for complaint. Henry VIII, again, had foreseen the kind of dangers which might arise were he to be succeeded by a child. He had provided against it with an Act of Parliament in 1536 which empowered his successor to repeal by a merely executive act ('letters patent' under the Great Seal) any Act of Parliament passed during his minority. Somerset dealt with this in due course by having the act repealed, which would have created a pretty conundrum for the judges if Edward had lived long enough to wish to take advantage of the original act.

In response to this widely shared view, Somerset and his government fell back upon the politically implausible but constitutionally impeccable thesis that royal power was royal power, irrespective of the psychological or medical condition of the monarch. If a law or writ or injunction was made or issued in the king's name, it was enforceable in the appropriate court and it was morally binding under the presumption of that obedience which all loving subjects owed their prince – a presumption which, since 1535, had been elevated to the level of a paramount divine obligation. They proceeded to enforce their interpretation with all the means at their disposal. Stephen Gardiner, who had taken every opportunity of harassing Somerset, was required to show his bona fides. He was to preach on Friday 29 June 1548 from the prestigious pulpit set up in the gardens of the palace of Whitehall in the latter years of the previous reign. A few days before the sermon, William Cecil arrived with a message from Somerset advising him that it would be sensible to include a few words on the subject of the reality of the royal authority of the boy king. Gardiner upheld Edward's authority, but did not speak of the question of age, and his affirmations of the Mass and of clerical celibacy were taken by Somerset as mere provocation. He was arrested later that day and taken to the Tower. The following year, one of the most outspoken of the conservative bishops, Edmund Bonner of London, was summoned before the council and ordered to preach an appropriate sermon at Paul's Cross on 1 September 1549. Like Gardiner before him, Bonner spoke strongly in favour of traditional doctrine; like Gardiner before him, he ignored the hint that he should speak specifically to the question of the authority of a boy king; and like Gardiner before him he was duly imprisoned – though in the Marshalsea rather than in the Tower.

Somerset has been praised in fulsome terms for his religious toleration on the grounds that he dismantled much of the Henrician machinery of censorship and repression. This judgement could hardly be farther from the truth. His chief purpose was to pave the way for religious changes which would otherwise have been unlawful. Proclamations against contentious and divisive preaching may have seemed even-handed, but it soon became clear that it was Catholic preaching that was contentious and divisive, while Protestant preaching (except at the radical extreme) was by definition moderate and conciliatory. The repeal of the draconian heresy and treason laws of the previous reign left the prerogative powers of the Crown untouched and was far from evenhanded in its effects. It was still treason to deny the royal supremacy, but denying transubstantiation was no longer a death-penalty offence. And if it was found necessary to prosecute extreme religious deviance, it could still be done: the radical Anabaptist Joan Boucher was burned in May 1550. The only repression that ceased was the repression of evangelical views. The ordinary powers of the Church and the Crown were more than adequate to silence the voice of religious conservatism.

English religion was already very different in 1548 from what it had been when Edward ascended the throne, but more was to come. As long as the chief religious service was the Latin Mass and as long as it was celebrated by a caste of priests set apart from ordinary men by celibate life and sacramental anointing, then the heart of Catholicism was still beating even if the body was horribly mutilated. But 1548 saw Cranmer issue an English form of words for the rite of communion in the Mass, while liturgical ceremonies such as ashes (for Ash Wednesday), palms (for Palm Sunday) and the veneration of the cross were abrogated. Over the winter of 1548–49, Cranmer finished his draft of a complete English form of worship, the *Book of Common Prayer*, which was formally imposed by the Act of Uniformity (January 1549), with effect from Whit Sunday, 9 June 1549. In the interim, another statute was passed allowing priests to marry – to the horror and disgust of many of their parishioners.

The air of inevitability with which the eventual success of the English Reformation has retrospectively invested its earlier stages has blinded posterity to the magnitude of what was done in the summer of 1549. It was not so much a matter of the doctrinal implications of the change, although we should not underestimate the significance of abandoning the Latin Mass, the liturgy of Europe for a millennium and of England for its entire history thus far, in favour of an entirely new English service with a very different underlying theology. It is more the sheer practical and technical aspects of the operation. Nothing like it had ever been envisaged, let alone attempted, in the entire history of Christianity. Medieval liturgical change, transmitted by manuscript, took place gradually, spreading by hand from one copy to another. Thus the feast of Corpus Christi spread throughout the Catholic Church in the course of the thirteenth and fourteenth centuries, and not overnight. In a world in which a rapid copy of a substantial text took weeks, and a fine, lovingly crafted copy took months, liturgical change could not be other than slow and piecemeal. Moreover, because of the vast areas covered by the Catholic Church, and its long duration in the world (the papacy had a longer continuous historical pedigree than any other political institution in western Europe), medieval liturgy was typified by regional and local variations.

It was only the invention of print that made Cranmer's unprecedented enterprise conceivable and feasible. Not even the Protestant reformations on the Continent had attempted anything on such a gigantic scale. Lutheran liturgies were often little different from their Catholic predecessors, while Zwinglian and Calvinist liturgies had thus far been imposed only upon a local basis, within a city and its hinterland. Yet, thanks to print, it was possible for a brand new religious service to be celebrated in the 8,000 or so churches of England on one and the same Sunday in accordance with a government decree for which there was little, if any, popular support. The mere success of this measure is a tribute to the capacity of Tudor administration.

The introduction of the new liturgy in the summer of 1549 marked a total break with the past. Cranmer's elimination of all mention of sacrifice from his English liturgy was perhaps the most drastic theological move (although his own views on the 'real presence' of Christ in the consecrated bread and wine of the eucharist were already somewhat shaky, the first *Book of Common Prayer* gave no indication of any change here). But, as Eamon Duffy has observed, the real religious impact was the shattering of the everyday liturgical experience of men and women. The shift from Latin to English made almost all church music redundant at a stroke. King's College, Cambridge, with the king's zealously Protestant tutor, John Cheke (by this time Sir John Cheke) at its head as Provost, actually disbanded its choir within a year or so, as it was no longer needed. The vast majority of feast days were no longer to be celebrated. Masses were no longer provided for special devotions or intentions. The central moment of the medieval Mass, the elevation of the consecrated body and blood of Christ for veneration by the congregation, was abolished. The symbol of peace and harmony, the 'pax', was no longer to be passed around among the congregation. No more than one Mass was to be celebrated per day in any particular church, and then only at the high altar: the chapels and side-altars of the medieval parish church, the focus of so much communal and family pride and investment in the preceding centuries, were rendered immediately obsolete.

THE REBELLIONS OF 1549

The promulgation of the *Book of Common Prayer* on Whit Sunday 1549 also marked the end of the first phase of Edward's reign, for, as the Yorkshire parson Robert Parkyn put it, in a little personal chronicle of the English Reformation, 'after the said Pentecost... began a commotion or insurrection of people in the south parts as Cornwall and Devonshire'. His own north country, unfortunately for the Catholic rebels of the south, remained largely quiescent throughout the turmoil, although a few thousand men took up arms in the vicinity of Scarborough before being dispersed with the offer of a pardon. The north as a whole had learned its lesson back in 1536. Lesser protests against the new Church service were made in many other areas, notably around Oxford, but it was in the south-west that protest assumed the threatening dimensions of a full-scale rebellion. By the beginning of July, the rebels controlled much of Devon and Cornwall, and were laying siege to Exeter. Their demands, which were predominantly religious, focused on the restoration of the Latin Mass and of traditional liturgical ceremonies, but also voiced a particular reluctance to accept fundamental change during a royal minority. A reply to these demands was published in the king's name on 8 July. Predictably, it takes its stand on the authority of the royal person, and emphasises that this authority is not diminished one jot by the king's youth:

> Be we of less authority for our age? Be we not your king now as we shall be? Shall ye be subjects hereafter, and now are ye not?... We are your rightful king, your liege lord, the sovereign Prince of England, not by our age, but by God's ordinance, not only when we shall be twenty-one years of age, but when we were of ten years. We possess our crown not by years, but by the blood and descent from our father King Henry the Eighth.

We should probably not imagine that Edward wrote this himself – although by now he was probably capable of it. But at twelve years of age, he would certainly have been capable of endorsing its strongly royalist sentiments and making them his own.

The government's problems were by no means confined to the south-west nor even to the religious conservatives. For at the same time, social and economic grievances provoked another rising among the countryfolk of East Anglia under the leadership of Robert Kett. This is sometimes seen as a Protestant revolt in contrast to the essentially Catholic revolt of the West Country, largely because leading Protestant clergymen, such as Dr Matthew Parker (later to be Elizabeth I's first Archbishop of Canterbury) and Dr John Barrett, the foremost Protestant preacher of mid-Tudor Norwich, went out of the city to the main rebel camp on nearby Mousehold Heath, and celebrated Prayer Book services there. It would be safer to see this as a cannier revolt.

In fact, the shock of the Prayer Book probably sparked off all the protests that summer, whether or not their grievances were religious. The East Anglian rebels, like all Tudor rebels, were anxious to emphasise their loyalty – all Tudor rebels laboured under the huge disadvantage that in a true monarchy, as in a one-party state, effective opposition to the regime could only be interpreted as treason – and perhaps felt that their social and economic grievances might be listened to more sympathetically if they were not combined with a challenge to what was in effect the government's headline policy: religious reform. East Anglia was as yet hardly a hotbed of Protestantism.

One or two towns (such as Colchester, Ipswich and Norwich) had influential and growing Protestant minorities. But the revolt was primarily rural, and Protestantism had made little headway in the countryside. The generally Catholic sympathies of the region were evident a few years later in the massive support it gave to the cause of Mary Tudor in the succession crisis of 1553.

Kett's strategy was a shrewd one, for Somerset did indeed respond with some genuine sympathy for the East Anglian grievances, and seems to have been reluctant to take the gloves off. But his aristocratic colleagues, fearing for the gains they had made over the last few years, were less squeamish. Lord Russell led a force of German and Italian mercenaries against the western rebels, cutting them down in their thousands in August. Ironically, the mercenaries were themselves Catholics, though the idea that they might have proved sympathetic to the rebel aims had they known them is a trifle naïve (the rebels cannot have looked like a promising paymaster). At much the same time, the Earl of Warwick delivered a similar object lesson in the virtues of obedience to the rebels of Norfolk. The government's victory is no surprise. Without magnate leadership, risings of this kind were doomed to failure, and these risings had nothing like the gentry and noble leadership that had taken over the Pilgrimage of Grace. The two regions which experienced the worst disorder in 1549 were the two regions whose traditional power relationships had been disrupted by the overthrow of their magnate dynasties. East Anglia had been dominated for most of the Tudor era by the Howards, who had been taken down in 1546, and the West Country had traditionally looked to the power of the Courtenays, Marquesses of Exeter, who had been taken down in 1538. Had the traditional leaders been in place, then as long as those leaders remained loyal the chances are that the first stirrings of revolt would have been promptly suppressed. The fact that Howard and Courtenay were both in the Tower meant that there was nobody available either to suppress the risings promptly or to provide them with the organisation and legitimacy which might have made them a real challenge to the regime.

THE FALL OF SOMERSET AND THE RISE OF NORTHUMBERLAND

The Duke of Somerset, overtaken by events and his colleagues, found his grip on power irretrievably weakened. Once the disorders had been suppressed, Somerset was slow to wake up to the manoeuvres of the Earl of Warwick, John Dudley. When he finally did so, early in October, he attempted to cling on to power by taking control of the king's person and printing an appeal to the people to come to the aid of their king and his Lord Protector. First he battened down the hatches at Hampton Court, preparing for the worst. But except for those holed up with him, his former colleagues melted away. So, on the night of 6 October, he made a dash for the surer refuge of Windsor Castle. But the gentry did not rally to him, as in his vanity he had imagined they would, and the studied moderation of the Privy Council in London, under Warwick's shrewd leadership, made it impossible for him to do anything other than surrender – albeit with guarantees of his safety, property and honour. He soon found himself in the Tower.

The fall of Somerset was expected in many quarters to lead to the reversal of the drastic measures of Protestant Reformation which had been introduced in the previous two years. The religiously conservative politicians who had been politically marginalised since the fall of Wriothesley early in 1547 certainly thought so. Wriothesley himself made a political comeback, returning to the council table in October 1549, and, with the Earl of Arundel and others, threw in his lot with Warwick on the assumption that the disorder of 1549 and the collapse of Somerset's regime spelled the end for Cranmer's Reformation. For a brief moment, it looked as though Wriothesley would emerge from the ruck carrying the ball. It was reported that he was lodging close to the king, that 'every man repaireth to Wriothesley... and all things be done by his advice'. Yet circumstances were still against the conservatives, and the frustration of their hopes was almost inevitable. Dudley himself, though hardly a man consumed by evangelical fervour, had been broadly sympathetic to the cause of Reformation since the mid-1530s, mostly no doubt because of the modest veil it provided for the pillage of the Church. He abandoned his new-found conservative friends just in time to assume command of the reformers as they abandoned Somerset's lost cause. The fall of Somerset was thus strangely akin to the fall of Anne Boleyn back in 1536. On each occasion, adroit manoeuvring saved the cause of the Reformation, albeit at the cost of one or two heads.

As in the wake of Henry's death, so in the wake of Somerset's fall, the key moment was the exclusion of Wriothesley, now for a second time, from the Privy Council. Not much is known about Wriothesley's political style, but it begins to look as though he was short on leadership qualities. To lose one power struggle may be regarded as a misfortune; to lose two looks like mismanagement. His brief return to the council table was curtailed by illness, and by February 1550 he was once more on the sidelines. Among the conservatives who had served Henry VIII, only Stephen Gardiner had the ability and the ambition to lead a government. He remained in gaol. The primary objective of the conservative Privy Councillors over the winter of 1550–51 was to get him out. They failed, and with that failure went their hopes.

In the meantime, Warwick was consolidating his grip on the young king and thus on the reality of power – in the interests of which he was happy to dispense with much of its outward display. His regime differed in many respects from that of his predecessor. Most obviously, Edward was now encouraged to associate himself more closely with political discussions and actions. Warwick was careful from the start to foster in the boy a proper sense of his own place and person. Indeed, the first issue which Edward raised with the council on his own account was the fate of his fallen uncle. In an inspired example of *reculer pour mieux sauter*, Warwick seized the initiative by appearing to surrender it, calling upon his colleagues to respect this, the first royal wish proposed to them. Somerset was spared for the time being, and in February 1550 was released from the Tower. From April he was even back on the Privy Council, and a reconciliation between him and Warwick was sealed by the marriage of Anne Seymour to Dudley's eldest son, Lord Lisle. However, the following year Warwick began a relentless pursuit of Somerset, which culminated in the duke's trial on trumped-up charges of treason in December 1551. He gave as good an account of himself as the Earl of Surrey had done five years earlier, and to as little avail. Although the charge of treason was dropped, he was still found guilty on three counts of felony, and condemned to death just the same. Warwick, who had now been promoted Duke of Northumberland, made a show of interceding for Somerset's life, but in fact systematically misinformed Edward about the trial in order to ensure that the king signed the death warrant. As far as we can tell, Edward, who showed no cruelty in his nature, sought to preserve his uncle's life, but the execution was presented to him as an unpleasant but unavoidable duty. Clearing his conscience before his own execution less than two years later, Northumberland was to admit that he had falsified the charges against Somerset.

By thus owning up to his rather crude elimination of his rival, Northumberland set himself up for posterity as a villain, while his victim, Somerset, who was always careful to set his own actions in the best possible light, successfully imposed upon posterity his own valuation of himself as a benevolent statesman selflessly devoted to the common good. Only recently have historians challenged these enduring myths. While the 'Good Duke' of Somerset has been turned by 'revisionist' historians into not simply a villain but, which is worse, an incompetent villain, the 'Bad Duke' of Northumberland has undergone an equal and opposite transformation. He has emerged from the process as not merely a competent administrator but a talented statesman adept at consensus politics and genuinely concerned for reform. In short, the historical reputations of Somerset and Northumberland have been simply exchanged. What historians should really abandon is the notion that the two men were so very different. Somerset was a self-serving *arriviste* who feathered his nest at the expense of king and Church. Northumberland was just as self-serving as Somerset, but less hypocritical and more capable. Where Somerset's arrogance alienated powerful interests, Northumberland's superior management skills created more consensus behind his policies (which were for the most part cautious and sensible enough). But the net effect was the same. Northumberland, like Somerset before him, ruled the king and therefore the kingdom.

The events of 1549–50 left Northumberland understandably preoccupied with the security of his regime, and many of his measures were directed towards enhancing it. The most important of these was the introduction in some counties of Lords Lieutenant (an office which survives in largely honorific form to this day) to fill some of the gaps left by the disappearance or marginalisation of traditional regional magnates, gaps which had contributed to the troubles of 1549. Except in the controversial areas of religion and the succession, his policies were not so much initiatives as facing up to the inevitable. Peace with France was the only sensible course of action, and Northumberland secured a reasonable deal in exchange for the surrender of Boulogne in 1550. And in the context of fiscal exhaustion and economic slump, it was only sensible to try and retrench on expenditure, rationalise royal finances, and begin to remedy the catastrophic debasement of the currency by which first Henry VIII and then Somerset had staved off financial collapse through the wars of the 1540s.

FURTHER REFORMATION

The irresistible progress of the Reformation was signalled in the continuing harassment of Stephen Gardiner in 1550, a process recorded in some detail in the king's diary. In 1549 Gardiner had endeavoured to adjust to the changing times by working out an interpretation of the *Book of Common Prayer* which enabled him to maintain that it was compatible with a traditionally Catholic theology of the Mass. This required all the ingenuity at his command, and was far from Cranmer's intention. Steps were therefore taken to close the loopholes which Gardiner had opened. In summer, he was invited to sign up to a series of articles which would have committed him unequivocally to the Reformation programme. This he refused to do even in the face of personal orders from the king – and the diary at this point reveals the teenage Edward investing religious reform with his personal authority. He wrote of the bishop's refusal to assent to the 'books of my proceedings'. First Gardiner was deprived of the income from his bishopric, and then, as he still held out, he was subjected to lengthy judicial proceedings which began in December 1550. For all his adroit legalistic footwork, the trial ended in February 1551 with his removal from the bishopric of Winchester. He would not be released from the Tower of London until the reign of Mary Tudor. It is characteristic of Northumberland's ecclesiastical policy that Gardiner's successor at Winchester, the Protestant John Ponet, had to agree before being appointed bishop to surrender the entire property of the bishopric into the king's hands (through which it passed rapidly into the hands of Northumberland and his cronies), settling instead for an annual salary of a little over £1,300. If we did not know that these men were reformers, we might almost think the deal smacked of 'simony' (trading holy things for money).

Meanwhile, the pace of change quickened. In January 1550 the government ordered local authorities in Church and state to call in all old Catholic service books for destruction. Missals, breviaries, ordinals, hymnals, antiphoners, graduals, processioners – thousands upon thousands of volumes were consigned to the flames in what was probably the greatest episode of book-burning in English history. It was the accompaniment, of course, to the greatest single episode of vandalism in English history as the same imperative to dispose of 'idolatry' resulted in the systematic destruction of almost all religious images and pictures. The implementation of religious change depended heavily on the bishops and hierarchy of the Church, and the normal process of natural wastage was not giving a quick enough turnover in personnel in the higher echelons of the clergy. So the royal supremacy was now aggressively used to speed things up. Conservative bishops such as Day of Chichester followed Bonner and Gardiner into enforced retirement, and were replaced by reliable Protestants such as Nicholas Ridley and John Scory. Zealous bishops like Cranmer in Canterbury and Ridley in London went on to order the removal of the very altars from the churches. In November 1550, all bishops were instructed, as Edward put it, 'to pluck down the altars'. The altar, the place of sacrifice, was the ultimate symbol of what the Protestants rejected as the idolatry of Catholicism. With the altars gone, there was no longer any need for the apparatus of plate, vestments and ornaments which had adorned the old religious services, so in 1551 the Crown, partly inspired by theological correctness but more urgently driven by dire financial need, commanded the liquidation of the remaining movable property of parish churches for the benefit of the royal coffers.

The rapid progress of the Reformation represented not the implementation of a single programme but a continuous revolution. Cranmer's own theology was in flux throughout the reign, and had moved on beyond the first Book of Common Prayer probably even before it was brought into use in summer 1549. Assisted and advised by Protestant theologians from Europe who had taken refuge in England from adverse political conditions abroad, Cranmer was hard at work on a more radical revision of the liturgy, which resulted in the second Book of Common Prayer, issued in 1552. The firmly Protestant stance of this book was further clarified in a series of forty-two Articles of Religion, propositions on faith and worship which represented the official teaching of Cranmer's Church of England. Cranmer was a healthy man and could have lived another fifteen years. His religious views had been in non-stop development since 1530, and there is no reason to suppose that he had finished yet. The Catholics of England had been on the back foot most of the time since 1534, and since 1547 they had been cornered and silenced. A few lurked in impotent exile, others languished in English gaols, but the majority were evidently stunned beyond all thought of resistance. Without the brief vindication of traditional religion under Mary Tudor, which brought back the exiles, freed the captives, and heartened the hitherto silent majority, Catholicism in England would have disappeared as totally as it did in Zürich and Geneva.

The records of the latter years of Edward's reign, and in particular the political journal which he kept until the onset of his final illness, show him beginning to emerge as a political actor in his own right. The essays in political theory and practice which he wrote at the behest of his tutors are able enough efforts, although it is hardly realistic to look to them for signs of originality or insight, still less as hints as to how an adult Edward's kingship might have developed. These were humanist exercises, educational rather than political. But they do show that his political education was taken seriously by those who had control of him. His political journal from this time shows that he had real concerns of his own. Foremost among them was the religious intransigence of his elder sister, Mary. His journal abounds in records of discussions about her refusal to abandon the Mass, and about the religious offences and obduracy of her chaplains and servants. All the notes smack of that combination of dogmatic self-righteousness with ignorance of human values and political realities which is the peculiar prerogative of the adolescent. The intolerant zeal for which that same sister would became notorious is all too evident in Edward's anxiety lest his failure to prevent her hearing the Mass in her household would implicate him before God in what he regarded as her idolatry. 'To give licence to sin was to sin', he notes, from a conversation with a trio of worthy bishops, although he also notes their concession that 'to suffer and wink at it for a time might be borne, so all haste possible might be used'. We can see the same youthful inflexibility in Edward's refusal to attend the (Catholic) christening of the Spanish ambassador's son in autumn 1552. By 1550, he considered himself a 'true minister of God', as he wrote in a letter to his sister. Had he reached maturity, he would probably have imposed his theological will with even more determination than Mary, given his youthful vigour and his obviously superior intellectual capacities.

It has been argued, on the basis of this same journal, that Edward was less interested in theology and the content of religious belief and practice than historians of his reign have customarily believed, and that any concern the journal evinces with matters of religious observance was really concern about political loyalty. What really bothered Edward about Mary's stand, it has been argued, was not the intrinsic significance of her actions and omissions, but was rather her refusal to obey the royal will. It is certainly true that he resented the slight to his authority: 'It is a scandalous thing that so high a personage should deny our sovereignty', he wrote to her in 1551. Yet his appeal to doctrines of obedience was an attempt to outmanoeuvre her by appealing to a virtue she herself claimed to respect and value (she professed obedience to her father's will). Edward's fear that indulgence towards Mary amounted to giving licence to sin shows that his concern was a matter of conscience as well as of politics. His detailed account of the harassment and eventual dismissal of Stephen Gardiner, the elderly and experienced bishop of Winchester, gives a similar impression. Edward's astonishment that Gardiner should dare to refuse a direct command from his youthful and inexperienced sovereign is recorded with an almost endearing naïvety. True, the Tudor expectation of unquestioning obedience is seen here in its purest form, untempered either by frailty of sex (as under his sisters) or by dynastic insecurity (as under his father and grandfather). Yet Edward is evidently concerned with the religious content as well as with the political form of Gardiner's disobedience.

The attempt to separate religion and politics is the biggest misunderstanding in this view of Edward – as it would be for any issue of religion or politics in the Tudor century. Edward's concern was clearly for more than the outward obedience which satisfied his sister Elizabeth. The recurrent interest in religious affairs visible throughout his journal also testifies to a depth of religious engagement far greater than hers, though no greater than Mary's. His lengthy discussions of Mary's disobedience in his journal reveal not simply the tyrannical (or perhaps merely adolescent) expectation of unquestioning obedience, but also a concern for the state of his own soul if he allowed political pressure for freedom of observance for Mary to keep him from what he saw as the path of righteousness. Of course obedience was a paramount concern as well. But here he shows a typical Tudor trait. Enormous pressure had to be brought to bear on Edward to induce him to grant the Imperial demand that Mary be allowed to retain the Mass unmolested in her household.

Several sources report that Edward listened most attentively to sermons, and a later reference to a notebook of his (now lost) in which he summarised each sermon that he heard corroborates them. As early as 1550 the Spanish ambassador noted that nobody about court was readier than the king to argue for the new doctrines, and that the king was assiduous in noting sermons. Edward was particularly taken with the foreign reformers who had sought refuge in his kingdom. They eagerly bestowed upon him copies of their many books, which he just as eagerly perused. When one of them, Martin Bucer, died in 1551, Edward copied into his journal passages from a memorial volume which his tutor, John Cheke, collected and published in the great man's memory. Nor should it be forgotten that Edward himself wrote a book – a brief treatise against the authority of the Pope, remarkable not only because it was composed in French, but also because it shows that he inherited his father's taste for amateur theology. His own drafts for a revision of the statutes of the Order of the Garter, inspired perhaps by his attendance at the Garter ceremony on 23 April 1551, are the fruit of his realisation that this chivalric gathering still invoked the patronage of a Catholic saint, and a saint of dubious historicity at that. The Order's dedication was to be altered to the somewhat cumbersome 'Defence of the Truth wholly Contained in Scripture', and St George himself, along with his dragon, was to be erased from the Order's heraldry, to be replaced by a knight bearing a sword and a Bible: a suitable enough emblem for Edward's militant Protestantism.

If 1552 saw the Reformation reach new extremes, it also saw the beginning of the end. In April, the young king, who had hitherto enjoyed robust good health, fell seriously ill – 'of the measles and the smallpox', his physicians told him (an unlikely combination, although whatever it was, it left him very weak). Recovering somewhat, Edward was taken on a progress around the southern counties in summer 1552, perhaps undertaken partly with a view to furthering his recuperation. The personal appearance of the king was a traditional medieval technique of governance intended both to instil fear and respect into the hearts of those who had challenged central authority and to inspire the loyalty of his 'loving subjects'. Both Henry VII and Henry VIII had found it useful to parade themselves before their people in this way. In Edward's case, it was also part of the political nurturing of the young king by his ministers, a task which Northumberland took more seriously than Somerset before him – perhaps because he realised the significance of having to manage a youth rather than a mere boy. It says much for Northumberland's confidence in his own position and in his relationship with the king that he felt no need to accompany Edward on tour. Edward, freed for a while from Northumberland's tutelage, was able to meet some of his greater noblemen in their homes and see some of the major towns of his realm, such as Southampton and Portsmouth. The royal progress told Edward, as well as his subjects, that he was their king, and confirmed the general message about the reality of royal authority even during a minority which was vital to establishing the legitimacy of the regime's most contentious policy, the Protestant

Reformation, now nearing its high-water mark. However, the progress may have come too soon after his illness, for he became visibly drained as the weeks of activity went by, and the progress was cut short, to end in September. Soon after his return to London, his political journal peters out, and in February 1553 he once more fell seriously ill – never to recover.

That towards the end of his reign Edward was gaining in political maturity can hardly be denied. However, the argument must not be taken too far. The governmental initiative still lay firmly with the Duke of Northumberland, and it is impossible to allow, in what was still a personal monarchy, that the king could be fully politically mature until he had shown his mettle by dispensing with the services of his novice-master. Northumberland was Mazarin to Edward's Louis XIV, and Edward's emergence from political dependence and tutelage could only have been impressed upon his people by his emancipation, and there was no sign of this when Edward died.

THE SUCCESSION CRISIS

On the contrary, the final crisis of the reign, even as it saw Edward more directly and personally engaged in the political process than ever before, also showed that his dependence on the will and guidance of the Duke of Northumberland was still total. That final crisis concerned the succession to the throne, as it became obvious that Edward was dying and that his sister Mary was likely to take her rightful place as queen.

If Mary Tudor's courage under the pressure of the previous four years had shown Edward's regime one thing, it was that the English Reformation would not be safe in her hands. And if there would obviously be no room for Protestantism, there would equally be no room for Northumberland under the new dispensation. As it was Northumberland who stood to lose most from Mary's succession, it was he, not surprisingly, who did the most to prevent it. Playing upon the dying Edward's own religious anxieties and commitments, and making sure that neither Mary nor Elizabeth could secure any access to the royal presence, he set the king to considering a change to the arrangements Henry VIII had enshrined in his will and in statute. The religious question, however politically central, could hardly constitute grounds for frustrating both the conventional order of inheritance and the will of King Henry. But Mary's technical illegitimacy under English law was a far more potent weapon. Under common law, bastards simply could not inherit, and it was easy to argue for Mary's exclusion on these grounds.

If this proved too much, and also excluded Princess Elizabeth, Northumberland would not be weeping long. While the Protestant religion might be safe in Elizabeth's hands, Northumberland knew that his own career would be finished. He could never have attained the hold over her that he had established over the boy king. With the Stuarts, descended from Henry VIII's elder sister, passed over in the 1544 Act of

Succession, that left Jane Grey next in line. Jane was the eldest granddaughter of Henry's younger sister, Mary, the French queen and Duchess of Suffolk. She had previously been contracted in marriage to Northumberland's eldest available son, Guildford, a boy much the same age as Edward (with whom Jane's name had also been linked in the past), and on 21 May 1553 the wedding was celebrated.

It should not be imagined that the attempt to divert the succession was simply a matter of Northumberland imposing his will upon the king. Northumberland enjoyed the full support of Edward in what was done. This was doubtless one of those cases in which, as a French ambassador once remarked, Edward anticipated the wishes of Northumberland and acted freely in order the better to please him. The confidence in the power of the mere will of the king, expressed in letters patent, to outweigh a clear Act of Parliament is redolent of that undiluted doctrine of kingship which had been instilled into the boy. This last, and in the event frustrated, action of his reign was more fully his work than anything that had gone before. It is unlikely that the mere machinations of Northumberland could have imposed upon his colleagues and potential rivals a settlement so obviously advantageous to himself, even were the Protestant faith itself otherwise at risk. It was the manifest and urgently expressed will of the dying king which induced the Privy Councillors and officers of the Crown to consent to the deed.

The Crown's legal advisers were particularly reluctant to follow the king's orders and draw up letters patent embodying his will. The Lord Chief Justice, Sir Edward Montague, pointed out that the proposed course of action would not only be unenforceable in law (as letters patent could not prevail over statute) but would also involve all subjects who pursued it in treason under the terms of Henry VIII's Act of Succession. However, a personal interview with Edward on 15 June, in the presence of Northumberland and his supporters, caused him to act against his better judgement. Montague was, frankly, overborne. Faced with the express command of his sovereign, he literally had no choice. At least he could find a shadow of justification in the fact that the king announced an intention of confirming the proceedings in Parliament if possible. This brought the whole affair within the scope of the king's power to make law by proclamation in the absence of Parliament (a power which the common law recognised subject to subsequent parliamentary confirmation). Montague's submission salved many other troubled consciences. Cranmer, for example, had hesitated to sign, recalling that he had previously sworn to uphold the succession of Mary after Edward, and fearful of incurring the guilt of perjury. However, the capitulation of the judges gave him the wherewithal to absolve his own conscience, and, as so often in his life, he washed away one oath with another.

The letters patent drawn up by Montague and his colleagues, dated 21 June 1553, made the best of a bad job, attempting to counter Henry VIII's last Act of Succession (1544) by invoking against it 'divers acts of parliament remaining in their full force' which confirmed the illegitimacy of Edward's sisters. The statutory rights of Mary and Elizabeth were therefore brushed aside on the grounds that 'being illegitimate and not lawfully begotten' they were 'to all intents and purposes... clearly disabled to ask, claim, or challenge the said imperial crown' of the realm. Appeal was also made to the risk that, should either of them marry a 'stranger born out of this realm', then he might 'practise to have the laws and customs of his... native country... practised... within this our realm... to the utter subversion of the commonwealth'.

Meanwhile, Northumberland did his best to broaden the basis of support for his coup. Key figures were won over with grants of land and office, and the letters patent were circulated widely among the court and London élite for signature. The French ambassador was approached with a view to providing military aid if need be. As the succession of Mary could only bring England back into the Habsburg camp, French support was promptly forthcoming.

As was by now becoming traditional, news of the Tudor king's death on 6 July 1553 was kept a close secret by the ruling élite as it sought to tighten its grip on power during the transition. For once, the tactic misfired. The delay in the proclamation of Edward's designated heir, Jane, gave Mary the opportunity to mount her own bid for the throne from the East Anglian heartlands of her princely estates. Within a fortnight, Edward's 'devise' was frustrated, and Mary, despite everything, was on the throne. History, for a few years, would be different, even if the Marian Reaction would prove as shortlived as the Edwardine experiment. The so-called 'nine days' of Queen Jane were not a reign at all, just the unravelling of a coup – a coup which had every chance of success, except that its intended victim, Mary Tudor, had never fallen

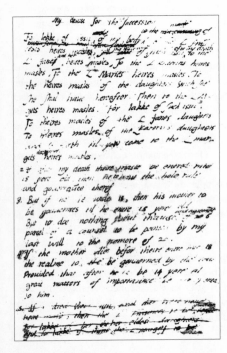

Edward VI's 'devise for the succession' of June 1553. There are six paragraphs in the Devise, which is entirely in the handwriting of the youthful king. The 's' in 'L. Janes' is seen to be deleted by a stroke of the pen, and words 'and her' to be interpolated above the line. This amendment shows the plan changing from a preference for male heirs if possible to a transfer of the crown to Lady Jane in person (this privilege is not accorded to her younger sisters). It thus tightens the grip on power of her father-in-law, the Duke of Northumberland.

into the hands of her enemies. Jane herself had no role in the events that unfolded around her.

Had Edward VI survived, the history of England and of Europe would have been vastly different. Although Mary Tudor, like many others as Catholic as she, persuaded herself that the Protestant Reformation was little more than a self-seeking conspiracy by a court cabal, and that Edward would repudiate it upon attaining his majority, she was quite wrong. This is not to deny that the Protestant Reformation in England was a self-seeking conspiracy by a court cabal – even dedicated Protestants like Hugh Latimer and Thomas Lever said as much, in sermons preached to the court! – but it was much, much more. For a start, it was an evangelical religious movement offering a new heaven and a new earth, capable of inspiring its followers to virtuous lives and heroic deaths. As Mary was to find, the removal of the cabal and the withdrawal of royal support did not mean that Protestantism would simply melt away like a morning frost. Even more importantly, Protestantism was in a real sense Edward's religion. There was no way that he would have repudiated it had he grown up. And once the young zealot had taken personal control of his government, there is every reason to believe that the Protestant politics of Somerset and Northumberland would have been the keynote of his reign. He had been groomed by Cranmer, Somerset and Northumberland to be the champion of European Protestantism, a sort of evangelical crusader. Even allowing him the modest life expectancy of his father and grandfather, around fifty years, he might have ruled England until the 1580s.

A solidly Protestant England, united under a vigorous Tudor king, would have been well placed to take full advantage of the religious and political chaos which spread through France and the Netherlands in the later sixteenth century. Of course, not even under a vigorous and mature king could England have threatened the hegemony of Spain under Philip II. But it would certainly have shifted the balance of power, it would probably have driven Spanish power back to the Pyrenees, and it might possibly have established the total dominance of Protestantism in northern Europe. With England's political leadership and full royal support for the international vision of Thomas Cranmer, who under these circumstances would have become the veritable patriarch of European Protestantism, the history of Protestantism itself might have been very different, a solid ecclesiastical block in the north ranged against the Catholicism of the south and the Orthodoxy of the east. As for England itself, thirty years under a king as zealous as Edward would have resulted in a Protestantism as dour and grey as anything ever seen in Scotland or Switzerland. 'Merry England' would have come to an even more complete and sudden end. There would have been no more cakes and ale, no Shakespeare, no Anglican choral tradition... The future of England, to use some words at this time still to be coined, would have been not 'Anglican' but 'Puritan'. Yet it was not to be. For Mary Tudor would in fact inherit the throne, and would thus save not only English Catholicism, but even much that would later be part of Anglicanism, much that we find it difficult to conceive the history of England without.

4

MARY TUDOR

A SURPRISING ACCESSION

The oddest thing about Mary's reign, like that of her grandfather, was the fact that it happened at all. A hundred years before, the accession of a woman to the English throne was all but unimaginable. Sir John Fortescue, the most influential constitutional thinker of fifteenth-century England, had flatly denied that a woman could wear the crown. Nor was her sex the least of the obstacles in Mary's path. Untrained for rule and unmarried, declared illegitimate and excluded from the succession in 1534, subsequently restored to it in 1544 (though with no revocation of her illegitimacy), a convinced Catholic who by 1553 stood almost alone against the religious policy of the Protestant regime, Mary looked likely to be baulked of her rights when the Duke of Northumberland married off Lady Jane Grey to his son, Guildford Dudley, and Edward VI willed the crown to Jane by virtue of her descent from Henry VII. The fact that the duke hoped to frustrate the accession of one woman by running another as her rival is a commentary on how much things had changed, as well as on the lack of a plausible male alternative. The account of how Mary overcame these formidable obstacles, a veritable Renaissance history of *virtù* dominating *fortuna*, is the most romantic and appealing episode in what has generally been seen as an unappealing and drab reign.

As Edward lay dying, Mary was summoned by the council to London, but shrewdly set off in the opposite direction, making for Kenninghall, deep in Norfolk. This certainly saved her throne, and probably her life: had she been in Northumberland's power, nothing could have stopped him. When it came, on 6 July, the death of Edward VI was not so well-kept a secret as that of his father and grandfather before him. At a moment when, in the interests of Northumberland's coup, it was essential that secrecy be maintained, news of the young king's death leaked almost instantly, a sign that the apparatus of government around the duke was by no means unanimous about his imminent seizure of power.

So it was at Kenninghall that news of Edward's death first reached Mary on 8 July, sent by a gentleman and councillor, Sir Nicholas Throckmorton, whose religious sympathies were firmly Protestant. Mary was worried that the message might be a set-up. But on 9 July, with the news of the king's death confirmed, she had herself proclaimed queen – in fact beating the Duke of Northumberland to the draw: Lady Jane Grey was not proclaimed queen until 10 July. Mary at once despatched an imperious letter to the Privy Council in London, requiring them to endorse her claim. More practically, she summoned to her side the gentry of East Anglia, and they responded so promptly as to suggest that there had been some preparation, or at least some forethought, over the previous weeks. Besides the support of the gentlemen of her household, such as Robert Rochester, Henry Jerningham and Edward Waldegrave, she was joined by some of Norfolk's wealthiest and most influential knights: not only doughty backwoodsmen such as Sir Henry Bedingfield, but also Sir Richard Southwell, a veteran shire administrator and trusted servant of Henry VIII – the sort of substantial figure who brought experience and credibility, as well as more tangible resources, to the queen's camp.

Mary's letter to the council reached London on 11 July, causing consternation in the Dudley camp. Moving south into Suffolk, the next day she established herself in the formidable castle of Framlingham, where first hundreds and then thousands of men flocked to her standard. Jane had already been proclaimed at Ipswich, but Mary's approach and the groundswell of popular support for her cause changed the mind of another key figure, Sir Thomas Cornwallis, Sheriff of Norfolk and Suffolk. Although the initial moves on Mary's behalf were instigated and implemented by those who were clearly Catholic at heart, the bandwagon they started gained such momentum that even the Protestant leaders in the region had no choice but to jump on board.

Thomas, Lord Wentworth, who had led the Protestant Reformation in eastern Suffolk since the 1530s, was induced to lend his support – perhaps helped by his loyalty to the memory of Henry VIII, who had made him what he was. Peers as

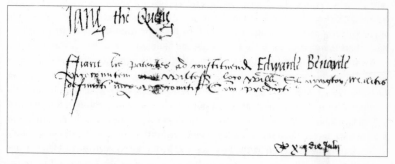

Warrant of Queen Jane for the issue of letters patent appointing Edward Benarde to be sheriff of Wiltshire, 14 July 1553. This has the signature 'Jane the Quene' and is one of the very few documents signed by Jane during her nominal reign of nine days. The name 'Edwarde Benarde', the sheriff-designate, is also in her hand.

well as knights and gentlemen were now answering Mary's call, and in London the duke and the Privy Council began to panic. Northumberland raised troops to march against her, hopeful that Lady Jane's father, the Duke of Suffolk, would lead them. But although his supporters were still right behind him, they were determined to remain there, at a safe distance. Northumberland was obliged to assume personal command, and headed north out of London on 14 July. Meanwhile, the summonses and letters despatched in Mary's name were working stronger magic than those despatched in Jane's, and the rest of the nation was taking Mary's side. The Thames Valley, the Midlands, the West Country and the north were all raised on her behalf. It was still Catholic families who took the lead. Troops were raised in her name by county luminaries such as Edward, Lord Windsor, in Buckinghamshire, Henry, Lord Abergavenny, in Kent and Sir Thomas Tresham in Northamptonshire.

Others were more cautious. Princess Elizabeth – who stood to lose as much as Mary from Northumberland's coup – amassed a substantial force of her own clients at Hatfield. She played a waiting game: if she did not rush to the aid of Jane, neither did she hurry to her sister's side. In the confusion of those days, other local magnates, such as Lord Rich and the Earl of Oxford in Essex, likewise hedged their bets. But such hesitation worked in Mary's favour. The longer the issue was undecided, the more Jane's cause looked like the overreaching ambition of a self-serving noble *arriviste*. While the zealous Protestants who had to be his main constituency were uncertain and divided over the competing claims of religion and dynastic legitimacy, the zealous Catholics rallied to Mary with the complete conviction of those who can see in events the divine vindication of their cause. Civil wars are usually fought between minorities, and Mary's minority was the more cohesive and the more determined.

The endgame was over in a few quick moves. Pausing only to sack Sawston Hall, where Mary had stayed on her flight into Norfolk, Northumberland made for Cambridge, where the vice-chancellor, Dr Edwin Sandys, unwisely lent him the university's support. On Monday 17 July he advanced boldly into Mary's heartland, Suffolk, reaching Bury St Edmunds. But on Tuesday, haemorrhaging troops all the way, he retired to Cambridge, beaten back by the mere rumour of the size of Mary's host: there is no particular reason to doubt the figure of 30,000 which was put upon it. Meanwhile, back in London, news from the rest of England convinced the rump of the Edwardine government to switch horses. The Duke of Suffolk broke the news to his daughter Jane on 19 July, and then proclaimed Mary queen on Tower Hill. London exploded with joy – as much out of relief at not facing an overwhelming military assault as out of loyalty to Mary. Bonfires were lit, bells were rung and impromptu parties filled the streets as people celebrated with the traditional symbols of that 'merry England' which the Protestant Reformation was already obviously out to suppress.

Meanwhile, Northumberland himself proclaimed Mary in the market square at Cambridge, before holing up in the house of his friend, Sir John Cheke, once Edward's tutor, and still Provost of King's College. In a rare moment of co-operation between town and gown, a large force led by the mayor surrounded Northumberland's refuge and put him under arrest. He was soon on his way to the Tower, with most of his family – and the hapless Dr Sandys.

Mary made a slow and stately progress towards London, disbanding her forces, and receiving the dutiful submission of all those who had not been swift enough to display their loyalty before Northumberland's ignominious surrender. Elizabeth, milking a difficult situation for all that it was worth, upstaged Mary by making her own entry into the city of London on 29 July, bringing 3,000 men with her – barely a tenth of Mary's army at its height, but a significantly larger retinue than Northumberland had been able to scrape together – before riding out to join the queen for her state entry on 3 August. But a touching display of sisterly solidarity was the message people chose to read, amidst their joy at being spared the horrors of civil war.

There were a few executions, of course. Northumberland was sent to the block, along with some of his closest associates, despite his timely and desperate reversion to the faith of his fathers. But mercy was, unusually, the rule. Even Jane Grey and her unfortunate husband were spared, at least for now.

Arrangements were swiftly under way for Mary's coronation, which would set the seal on her bloodless victory. The nobility thronged to greet their new sovereign. A dozen noble families were honoured in the traditional manner as their youthful heads or heirs were created Knights of the Order of the Bath. Stephen Gardiner, released from the Tower on Mary's arrival in August, celebrated the rites on Sunday 1 October 1553, and the traditional duties of ceremonial service to the monarch were performed at the coronation feast by the Duke of Norfolk and the Earls of Arundel, Derby, Devon, Shrewsbury, Surrey, Westmorland and Worcester. It was in fact a celebration of national reconciliation after the stresses of the summer.

A SINGLE-ISSUE REIGN

Mary Tudor had only one policy: to restore the Church of England in all its pre-Reformation glory. Her first public act on reaching London was to issue a proclamation announcing her own inability 'to hide that religion which God and the world knoweth she hath ever professed from her infancy', and permitting and encouraging (though not at this stage compelling) her subjects to profess it likewise. This policy expressed a single underlying political attitude: conservatism, a preference for the old ways. To restore Catholicism was, in effect, to turn the clock back. It is not difficult to appreciate how natural it was for someone whose life had been torn apart in her teens to hanker for the way things were. Even her wedding, a year later, was an opportunity for her to parade her old-world values. Her wedding ring, she let it be known, was 'a plain hoop of gold, with no stone in it... because maidens were so married in old times'.

Mary was a deeply religious woman, and nobody has ever impugned the sincerity and depth of her convictions, which were well known to her contemporaries. Among the clearest testimonies to this are the numerous religious books which were dedicated to her by authors and translators. By far the greater part of all dedications to Mary, whether as princess or as queen, were of religious texts. When Henry Parker, Lord Morley, broke with his usual practice by dedicating to her a translation of a secular work, Cicero's *Dream of Scipio*, he acknowledged that it might therefore come as a surprise to her, but justified it on the grounds that Cicero, though a pagan, was a man of exemplary virtue. Although one cannot always take a dedication as evidence of a recipient's beliefs or interests (for example, John Calvin dedicated his *Institution of Christian Religion* to Francis I of France, but one would hardly conclude from this that Francis was a Protestant!), when a person receives dedications overwhelmingly of one particular kind, it is reasonable to suppose that those seeking to give pleasure or to secure reward through these gifts had a fair idea of what would and would not be acceptable. Protestant authors did not bother dedicating books to Mary.

There was no room for compromise in Mary's mentality. The only compromise in her personal history was when, after the death of her mother, she had humbled herself to accept her father's proceedings: something she doubtless repented as a betrayal of herself, her mother, and her faith rather than reckoned a laudable or even an understandable means of self-preservation. Yet her attitude towards her father remained as queen what it had been as a princess – deeply ambivalent. She frequently lamented her womanliness, wishing she had the awesome charisma of her father so that she might properly rebuke the failings of her ministers and induce them to more zealous and effective service. The best she could do was to invoke her father's memory: despite the notorious burnings, she never struck terror into her subjects' hearts as her father had done.

If she had bent the knee before her father's supremacy, she was less than obsequious to the authority of those who ruled in the name of her younger brother. Throughout Edward's reign she had flouted the law by attending Mass in her private chapel, relying in part on her status as heir presumptive, and rather more on the diplomatic weight of her cousin, the Emperor Charles V, who for a while seemed set to turn the political tide of the Reformation in its very heartland, the Holy Roman Empire (essentially, modern Germany and Austria). Not that her position made resistance especially easy. Enormous pressure was brought to bear on her to give up the Mass. She was summoned for interviews with the Privy Council and with Edward VI in person, and was harangued at length by both. Representatives of the Council came to her palace at Havering to arrest her chaplains (fortunately for her they missed one, who, in hiding, ministered to Mary for the rest of the reign). During some of her interviews with the king and his advisers, Mary forthrightly proclaimed her readiness to die for her beliefs rather than give up the Mass. In that age of martyrdom, when the commitments and risks of religious conviction were so clearly appreciated by so many people, there is no reason to doubt that she would have proved as good as her word. Nobody ever questioned her courage, though some preferred to put a less favourable interpretation upon it. Thomas Cromwell was not far from the mark when, back in 1536, he described her as 'the most obstinate woman that ever was'.

RESTORATION OF THE MASS

Even as Mary made her way to London, her religious policy, which hardly needed explicit formulation, was being eagerly if illegally implemented by squires and parsons across the country. As Robert Parkyn noted in Yorkshire:

> In the meantime, in many places of the realm, priests was commanded by lords and knights Catholic to say Mass in Latin with consecration and elevation of the Body and Blood of Christ under form of bread and wine with a decent order, as hath been used before time.

Parkyn's unselfconscious assumption that humble priests would follow the lead of their social superiors tells us a lot about the reasons for the success of the English Reformation. But not everyone was so co-operative. Down at Adisham in Kent, the Cambridge graduate and zealous Protestant John Bland, a protégé of Archbishop Cranmer, resisted his parishioners' demands for the Mass, and was offered physical violence in return for his determination to uphold the law. Mary herself showed none of that precise legalism which was to accompany the reversal of her policy in the reign of her successor, Elizabeth. Mass was immediately restored in the Chapel Royal, and the Common Prayer service was used only for Edward's spartan obsequies. Within a few weeks she issued a proclamation which in effect suspended the statutory penalties for celebrating and attending Mass, and when her first Parliament convened on 5 October, the repeal of Edward VI's religious legislation was high on the agenda. It met with unusual resistance in the House of Commons. Some eighty votes were cast against it, although the 270 in favour carried it easily. The *Book of Common Prayer*, which many had dismissed as a 'Christmas game' on its first appearance in 1549, was outlawed in time for Christmas.

THE SPANISH MARRIAGE

If one single action of Mary's deserves the criticism which is usually heaped upon her reign, it must be her marriage to Philip of Spain. In both personal and political terms it was a disaster, although it is not clear that Mary herself realised this until the bitter end (and it was bitter indeed) – which may be a sufficient commentary on her personal and political failings. The sixteenth century, as we have frequently been reminded in recent years, was a patriarchal age. It was expected that wealthy, well-born women would marry, and there was no reason why Mary should not conform to that expectation. Indeed, to the extent that she had been educated for any role in life, it was for marriage to a foreign prince.

    Mary's education had of course been wider than that of most women of her time. Her mother had commissioned one of the leading Spanish scholars of the day, Juan Luis Vives, to design a programme of education specifically for her. The result was *The Education of a Christian Woman* (1524), which recommended not only the traditional female accomplishments of spinning and needlework, but a humanist academic programme of grammar and rhetoric. Mary was not to be hampered in her studies, as her great-grandmother Lady Margaret Beaufort had been, by ignorance of Latin. To some extent, she should be seen as the first in a line of Tudor bluestockings which included her younger sister Elizabeth and her cousin Jane Grey, although she was not their equal in learning (Elizabeth read Latin and Greek fluently, and even translated the classics for pleasure). Mary could speak French, Spanish and Latin, and could follow Italian. She could ride; she could sing; she could even play the lute and the keyboard. She was, of course, prodigiously devout in a conventional way. Although she read, and even translated, some Erasmus, there is no indication at all that she had any sympathy with the kind of criticism of the Church which by this time his very name stood for. Her patience in adversity, which she had ample occasion to exercise, suggests that she would have been inured to witnessing the serial infidelities that were almost expected of a royal husband. Had her life been happier, she might long before have left her native shores to bear the children of some Habsburg or Valois prince, living the sort of life outlined for her in another little tract commissioned by her mother, Erasmus's *Introduction to Christian Marriage*. As it was, the tortuous political manoeuvres of her father's reign had denied her the opportunities that had come her way. But, having secured the throne, there was apparently nothing to prevent her from fulfilling what she doubtless regarded as her maternal destiny: nothing, that is, except age and ill health.

For it is not necessary to descend into the murky underworld of psychohistory to conjecture that her experience as a teenager, when her father brutally rejected her along with her mother, combined with the unaccustomed hardships of life under virtual house arrest with her mother in the early 1530s, might have disturbed her sexual development as well as damaged her physical health. By the time Mary was in a position to find herself a husband, she was over thirty-seven years old, which even today would be considered a little risky for a first pregnancy. It was extremely late by sixteenth-century standards, and while it was not unknown for women to continue bearing children into their early forties, in her case the medical evidence is far from clear that she was still capable of conceiving. The immediate family precedents were not good. Her own mother's pregnancies had miscarried more often than not, with the last of them occurring in 1518, when she was only thirty-two.

In choosing a husband, Mary was in an unprecedented and unenviable dilemma, as her husband would necessarily become king. To marry an Englishman, however noble, would be to marry a subject and raise him to the throne, indeed to an eminence greater than her own. Yet to marry a foreigner would mean making a foreigner king. Neither option was ideal. It was one thing for a king to take a subject as a wife. This involved no disturbance to the social order, although, as was seen under Henry VIII, the political implications for the bride's family could be huge. The king's wife had no power, though she might exert influence. For a queen to take a subject as a husband was a different matter, as it would to a greater or lesser extent transfer power from her hands to his. And this is not to mention the affront both to Tudor pride (which ran undiluted in Mary's veins) and to national esteem in marrying beneath her own and her realm's dignity. Again, it was one thing for a king to marry a foreign princess, quite another for a queen to marry a foreign prince. A prince in line for (or already upon) a foreign throne might simply subordinate the interests of England to those of an international dynasty, while a younger son would no doubt regard the marriage as the opportunity to fulfil the political ambitions from which only the smallest accident of birth had separated him.

It is hardly surprising that Mary's Privy Council divided sharply over this novel problem, with the Lord Chancellor, Gardiner, preferring the domestic option, and William Paget urging a foreign marriage. The dispute spilled over into Parliament in November 1553. When the Speaker of the House of Commons led a delegation to lobby the queen against marrying abroad, the dilemma was laid out unmistakably. The Commons could not bear the thought of a foreign sovereign. But their suggestion that Mary marry a subject enraged her so much that she trampled on convention by answering for herself, instead of allowing the Lord Chancellor to answer for her. Haughtily intimating that royal marriages were a matter for the royal prerogative rather than for parliamentary debate, she dismissed their intervention as an impertinence. Her outburst may have been more calculated than it appeared, for later she gave a dressing-down to Gardiner, whom she suspected, not wholly without reason, of having briefed the Speaker of the House of Commons in advance of this meeting.

In the circumstances, a foreign prince was probably preferable to an English noble – for the only plausible domestic candidate was the inexperienced and unstable young Edward Courtenay, Earl of Devon, who had spent most of his life thus far in the Tower of London. At least a foreigner, as an outsider, brought a new element into the system rather than merely strengthening one part of it, and a prince of royal blood necessarily stood above aristocratic rivalries as a home-grown nobleman never could. It was one of the more unaccountable acts of the varied career of Bishop Stephen Gardiner that at this moment, when he was on the brink of supreme power under the queen, he urged the cause of Courtenay in the teeth of Mary's clear preference for a foreign husband.

When it came to bringing these general considerations down to the arena of political practicalities, Philip of Spain, in his late twenties yet already a widower, looked an excellent choice. The marriage would seal the traditional anti-French alliance between England and the Burgundian and Castilian dynasties that were united in his person. In itself the marriage summed up Mary's 'good old days' policy, for it represented a return to an alliance which, except at a few moments of crisis, had served England well since the time of Henry V. Mary's own sympathies lay firmly with the Habsburgs, who had shown themselves her friends, at times her only friends, throughout the 1530s and the 1540s. Finally, as in due course Philip would become fully occupied with his dominions abroad, he was likely to be a less destabilising influence on English politics than a foreign prince seeking to put down roots here.

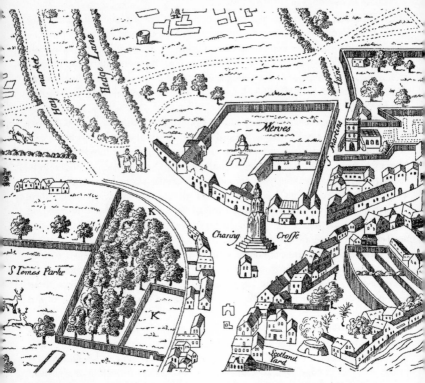

Plan of the Charing Cross area from the 'Ralph Agas' map. After a brief skirmish at Charing Cross, Sir Thomas Wyatt's troops headed east along the Strand and Fleet Street on Ash Wednesday (7 February) 1554, only to find the gates of the city of London barred against them at Ludgate.

Even when the queen's choice was made, and the council merely had to implement her decision, there was still much to be done, chiefly to frame the marriage treaty in order to protect English interests as far as possible against the risk of subordination to those of a foreign power. In so far as this could be done by treaty, it was done well. Strict limits were placed on Philip's intrinsic powers as king consort, and, in the absence of children, his powers would lapse with Mary's death. But there was nothing anyone could do to prevent Mary, should she see fit, from following her husband's policy advice. Everyone assumed that he would make a very real contribution by virtue of what was at the time viewed as the innate superiority of men over women and the legal and moral authority of husbands over wives.

WYATT'S REBELLION

The petition of the Commons against the Spanish marriage was a fair reflection of public opinion on the question, and some of the queen's enemies sought to exploit this. A small coterie of disaffected aristocrats planned simultaneous risings against the marriage across much of southern England. But their plans leaked out, precipitating premature action. Sir Thomas Wyatt made his move in Kent on 25 January 1554. A Protestant himself, as were others among the conspirators, his aims may have included not only halting or reversing Mary's religious policy, but even removing her from the throne. The involvement of Jane Grey's father, the Duke of Suffolk, would certainly suggest as much. But Wyatt based his call to arms on opposition to the queen's proposed marriage. Within days he was camped with several thousand men on the south bank of the Thames, looking to cross into the city of London. Although less success attended the efforts of his accomplices, the Duke of Suffolk in the Midlands and Sir Peter Carew in Devon, proximity to London made Wyatt's force a real threat. When some of Mary's troops, ineptly led by the decrepit Duke of Norfolk, defected to Wyatt, the situation looked desperate, and some of her councillors (including Gardiner, whose palace in Southwark was trashed by the rebels) lost their nerve. Mary, however, was no coward. Showing typical Tudor fortitude, she appeared at the Guildhall on 1 February and roused the assembled citizens to resist:

> Wherefore now, as good and faithful subjects, pluck up your hearts, and like true men stand fast with your lawful prince against these rebels, both our enemies and yours, and fear them not, for, I assure you, that I fear them nothing at all.

Her performance on this occasion is fully comparable to Elizabeth's at Tilbury in 1588, in the face of a more immediate (if less overwhelming) danger. London Bridge was held, and Wyatt had to move upstream to cross at the next bridge, at Kingston in Surrey. As his men approached London from the west, there was once more panic at court, but Mary's courage again rallied the fainthearted. The City was unmoved by Wyatt's appeal, and the queen's troops, under the Earl of Pembroke and Lord Clinton, were sufficiently well organised and motivated to pin down his force and secure his arrest.

The failure of Wyatt's Rebellion led directly to the execution of the unfortunate Jane Grey, who had hitherto been spared. The Duke of Suffolk's decision to throw in his lot with Wyatt cost not only his own life but also those of his daughter and son-in-law. Suffolk and his brother were brought to the Tower on 10 February, and Guildford Dudley and Jane Grey were sent to the block on Monday 12 February, within days of Wyatt's capture. The French ambassador, Noailles, claimed that many humble or innocent men were executed in the wake of Wyatt's Rebellion, but his evidence is not necessarily reliable. He had done his best to help prevent Mary's succession and was always prone to exaggerate anything to her discredit and to

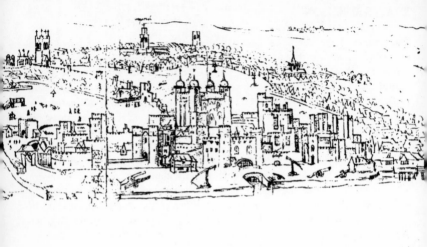

The Tower of London drawn by Anthony Van Wyngaerde in the 1550s. Lady Jane Grey was immured here from July 1553 until her execution in February 1554. Next month the Tower welcomed its most illustrious prisoner that century, Princess Elizabeth herself.

make the strongest case he could for the weakness of her position. Historians have perhaps paid too much attention to the reports of the ambassadors at Mary's court, be it to the unbounded hostility of Noailles or to the complacent and self-important optimism of Renard, the Spanish ambassador.

For a few weeks, moreover, it looked as though the chief result of the rising would be the execution of Elizabeth. Some of the conspirators had certainly hoped to see a marriage between Elizabeth and Courtenay, and to exclude the possibility of a foreign king by placing this English couple on the throne instead of Mary. No sooner had Wyatt's troops dispersed than Elizabeth was summoned to London. Before long, she was transferred from Whitehall to the Tower, where she was subjected to a series of intensive interrogations. Renard and Gardiner both urged Mary to execute her sister. Elizabeth had been highly circumspect, however, when the plotters had tried to make contact with her, and for all the suspicion and circumstantial evidence, nothing could be pinned on her. It was left to Wyatt himself to undo the damage. Consigned to

Instructions for my Lord Privei Seal

*furste to tell the kyng the whole state of this Realme,
wt all thynges appartayninge to the same asmuche as ye
knowe to be trewe.*

seconde to obey hys comandment in all thynges

*thyrdly in all thynges he shall aske your aduise to dect
your opinion as becometh a faythfull conceyllour to do*

Marye the quene

Queen Mary's instructions to Lord Russell, Lord Privy Seal, sent to receive and brief her husband, Philip of Spain, at Southampton in July 1554. The note is written in the queen's own hand, and signed 'Marye the quene'.

Passport for Richard Shelley to travel to Spain, signed 'Philippus' and 'Marye the quene', in the first year of their joint reign, with blanks for the day and month. Shelley was one of the envoys who were to take to foreign Courts the news of the birth of the son Mary believed that she was expecting. Letters announcing the news had been drawn up for them to carry, with blanks left for the date of birth.

the scaffold on 11 April, when the government had squeezed all it could out of him, he used his last moments to exculpate Elizabeth. The political difficulty of shedding royal blood in the teeth of such notorious and authoritative testimony to Elizabeth's innocence was evident. Even if Wyatt was lying – and he may have been – scaffold testimonies such as his, uttered when men and women expected imminently to face their creator, were popularly credited with almost gospel truth. Instead of facing trial herself, Elizabeth was in due course taken from London to Woodstock, there to spend the next year in the custody of one of Mary's 'good Catholic men', the dour and dutiful Sir Henry Bedingfield, one of her earliest supporters in the dark days of July 1553.

Wyatt's Rebellion did nothing to prevent Mary from marrying Philip. As was usual with the Tudors, opposition of this kind simply hardened her resolve. Philip landed at Southampton on 20 July 1554, and his marriage to Mary was celebrated at Winchester on St James's Day (25 July) – suitably enough, as St James was the patron saint of Spain. Philip's inferior rank to Mary might have been an embarrassment, but his father sorted this out by making over to Philip the kingdoms of Naples and Jerusalem from his own ample store of titles. Among other things, this meant that Philip and Mary enjoyed one of the most portentous royal styles ever to have been seen in English legal documents:

King and Queen of England, France, Naples, Jerusalem and Ireland, Defenders of the Faith, Princes of Spain and Sicily, Archdukes of Austria, Dukes of Milan, Burgundy and Brabant, Counts of Habsburg, Flanders and Tyrol.

Although hindsight and the demise of a hierarchical social order make this resounding sequence of titles seem absurd and somewhat ironical to the modern ear, at the time it was in and of itself a matter of high political importance. It was formally announced at their wedding, and subsequently printed and widely posted. Almost every chronicle of the time is careful to record it accurately, and it figures – in full – with remarkable frequency in the public and legal documents of Mary's reign. Amidst the high hopes and rejoicings of the wedding itself, it must have sounded like the inauguration of a new empire, perhaps even the dawn of a new age.

Philip's first meeting with his new wife had been as much a disappointment for him as it was a delight for her. There can be little doubt that, on the personal level, she had the better of the deal. Rather as Henry VIII had found with Anne of Cleves, the portraits Philip had been shown beforehand proved to have been somewhat flattering. Unlike his father-in-law, though, he was up to doing his conjugal duty even if he was unable to find it a pleasure. Moreover, he showed his wife every courtesy, and it soon became apparent that Mary, at least, was deeply in love with him. However, snidely praising his courage in adversity, Philip's attendants were soon muttering to the effect that Mary was old enough to be his mother. This was not quite fair (she was eleven when he was born in 1527) – but in 1521 she had, after all, been betrothed to Philip's father! (The betrothal was broken off in 1525.)

Philip II of Spain, engraving by F. Hogenberg, 1555. This portrait shows the prince as a young man after he had married Mary Tudor but before his father's abdication. So he is described in the frame as King of England and France (a title then still claimed by English kings) but as Prince of Spain.

Sixteenth-century kings did not, however, necessarily expect sexual fulfilment from marriage, and often expected to find it elsewhere. Philip seems not to have been a habitual philanderer, although it was well known that he was rather taken with Mary's pretty young sister, Elizabeth, when he first saw her – the offer of marriage which he extended, more in hope than expectation, after Mary's death probably had a personal as well as a political motivation – and his eye certainly fell on some of the young ladies at court, though not always with the desired results. One of these girls, Magdalen Dacre, a strikingly tall and pretty young blonde, told how one day, when she was washing herself, Philip, passing by outside, caught sight of her through a window and optimistically reached in for a grope. Snatching a handy stick, she whacked his arm with it, causing him to express (doubtless after one or two other exclamations) some rueful praise for her maidenly modesty.

Biologically, Mary's decision to marry a foreign prince who, as the years passed, was likely to spend more and more time abroad was a disaster, and arguably a foreseeable one. At her age, given her record of ill health and her pressing need to secure the succession, Mary needed a husband in constant attendance to maximise her chances of conception. Philip, who in the event landed only twice upon English shores and spent only a year and a half in England during his four years of marriage to Mary, was much less likely to father a Tudor heir. That said, most of that time spent in England was in his first visit, which lasted from July 1554 until September 1555. And within a few months of their marriage, Mary was showing all the signs of early pregnancy.

RECONCILIATION WITH ROME

From the start of her reign, Mary was determined to restore the old religion in its fullness, and before she even arrived in London she had sent letters to Pope Julius III with a view to reconciling England with Rome. But this was not going to be an easy process. Mary had steadfastly held to the Mass under Edward, so it was no surprise when she promptly set about dismantling the Edwardine Reformation. But, after initial recalcitrance, she had succumbed to her father's royal supremacy in 1536, and nothing she had said or done since had led anyone to expect that she would wish to undo that as well. One wonders whether she made some private vow in the turmoil of July 1553, promising to restore papal supremacy if God granted her victory. If so, she made no attempt to do so in her first Parliament, and in the first version of her royal style to be promulgated, on 1 October 1553, she retained the title of Supreme Head like her brother and father before her. Nevertheless, by the end of the year her intentions were becoming apparent, for the title of 'Supreme Head' was quietly dropped from official documents.

The man chosen to effect the reconciliation was Cardinal Reginald Pole, a cousin of Henry VIII who had been in self-imposed exile since the early 1530s. Educated at Oxford and then Padua, Pole had initially assisted in Henry's pursuit of his divorce from Catherine of Aragon, before resuming his theological studies in Italy rather than involve himself any further. Henry's advisers were still hoping to win his support for the break with Rome in 1535, but after the executions of Fisher and More he had penned a *Defence of the Unity of the Church* which argued at length against the divorce and the supremacy, asserted the rights of the papacy, and urged the king in no uncertain terms to repentance. Pole's promotion as a cardinal in 1536, followed by the publication of this tract in 1537, burned his boats with Henry. Cardinal Pole was twice entrusted by Pope Paul III with implementing Henry VIII's excommunication (first early in 1537 in response to the Pilgrimage of Grace, and then again early in 1539 in response to the burning of Becket's bones). He had also played an important part in reforming efforts in the Catholic Church, both in Rome itself and at the Council of Trent (ironically, Pole was actually more sympathetic than Henry VIII to the theology of Martin Luther). He was therefore the obvious choice for appointment as papal legate to England in response to Mary's request to return her country to the fold. However, his path was far from smooth, and it would be more than a year before his mission could even begin.

The great obstacle to reconciliation with Rome was not a matter of principle but a question of property. The plunder of the Church in which almost the entire ruling class of England had eagerly participated since the break with Rome was, under the canon law of the Roman Catholic Church, a sacrilege which entailed instant excommunication. Political realists – including King Philip and Bishop Gardiner – knew full well that reconciliation would be contingent on a papal dispensation confirming them in possession of their loot. Idealists and rigorists – such as Queen Mary and Cardinal Pole – were inclined to be less accommodating. The realists prevailed, and when Cardinal

Reginald Pole finally came to England, he grudgingly brought a dispensation with him. Once Parliament had hastily repealed Henry VIII's act of attainder against him, Pole crossed from France, and made his way to London, where he was greeted by King Philip at Whitehall on 24 November 1554. On 28 November Parliament convened, not in its usual place, but in the Great Chamber of Whitehall Palace, as the queen was ill and did not wish to go outdoors. After a brief speech from Lord Chancellor Gardiner, they listened to a lengthy sermon from Cardinal Pole, which recapitulated the Christian history of England and emphasised the providential benefits of communion with Rome, and the providential price of schism. Next day, Parliament met in its own chambers to debate the issue, and agreed, with only one dissenting voice, to return to the Roman obedience. No condition was explicitly attached to this measure, but everyone knew the real political price was the dispensation to retain Church lands. The gentry and nobility of England drove a hard bargain for their souls.

On Friday 30 November, Parliament once more convened in the Great Chamber at Whitehall, for a ceremony unique in parliamentary and ecclesiastical history, the granting of absolution for national schism through a nation's representative institution. Gardiner, as Lord Chancellor, presented to Philip and Mary a petition for absolution, begging them in turn to present it to the cardinal. This brief but pithy document expressed repentance for the passage of laws against the Holy See, promised to repeal them, and concluded with the pious hope that:

we may as children repentant be received into the bosom and unity of Christ's Church, so as this noble realm, with all the members thereof, may in this unity and perfect obedience to the See Apostolic and popes for the time being, serve God and Your Majesties to the furtherance and advancement of his honour and glory. Amen.

Cardinal Pole had his papal authorisation read out in full, and then solemnly granted absolution to the assembly.

The moment of national absolution was made doubly significant by the announcement of a landmark in Mary's pregnancy, the quickening of her child. Upon meeting the cardinal, Mary claimed, she felt the child leap in her womb as John the Baptist had done when the Virgin Mary greeted his mother, Elizabeth. The cardinal had played his part by greeting her with the words of Elizabeth to Mary, 'Blessed art thou among women, and blessed is the fruit of thy womb'. This news was formally announced in St Paul's on the day of Cardinal Pole's address to Parliament and the bishop of London ordered public prayers and processions of thanksgiving for the quickening of the child and of intercession for a healthy pregnancy and safe delivery. With hindsight, the element of wishful thinking in this excessively happy timing is all too clear. But at the time the announcement must have seemed, as it was meant to seem, like a glorious divine vindication of Mary's policy, indeed of her entire life. The schism had begun with the birth of a child who had displaced Mary from the succession. Now Mary had reclaimed her birthright, and would seal the end of the schism by giving birth to her own child.

Her hopes, however, were doomed to frustration, although it is worth recalling that while hindsight speaks, correctly, of Mary's 'false pregnancy', it seemed real enough at the time to all except her bitterest enemies, such as the French ambassador. In April 1555 Mary retreated into the privacy of Hampton Court in order to prepare for labour, and at the end of the month a rumour swept London to the effect that she had given birth to a son. It was of course false, but there were still no doubts about the queen's condition. In May, letters were drawn up to announce the news of the birth to the courts of Europe, and ambassadors were appointed to deliver them. But when the apparent onset of labour in early June proved illusory, doubts began to spread rapidly about the entire pregnancy. Soon only Mary still believed, and by August even she had given up hope. Philip's departure on business to the Netherlands later that month was the nearest thing to a public announcement that the pregnancy had been false. He would not have left had his wife been imminently expecting a child. He was not to return for nearly two years. After the disappointment of 1555, few were convinced when, around New Year 1558, news of a royal pregnancy was announced for the second time.

REBUILDING TRADITIONAL RELIGION

The consistent belittling of Mary's achievement by unsympathetic historians has extended to complaining that she did not inaugurate a 'Counter-Reformation' in her realm – a criticism which boils down to not establishing the Jesuits or presiding over a period of devotional creativity such as that represented a little later in Spain by the likes of St Teresa of Avila and St John of the Cross. As so often with the reporting of her reign, prejudice and hindsight have combined to blind historians to much of what happened, and to make them misinterpret whatever was not missed. Eamon Duffy's work on the Marian Restoration has uncovered evidence of effective religious renewal which historians have hitherto simply ignored. Cardinal Pole's legislation for the English Church, produced at a synod held in London under his authority as papal legate in 1556, laid a firm foundation for reform. The book of homilies (modelled on Cranmer's homilies of 1547, but now promoting Catholic rather than Protestant doctrine), the detailed explanation of Catholic doctrine (modelled on Henry VIII's King's Book of 1543, but correcting it where necessary), and the 'primer' or prayer book for the laity (also modelled on examples from Henry's reign) were all widely printed and circulated. The judicial separation of hundreds of parish priests from their recently acquired wives (now legally reclassified as concubines and more commonly vilified as whores) was not simply a human tragedy (perhaps not at all in some cases) but a remarkable administrative achievement, entirely typical of general Tudor effectiveness in managing the Church.

Even Mary's extraordinary record of founding religious houses is turned against her, as the fact that 'only' six monasteries were functioning by the time she died (compared with over 800 when she was born) is made a mark of failure. This hostile judgement is particularly unthinking. Henry VIII had foreclosed on half a millennium of monastic heritage in barely five years, but founding religious houses was a lengthy and expensive business. Has anyone else ever founded six monasteries in five years? Henry V, one of England's greatest kings, had planned to found three religious houses – one of Celestines, one of Bridgettines and one of Carthusians – but only the latter two were ever established, and neither was complete when he died after a reign of eight years. Moreover, Mary's foundations were made in a period of great fiscal stringency (and for that reason were not as well endowed as they had formerly been). Indeed, she was criticised for wasting money on monks and nuns at a time when the currency was debased, inflation was rampant, and the expenses of war were imposing a huge tax burden on her people.

The houses she refounded were: the Dominican friars at Smithfield and the Observant Franciscan friars at Greenwich (April 1555); Westminster Abbey (November 1556); the Charterhouse at Sheen (January 1557); the Bridgettines of Syon (April 1557); and the Dominican Nuns at King's Langley (June 1557), who shortly before Mary's death were given back their original house at Dartford (September 1558). In addition, Mary re-established the Fraternity of Jesus in St Paul's Cathedral (July 1556) and the Savoy Hospital (November 1556). Several of these houses had royal and personal associations which were important for the queen. Greenwich had been founded by Henry VII (as had the Savoy), and had shown steadfast support for Mary and her mother in the early 1530s. Syon and Sheen were Henry V's foundations (she highlighted this connection in her will), and both had been loyal to Catherine and Mary in the crisis of the 1530s. Finally, Westminster Abbey was still the temple of the English monarchical cult, and in March 1557 the new abbot, the congenial John Feckenham, restored the shrine of St Edward the Confessor, which had stood at its spiritual heart until 1538. Mary's will bequeathed huge sums to these houses, but her legacies, like much else in her will, were not honoured by her successor. In particular, Mary was anxious to bring the body of her mother to rest in the Tudor mausoleum, Henry VII's chapel at the back of Westminster Abbey. But Catherine of Aragon still lies in Peterborough Cathedral.

It was hardly to be expected, in the climate of doubt and insecurity created by the kaleidoscopic religious changes of the preceding twenty years, that Mary's lead would inspire a wholesale and instant resurgence of English monasticism. Even those who endowed chantries and Masses for the sake of their souls in her reign often expressed shrewd doubts about the long-term security of their investments, and sought to secure them against state depredations should the devotional climate cool once more. Yet Mary did set an example, and by the time she died, there were signs that it was beginning to be followed. If the Counter-Reformation had gone on to succeed in England, then it would have depended heavily, as it did in Europe, on a revival of monasticism and on the rise of new religious orders (such as the Capuchins, Jesuits and Discalced Carmelites). But the Counter-Reformation in Europe was a matter of generations, not of years. Mary could hardly have done any more, and might well have done a great deal less.

THE BURNINGS

Mary's Catholic Restoration is, understandably, best known for the burnings. The execution of nearly 300 Protestants between 1555 and 1558 has forever scarred the memory of her reign. The statute *De heretico comburendo* ('on the burning of heretics'), originally passed in 1401 to provide for the punishment of Lollards, and used against Protestants by Henry VIII, had been repealed by the Duke of Somerset in 1547. It was restored to the statute book in 1554, after an initial defeat in the House of Lords, with effect from 20 January 1555. Throughout 1554, with the connivance and perhaps at times the encouragement of the government, diehard Protestants had been fleeing the country in their hundreds in order to practise their religion freely abroad. Now, those who had remained or had been kept behind were in peril of their lives, as the renewed law took immediate effect. The first victim was John Rogers, a leading Protestant preacher who had published an edition of the Bible back in 1537. Rogers had been in custody for most of Mary's reign, and was now hurriedly tried, convicted and sentenced. He went to the stake at Smithfield on 4 February 1555. A series of high-profile victims later that year included the former bishops John Hooper (sent to die at Gloucester on 9 February), Hugh Latimer and Nicholas Ridley (burned together at Oxford on 16 October).

Although it is arguable that the burnings made rather less of an impact at the time than they have done subsequently, the fact remains that they represented systematic repression on a scale unprecedented and unparalleled in English history. Much is debated about this tragic episode, chiefly whether it did more harm or good to the Marian regime, and whether it was likely to achieve the destruction of English Protestantism. Perhaps the most interesting and obscure question about the burnings, though, is who was ultimately responsible for them. John Foxe, who singlehandedly shaped the historical image of the reign as we know it, had no doubts. Enthralled by that passionate devotion to monarchy which marks so much of the politics of Tudor England and the theology of early English Protestantism, Foxe exonerated Mary herself and placed the blame squarely on her bishops, men such as Reginald Pole of Canterbury, John Christopherson of Chichester, and above all Edmund Bonner of London. But whereas Foxe himself saw all those involved in the persecutions as equally guilty of shedding the blood of innocents, the evidence he himself provides shows that responsibility was by no means so evenly distributed. Those three dioceses of London, Canterbury and Chichester in fact witnessed by far the greater part of the burnings. Yet it is far from clear that this reflected the bloodthirstiness of their bishops. Reginald Pole was not, as far as can be ascertained, a vindictive man. Even Foxe says very little against him. John Christopherson was a careful scholar, and although this is no guarantee against psychopathic cruelty, there is no reason to

Opposite: Title page from the 1570 edition of John Foxe's *Acts and Monuments* (usually known as his 'Book of Martyrs'), famous for its detailed accounts of the Protestant victims of Mary's reign. On the left martyrs, burning at the stake, praise God while, on the right, monks kneel at the Mass – which Foxe believed to be idolatry.

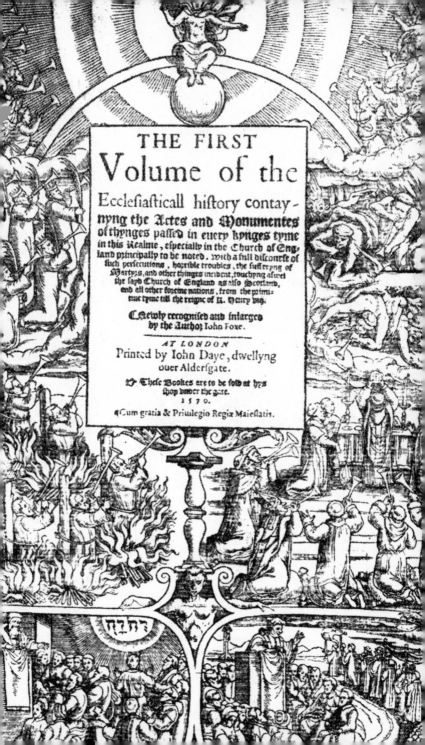

THE FIRST
Volume of the
Ecclesiasticall history contay-
nyng the Actes and Monumentes
of thynges passed in every kynges tyme
in this Realme, especially in the Church of England principally to be noted. With a full discourse of
such persecutions, horrible troubles, the sufferyng of
Martyrs, and other thinges incident, touchyng aswel
the sayd Church of England as also Scotland,
and all other foreine nations, from the primi-
tiue tyme till the reigne of K. Henry viij.

Newly recognised and inlarged
by the Author Iohn Foxe.

AT LONDON
Printed by Iohn Daye, dwellyng
ouer Aldersgate.

These Bookes are to be sold at his
shop vnder the gate.
1570.

Cum gratia & Priuilegio Regiæ Maiestatis.

The burning of Bishop John Hooper at Gloucester, 9 February 1555, from Foxe's *Book of Martyrs*.

conclude that he was any more or less keen on the execution of heretics than any of his episcopal colleagues.

In the case of Bonner, a vein of personal animus may have been present. Bonner had spent much of the previous reign in prison, and under Henry had been vexed for years by the advance of Protestantism in his diocese. He might well have rejoiced in the unexpected chance to repay his enemies, and Foxe relates a number of anecdotes which suggest that, in his case, it was often personal rather than merely judicial. Yet, as Eamon Duffy has recently shown from evidence reported by Foxe, even Bonner was driven on by orders from above. When a critical crowd gathered at one burning, Bonner produced a letter from the queen ordering him to stop procrastinating and get on with the job. The huge proportion of heretics burned in London reflects not simply the zeal of his diocesan staff, but the fact that many heretics were brought

⸀The burning of Tho.Tomkins hand by B.Boner,who not long after burnt also his body.

Edmund Bonner (Bishop of London, 1539–59) as Protestants saw him thanks to Foxe's *Book of Martyrs*. Here he is shown tormenting a captive Protestant by applying a candle to his hand. As around sixty out of nearly 300 Protestant martyrs under Queen Mary were burned in London, Bonner understandably held a prominent place in Protestant demonology. Yet he was also active in some of the more positive aspects of the restoration of Catholicism, and in 1559 he led Catholic resistance to Elizabeth's alteration of religion. He was then consigned to the Marshalsea prison, where he died in 1569.

to London for trial and execution. This was no doubt because, as London was manifestly the capital of English Protestantism, it was the place where the deterrent effect of the burnings would be maximised. If burning was largely *pour encourager les autres*, those others were more numerous in London than anywhere else.

In the end, the burnings were simply the execution of the law of the land. That law, reinstated by Mary, reflected the widespread sense that heresy was a heinous offence. The notion that national unity presupposed religious uniformity was a commonplace that hardly anyone thought to challenge. There seems no reason to doubt, however, that the chief responsibility for the vigour and intensity of the repression lay with Mary. Even her husband is reported to have advised more moderation, and to have been ignored. Mary displayed a common Tudor trait in her somewhat self-righteous, legalistic and implacable rigorism. Mercy was a rare virtue among the Tudors. Justice, or what passed for it, was more their line, and when their consciences were clear they were particularly dangerous. In this case, Mary's sense of justice rested in turn upon a sense of duty: the sixteenth-century Catholic

The burning of Hugh Latimer and Nicholas Ridley at Oxford, 16 October 1555, from John Foxe's *Book of Martyrs*. The preacher, Dr Richard Smyth, now rejoicing in the discomfiture of his enemies, had been obliged to recant certain Catholic beliefs at almost the same spot eight years previously. He had fled the country in 1549, and in 1559 he hurriedly left once more.

Church left monarchs in no doubt as to where their duty lay with regard to heresy. We should see her policy as deriving from a sense of duty rather than from personal vindictiveness. Her reintroduction of the law against heresy was part and parcel of her generally conservative and restorationist policy. As things had been, so should they be once again.

Only in the case of Thomas Cranmer do we see Mary settling a personal score. Cranmer, in pronouncing the sentence which annulled her mother's marriage to Henry VIII, and later in drawing up the liturgy which had replaced the Mass under Edward VI, had done more than any other single individual to destroy Mary's world. His support for Jane Grey had left him wide open to a charge of treason, on which he was duly tried and convicted in November 1553. Perhaps a cannier monarch would have seized this opportunity to destroy him, but Mary spared him to await trial in due course for heresy – a decision which is probably testimony both to her sincerity and to her understandable desire for vengeance. In the long wait before the revival of the necessary statute, Cranmer, along with Latimer and Ridley, was next subjected to the ignominy of having to defend his doctrines against a team of skilled debaters in front of a hostile audience in Oxford University (April 1554). In 1555, Cranmer could not be dealt with as expeditiously as his colleagues because, as archbishop, he could be tried only under special authority from the Pope. Formal proceedings against Cranmer commenced in September 1555. His inevitable conviction also had to be notified to Rome for confirmation, which was forthcoming in December, so it was not until February that the prospect of the stake was absolutely unavoidable. Under this pressure, Cranmer was relatively easily induced to recant his Protestant beliefs. He knew that in England a first offender who recanted was customarily let off with a penance (albeit often a humiliating and public penance). Burning was reserved for the obdurate and the relapsed. The decision to deprive him of the benefit of this custom can only have come from the very top.

MARY AND GOVERNANCE

It has become a commonplace to portray Mary's reign as one of weakness and poor government. In a scathing and comprehensive indictment of her regime, Geoffrey Elton not only dismissed her religious policy as divisive and unpopular, and her central government as hamstrung by a factious and unwieldy council, but also argued that by 1558 she had alienated the nobility and gentry to such an extent that her council was having serious difficulty in implementing the simplest decisions and executing the most basic governmental functions. On the contrary, the deliberately old-fashioned approach of the Marian regime was combined with a real commitment to firm government, subordinated of course to the paramount aim of rebuilding the old faith. The regime was fully aware of the importance of controlling the religion of the élite in the battle to define popular religion. Hence the incessant talk in government papers of 'good Catholic men' and 'honest Catholic men', and the pervasive desire to ensure that government was in the hands of these good, honest Catholics. The writs for Mary's parliaments used to call upon the shires and boroughs to return 'good Catholic men' to the House of Commons. In January 1556, the Privy Council wrote to the burgesses of Coventry, enclosing a shortlist of suitable candidates for the post of mayor, and advising them to elect one of those 'Catholic and honest persons'. There was certainly divisiveness here. It was one of the first times in English history that the question 'is he one of us?' became a political test. But only a minority was to be positively excluded, so the test did not disable government. More to the point, the Privy Council's concern with the personnel of government at the local level shows real political grip.

THE PRIVY COUNCIL

The peculiar circumstances of Mary's accession were largely responsible for what has long been one of the most vehemently criticised features of her regime: the unmanageable scale of her Privy Council (criticism of its size was first voiced by the Spanish ambassador to her court). Her counter-coup against Northumberland had been managed by a cabal of East Anglian gentry of distinctly Catholic sympathies. Northumberland, for a few days, had retained the support of the nobles and professional administrators of Edward VI's council. However, as these men sensed the direction of events, they slipped quietly away, and were welcomed, wisely enough with open arms, into Mary's camp. Once she had reached London, she had little choice but to leave most of these experienced royal servants in those political offices whose weight they had, however tardily, thrown into the balance on her side. To have dismissed them would have meant immediate administrative chaos and ultimate political disaster. The last thing she needed was a potential opposition party consisting of some of the most able and powerful politicians in the kingdom. Her East Anglian retinue, brimming over with goodwill and inexperience, could hardly be intruded *en masse* into the administrative heart of the Tudor state at a time of financial crisis. On the other hand, their claims upon Mary's favour were even more pressing than those of Northumberland's former if unwilling allies, and they predictably enough moved swiftly into the household offices which entailed personal attendance on the queen. Those whom she admitted to the council in fact proved capable enough men. Both groups were represented on her Privy Council, joined by a handful of other weighty figures, such as Gardiner and Tunstall (restored respectively as bishops of Winchester and Durham), who had spent much of the previous reign in custody. In practice, Mary's council was dominated by the old Tudor hands like Gardiner, Paget, Winchester and Bedford, the lasting legacy of Henry VIII's nose for talent.

Some have seen in the scale of Mary's council an infallible recipe for faction and division, yet in fact the whole issue of scale is something of a red herring. As in the reign of her grandfather, the title of councillor was often merely honorific, a sop to the noble and influential. Most Privy Council sessions had between eight and a dozen men present, a perfectly manageable number. Faction there was, at times, yet it was not a matter of numbers but of personal rivalry (between Gardiner and Paget) and genuine disagreement over policy. Her decision to marry Philip complicated her problems considerably – not only because opinion on the marriage was divided, but also because, when Philip was in the country, he became an alternative focus for political activity. For example, when William Paget found himself out of favour with Mary early in 1555, he turned his attention to briefing Philip. But a degree of faction was probably unavoidable under the circumstances of the 1550s, amidst uncertainty over the succession and deepening religious division. Even under the strongest kings, the heir to the throne is likely to attract in one way or another the support or at least the interest of a group looking to the future. As long as Mary, already middle-aged, remained without a child, and the heir presumptive to the throne was her younger sister Elizabeth, it was inevitable that a portion of the political nation, especially that portion more sympathetic to religious reform, would look to the daughter of Anne Boleyn rather than to the daughter of Catherine of Aragon. On one or two well-publicised occasions, conciliar divisions spilled over into Parliament, to the embarrassment of the queen. Yet it is hardly fair to regard these as any more of an indictment of government than the ill-concealed rows in the next reign over Elizabeth's relationship with Robert Dudley or her long courtship with the Duke of Anjou. If Elizabeth's reign had ended in 1569, then historians would probably, if unfairly, also characterise her council as plagued by faction. Mary mostly got what she wanted. There is no evidence that her government was crippled by faction.

The real problem with Mary's regime was neither the scale of her Privy Council nor the innate competitiveness of her councillors. It was her failure to identify a chief minister in the mould of Wolsey, Cromwell or Burghley: perhaps, at a deeper level, her failure to see the need for one. If there was a single political development of the era with lasting historical significance, it was the emergence of the chief minister, of a full-time professional to co-ordinate the increasingly burdensome paperwork of power. Occasionally monarchs such as Philip II or Louis XIV might cast themselves in this role, but most of them had neither the talent nor the inclination for it. There are some signs that Mary shared her husband's taste for getting to grips with the paperwork. But there are no signs that she had the sort of grip on events and understanding of politics necessary to make sense of it. The most successful Tudors, Henry VIII and Elizabeth, owed much of their success in government to their ability to pick men who could do that for them. Mary lacked that gift.

Yet Mary's background and situation made it impossible for her to select a chief minister in the way that her father had done. The field was inevitably restricted to those with talent and experience, most of whom were already in her government. And with none of these men could she ever enjoy that degree of trust essential to the relationship between monarch and chief minister. For they had all been compromised by service to her father or her brother. If they had not played a leading part in destroying the world of her childhood in the 1530s, tainting her mother with incest and her with bastardy, then they had browbeaten her over religion around 1550. Several had done both. She might appreciate political realities enough to understand that she could never govern without these men, the Gardiners, Pagets and Paulets. But she never liked them. During her disputes over religion under Edward, she had repeatedly and scornfully reminded them that they had been created out of political nothingness by her father, and she shared enough of the prejudices of the old nobility to think rather little of men who had clawed their way up the greasy pole. The two men she did trust, King Philip and Cardinal Pole, though both talented, could never fit the bill. Neither the foreigner nor the exile had the close ties among the English political élite vital to success in such a role. Besides this, Philip was mostly out of the country, while Pole was too idealistic and unworldly to act effectively as a chief minister, and in any case had no desire to do so.

MARY AND THE NOBILITY

Although the role of the nobility was changing in Tudor times, good relations with the nobility remained the essence of kingship. Mary was on excellent terms with her nobles, not so much because of any special talent in the management of men as because of her unmistakable commitment to aristocratic values and prejudices. The fundamental conservatism of her reign was as much social as religious. And as the social order had not been challenged to the same degree as the religious order, its conservation was less innovative. Part of the explanation for the size of Mary's council seems to lie in her implicit acceptance of the aristocratic account of power and counsel. As we have seen, she shared the ancient nobility's disdain for the low-born careerists whom her father had brought into his service and even raised to the peerage. By being generous with the title of councillor she satisfied noble aspirations without overburdening the machinery of central government with dead souls. The Duke of Norfolk and the Courtenay heir to the earldom of Devon were both released promptly from the Tower, and the repeal of acts of attainder against their families were among the first statutes of the reign. The ancient Norfolk proved a broken reed during Wyatt's Rebellion, and young Courtenay's lack of wisdom and experience was woefully exposed by the same crisis. But aristocratic sensibilities, ruffled by religious change and political upheaval, were soothed by such gestures. The ancient house of Percy, once 'cock of the north', humbled and expropriated by Henry VIII in the wake of the Pilgrimage of Grace, was restored to something of its former power and glory in the north, and regained from the upstart Dudleys the title of Northumberland, albeit reduced once more to an earldom. Across in Ireland, the Fitzgeralds, smashed by Henry VIII in the 1530s, were brought back inside the charmed circle and enjoyed once more the island's premier earldom of Kildare. Although ethnic conflict between the English and the Irish remained the running sore of politics there, Mary's reign healed some of the emerging divisions between the new English, officials and settlers sent over from England, and the old English, descendants of the Anglo-Norman conquerors.

Far from being alienated from her regime, the nobility and gentry were loyal and often enthusiastic supporters of the Crown. Very few joined in any plots against her. The southern earls (Arundel, Bedford, Huntingdon and Pembroke) were unhesitatingly loyal in the crisis of early 1554, as were barons such as Clinton and Abergavenny. The Earl of Westmorland acted swiftly to crush the ill-fated invasion of Thomas Stafford at Scarborough in 1557. There was no difficulty finding gentlemen to fight in the campaigns of the French war of 1557–58. The continuing development of the Lord Lieutenancy guaranteed many peers a central place in the emerging system of county government. Nobles flocked to the ceremonial occasions of Mary's reign, such as her coronation and her wedding, which provided them with the chance to display their national political importance before a domestic and an international audience. Six of England's earls were named among her executors.

One of the indexes by which historians seek to measure the success or failure of monarchs is the frequency with which they faced revolts or rebellions. The reign of

Mary is often singled out for its problems in exacting obedience and enforcing order. Her reign can be presented as a succession of plots and risings, and if these are made the evidence of weakness, then the case for her weakness is proven. Yet this is far from fair, and another example of the double standards that can still flaw historical judgement. The almost continuous series of plots which plagued Elizabeth in the 1580s and 1590s is quite rightly interpreted as evidence not for the weakness of the regime but for the desperation of its opponents. Realising that Mary's Protestant opponents were less numerous, less influential and less strongly supported from abroad than Elizabeth's Catholic opponents can help us put the events of Mary's reign in perspective. On only one occasion after her accession was Mary seriously threatened by a rebellion: when Sir Thomas Wyatt led what was meant to be a national rising, but turned out to be just another Kentish revolt. Coming as it did so early in the reign, it is no fairer to condemn Mary on this account than it would be to condemn Henry V on account of the Oldcastle Rising of 1414 (which, like Wyatt's revolt, combined religious dissidence, a rather limited noble discontent, political dissatisfaction with the regime, and ineffectual aspirations to nationwide conspiracy). Each of the other four Tudor monarchs faced larger rebellions than Mary ever did.

PROPAGANDA

Notwithstanding the endlessly repeated (and statistically far from well founded) assertions that Mary did not understand the power of the press and was outgunned by exiled Protestant propagandists, her regime was effective enough in putting across its message – essentially, religion and obedience, much like the message of any other Tudor monarch. It is true that exiled Protestants printed much more theological controversy than Catholics, but it is less clear how widely this circulated, or how effective it was. It was not enough to print books: they had to be delivered to their readers. There is not much evidence to suggest that the refugees' printing effort had an enormous impact on the domestic market. As with the prodigious propaganda efforts of the Catholic refugees in Europe under Queen Elizabeth, such literature was more to do with sustaining the spirits of an embattled minority than with recruiting mass support. The Marian authorities were quite happy to concentrate on mass-producing devotional, liturgical and instructional texts which would do more than polemics to rebuild and fortify Catholic attitudes.

A more justifiable criticism of Mary is that she lacked her sister's flair for showmanship. Her entry to London was inevitably part victory parade and part military column, as it was a show of strength as well as a display of dynastic legitimacy. So her retinue of 10,000 made the most important point. But while few events of this kind fall entirely flat, hers certainly left no golden moments in the popular memory. Her coronation celebrations were equally staid and somewhat old-fashioned. Wine flowed from the fountains, and rejoicing was inevitable. But there was nothing beyond the script, no impromptu rapport with the London crowd of the kind which came naturally to Elizabeth. The ceremonies themselves were more a matter of medieval munificence than Renaissance inventiveness. Sheer expense and opulence of dress and décor were emphasised rather than the emblematic pageantry sometimes seen under Henry and more often under Elizabeth. Not that Mary was without some sense of herself and her image. In a typically Catholic fashion, she took her patron saint, the Blessed Virgin Mary, as her role model. Some of her more imaginative propaganda exploited this association, as did Mary herself from time to time – notably in her account of her reception of Cardinal Pole. In Edward's reign, her entourage had ridden into London to escort her to a meeting with the king, all wearing rosaries as a kind of badge of allegiance to both Maries. In Mary's reign, Elizabeth rather pointedly refrained from making any use of the ornate rosary with which her sister presented her.

The adequacy of Mary's governmental machinery is best assessed in the perspective provided by the incoming government of her successor, Queen Elizabeth. One thing the new regime was quite clear about was the existence and effectiveness of that body of 'good Catholic men' upon whom Mary's council had relied in local government. In sizing up the prospects for a Protestant religious settlement, Elizabeth's advisers saw Mary's appointees as a major political obstacle, foreseeing the discontent of:

> all such as governed in the late Queen Mary's time, and were chosen thereto for no other cause, or were then most esteemed, for being hot and earnest in the other religion.

They also noted the preponderance of 'the papist sect' among the judiciary and the justices of the peace in the shires. Mary's government chased Protestants out of public office far sooner than Elizabeth's got rid of Catholics (who were still being purged from many positions and institutions in the 1570s), and in consequence its religious policy took effect more quickly at the local level. The Elizabethan authorities had a harder time getting rid of Catholic liturgical gear in the 1560s than the Marian authorities had reinstalling it in the 1550s. While Elizabeth deserves credit for not engaging in savage repression of Catholics in the 1560s, it is not clear that her government could in fact have implemented such a policy.

None of which is to suggest that Mary's reign was some oasis of good governance. Both the threat and the use of torture are mentioned with disturbing and revealing frequency in the minutes of the Privy Council. And it was not just the execution of heretics that the council encouraged. Local authorities were again and again urged to hang traitors, murderers, highwaymen, pirates and other felons. There is a sense of insecurity about all this. Yet it is not so very different from the domestic policy of the Duke of Northumberland, so many of whose administrative colleagues were still in post. And we should probably trace this neither to malice nor to incompetence, but to hard times. The Elizabethan regime of the 1590s was rather similar to Mary's in its feel, and for much the same reasons. England in the 1550s was barely beginning to recover from the fiscal squeeze and currency devaluations which had financed the wars of the 1540s. Poor harvests and recurrent epidemic disease slowed recovery, and there was little as yet to replace the monasteries in dealing with the problem of the poor. The return of war in 1557–58 only made things worse. Yet government coped, if barely. The revaluation of customs duties in 1558 may have been a desperate fiscal expedient – but it was successfully implemented. The burning of heretics became the acid test for Mary's government. It was unpopular and it often needed to be forced upon unwilling shire and diocesan functionaries. Yet it continued right to the end. It was cruel. But it was not incompetent, and it was not in any sense the sign of a regime in meltdown.

THE WAR WITH FRANCE

The war with France which occupied the last year of Mary's reign was the only episode in which her marriage to Philip had direct and damaging policy implications for her kingdom. Again, Mary has been criticised unduly for this entanglement, largely because of the fortuitous loss of Calais in January 1558. The decision to go to war was driven primarily by her husband, in pursuit of his own ambitions in the Netherlands. It was disputed bitterly by her Privy Council, many of whose members rightly saw no English interests at stake. Cardinal Pole urged peace as a matter of principle. Philip had to return briefly to England to lobby for war, and the argument was only swung when the French foolishly backed a hopeless plot against Mary, arming a noble adventurer, Thomas Stafford, who landed at Scarborough in April 1557, seized the castle, and was captured within a couple of days. War was now a matter of honour, and was by no means a transparently doomed policy. War with France was, after all, a return to the best traditions of English monarchy stretching back over 200 years. There was no problem in recruiting young nobles and gentry to fight alongside the Spanish against the old enemy. For example, the three surviving Dudley brothers all served in this war, and Robert's service as Master of the Ordnance secured his family's restoration in blood. Mary's critics sometimes seem to overlook the fact that the Anglo-Spanish alliance actually won the war at the decisive battle of Saint-Quentin (August 1557).

It was the loss of Calais, which had been in English hands since the reign of Edward III, that spoiled the party. In the long term, it was a blessing in disguise, but at the time the disguise seemed pretty effective. The fall of Calais was a national humiliation of the first order. Mary, as the personal embodiment of the nation, inevitably felt it as a personal affront. Yet the loss itself was probably sealed only by her death. If Philip had still been, with Mary, upon the throne of England during the peace negotiations of 1559 at Cateau-Cambrésis, he might not have been so ready to abandon the English bridgehead in France. Had she lived, Mary would certainly have strained every nerve to regain it. After her death, the fall of Calais came to be seen as a providential judgement against her for her persecution of the 'gospel' (though why God should have given Calais to the French, who were burning almost as many Protestants as the English, is anybody's guess!).

Ironically, the war with France also impeded the policy closest to Mary's heart – the restoration of Catholicism. For Pope Paul IV was bitterly opposed to Habsburg hegemony in Italy, and was therefore a bellicose ally of France against Philip II. Pope Paul added to political enmity a personal hatred of Cardinal Pole (they had been rivals in the papal curia throughout the 1540s), whom he summoned to Rome on bizarre charges of heresy. Mary refused to hand him over, and was obliged to invoke the kind of arguments which her father had deployed in the early days of the break with Rome in order to justify her disobedience. The Pope, in return, refused to approve any new appointments to replace the bishops who were then dying off at an alarming rate.

THE END

Philip's second visit to England (March to July 1557) was essentially political, but had its personal aspects. To a modern eye, the marriage of Philip and Mary might well seem to have been over, yet they presumably slept together, as a little later Mary once more fancied herself pregnant. Scepticism was widespread, and no one but Mary was surprised when the due date, in April 1558, came and went with no sign of labour. The symptoms of pregnancy changed imperceptibly into the symptoms of what was to be her final illness. She had made her will in March, in the expectation of facing the perils of childbirth. Thereafter, she prepared her soul for death. But neither her husband nor her councillors could induce her to provide for the succession. In fact, there was no option now but to recognise Elizabeth, which Mary simply could not bear to do. Right at the end, she acknowledged the inevitable, and sent a message and her blessing to her sister, hoping against hope for the preservation of her religion.

Mary Tudor died on 17 November 1558. Although she had been sickening for a long time, she may very well have been killed by the virus that was decimating her people, an early variety of influenza which in the two or three years around 1558 carried off as much as a fifth of the English population. There could not have been a worse time to die. The loss of Calais, the costs of war, and the social and economic dislocation consequent upon epidemic disease and poor harvests meant that her five years on the throne closed in an atmosphere of gloom and crisis which has unfairly coloured later perceptions of her entire reign.

In the end, Mary failed. She did not save England for Roman Catholicism. But she did not fail completely. She did save Roman Catholicism in England. Until her successful bid for the throne stopped the rot, Catholicism in England had been in retreat for six years and under pressure for twenty. Although much of the structures and practices of Catholicism survived under Henry VIII, the royal supremacy and its consequential subordination of religious truth to the royal will had sapped its inner strength. That is why resistance was so limited and ineffective under Edward VI.

What Mary's reign did was to restore the Catholic sense of identity. Indeed, her reign arguably created the Catholic sense of identity, at least in the English context, as it was in her reign that the words 'Protestant' and 'Catholic' first took on the mutually defining and mutually exclusive senses they still carry in English.

Mary might not have expected death as early as it came for her, but could perhaps be criticised for failing to provide for the security of her achievement. Whether she really understood that she would never bear children is doubtful. Did she know enough of the ways of the flesh to work it out for herself? Even if any of her ladies in waiting had the courage to tell her, she would not have been able to cope with such a final dashing of her hopes, the entire destruction of her sense of identity and purpose. So perhaps she should not be blamed too harshly for failing to provide against a contingency which she could not bear to contemplate. Nor does her political career give reason to believe that she would have been able to solve the problem. She was not ruthless enough to destroy her sister (the suggestion of some of her councillors, hardened by service to Henry VIII), and she had perhaps learned from their brother's attempt to frustrate their succession that, failing an heir of her own body, nothing short of death would keep Elizabeth off the throne. Elizabeth, like Mary, was to face the challenge of ruling as a woman in a man's world. Famously, she would do so by developing the persona of the Virgin Queen. Mary Tudor sacrificed her virginity in the hope of motherhood. Having modelled herself upon Our Lady, Virgin and Mother, her personal tragedy was to end up neither the one nor the other.

5

ELIZABETH I

Elizabeth's accession was neither as theoretically improbable as her grandfather's nor as practically troublesome as her sister's, but it was not without its curiosities and potential problems. As the daughter of Anne Boleyn, born while Henry VIII's first wife, Catherine of Aragon, was still living, Elizabeth was illegitimate under the Catholic canon law which Mary had restored in England. If that was not enough, she was also strictly speaking illegitimate under the law of the land. The vicissitudes of Henry VIII's succession laws had seen Elizabeth first in line for the throne under the first Act of Succession (1534), then bastardised and displaced by the second act (1536), before being restored as third in line for the throne under the third act in 1544.

However, the massive repeal of Henry's laws which had taken place under Mary had left Elizabeth in a kind of legal limbo from which there was no escape. Elizabeth could hardly pass an act retrospectively remedying this mess without acknowledging that she was illegitimate, which would have implied that she could not lawfully have taken the throne in the first place. This dilemma, while constitutionally amusing, was not of great moment, and was passed over in tactful silence. In the event, Elizabeth's accession was domestically untroubled, as the arrival of a young and probably fertile queen offered the realm new hope in the gloom which had overwhelmed Mary's last year. Mary's final illness gave both Elizabeth and the English élites ample time to prepare for the transition. The loss of Calais, the epidemic of influenza, and the phantom pregnancies which were all the fruit of her unpopular marriage with Philip II had dissipated the stock of popular support which had swept Mary to power five years before.

However welcome Elizabeth may have been domestically, there were also foreign interests to be taken into account, primarily those of her cousin, Mary Queen of Scots, whose legitimacy none could call into doubt, and who was married to the Dauphin of France (soon to become King Francis II). Although tacitly excluded from the throne by Henry VIII's legislation, in terms of blood and lineage Mary Stuart certainly had the best claim after Elizabeth. Indeed, doubts about Elizabeth's legitimacy might have cho spiritus

72 Igitur da mihi domine prudenti-
am celestem. vt discam.querere. et
inuenire te, et amare te super oīa.

73 Da mihi gratiam abducere &
me ab illis qui me adulantur. et
patienter illos ferre qui me adu-
vexant

74 Quando tentatio, et tribulatio ꝝ
veniunt, digneris succurrere mihi
domine. vt omnia vertentur mihi
in spirituale solatium et semper
feram patienter. ac dicam: bene-
dictum sit nomen tuum

fragilite laquelle tu congnois le
micubx

Ayes mercy de moy. et me   74
delyure de tout peche et iniqui-
te accellefin que ie ne soye acca
ble d'iceux

Il m'est souuentesfois fort gri   75
ef. et cela quasi me consond. de
ce que ie suis sy instable. sy feu-
ble et fragile, pour resister aux
motions iniques: lesquelles. co
bien qu'elles ne me causent de
consentir. ce nonobstant me sot
leurs assaulx tresgriefz.

Prayers written out by Elizabeth (then aged twelve) in a little volume she presented to her father, Henry VIII, as a New Year's gift for 1546. Her excellent italic hand betrays the influence of the talented humanist tutors employed by the king to teach her and her younger brother Edward.

provided Mary – or to be precise the powerful and numerous aristocratic dynasty of the Guise, her cousins, who dominated her and her young husband – with a pretext for launching a rival claim to the English crown. The natural anxieties of the Elizabethan regime were hardly assuaged when the young princely couple started to quarter the English arms with those of France in their heraldic emblems. Elizabeth's ambassador at the French court, Nicholas Throckmorton, was instructed to deplore this in no uncertain terms, and Elizabeth herself took the gesture as a personal insult as well as a political threat. Her moral ground was perhaps not quite as strong as it might have been, given that she, like all her predecessors since Edward III, quartered the fleur-de-lys of France with the lions of England in her coat of arms, and claimed the crown of France as part of her formal title. But the English claim to France had been heavily discounted through over two centuries of conflict, whereas the French claim to England was an unsettling new move on the diplomatic chessboard.

The ominous attitudes struck by France, however, were counter-balanced by Philip II of Spain, who, now he was rid of a wife for whom he had never felt great affection, briefly entertained the possibility of prolonging his short reign as king of England by marrying his deceased wife's sister – whom he had always found more attractive. There was never much prospect of this, as the marriage would have been the mirror image of that between Henry and Catherine of Aragon, on the intrinsically incestuous character of which rested Elizabeth's own claims to legitimacy. His polite offer was equally politely refused. Despite the disturbing direction of Elizabeth's

Above: The Entrance of Queen Elizabeth. Queen Elizabeth's accession (or 'entrance') came to be celebrated as a religious festival. This allegorical representation of the accession, from a later work commemorating God's mercies to Protestant England, depicts the new queen bringing justice and piety (represented by the sword and the Bible) to her realm.

Opoosite: A sketch of Elizabeth in one of the commonest of her portrait poses, holding a fan.

religious policy, though, Philip was especially anxious to maintain good relations with England during the peace negotiations following the cessation of the recent war with France. And he could not afford to let Elizabeth's right to the throne be called into question, as this might open England to the prospect of a Stuart succession and an alliance with France. Following his example, Catholic Europe therefore recognised Elizabeth.

The accession of a new queen of very different background and attitudes from her predecessor inevitably meant changes at the heart of government, on the Privy Council. It was the end of the road for those who owed their places on the council to their role in placing Mary on the throne. Elizabeth, like Mary before her, brought her own personal retinue to the council, such as her long-serving steward, Sir Thomas Parry, and her cousins Sir Francis Knollys and Sir Richard Sackville. That retinue also provided her most important appointment, her Secretary, William Cecil, who had been surveyor of Elizabeth's lands since 1550. Too closely implicated in the Edwardine regime ever to get far under Mary, he had looked to the rising star of Elizabeth for some time. Cecil brought his own network of kinship and friendship into her service. His brother-in-law, Nicholas Bacon, was given custody of the Great Seal as Lord Keeper. And the clergy who were called upon to advise on religious questions, and were soon to be promoted to the high places in the new Church, were often drawn from the circles in which he had moved in his youth at Cambridge, particularly from his own college, St John's. It is well known that many of Elizabeth's councillors were connections of the extended Boleyn family. Even Thomas Parry, for example, was married to the widow of Sir Adrian Fortescue, one of Anne Boleyn's many cousins, and that family in turn provided her in later years with Sir John Fortescue and Sir Thomas Bromley. The vast Howard clan, which provided still more of her servants (most notably Howard of Effingham) was also part of that family network. Yet this should not lead to suspicions of unthinking nepotism. Providing for relatives, if one was able to do so, was on the contrary considered a moral obligation at that time. And none of those relatives whom Elizabeth selected for high office disgraced it. The Boleyn and Cecil kin-groups were reasonably talented, and Elizabeth should be credited with something of her father's gift for talent-spotting.

Throughout her reign, though, there was another line of courtiers and officials who owed their careers not to their family or other prior connections with the queen or Cecil, but to their enjoyment of the queen's special favour. The Earl of Leicester (Robert Dudley), Sir Christopher Hatton, the Earl of Essex (Robert Devereux) and Sir Walter Raleigh all won that favour initially through their personality or their figure rather than through useful service. Double standards inevitably affect the historical judgement here. When a king's roving eye fell upon shapely young women at court, the implications might include another royal bastard and perhaps even some dividends in land and office for the young lady's family, but only rarely did it redraw the political map. On those occasions when a royal mistress had intervened in politics, she had inevitably aroused fierce resentment (as for example Alice Ferrers in the declining years of Edward III). Thus for a gentlewoman to catch the king's eye might mean personal advancement, but was not an obvious channel for political ambition. For an able young gentleman, catching the eye of the unmarried queen was a much more obvious path for ambition. Elizabeth should not so much be criticised for recruiting some of her closest political advisers this way as congratulated for choosing from the throng of those fighting for her attention only those that were worth promoting. The Earl of Oxford, a worthless wallflower, made no political impact despite the initial appeal which he had for the queen. He was certainly one of the most colourful personalities of the age. But a deep vein of instability flawed his character. From the curious episode of his youth in Cecil's household – when an unfortunate cook was deemed by a coroner's jury to have committed suicide by running upon the earl's sword! – to his short-lived conversion to Roman Catholicism, his ill-fated marriage to Cecil's daughter, and his scandalous affair with the nymphomaniac Ann Vavasour (one of Elizabeth's Maids of the Bedchamber), his career was an object-lesson in political failure. If the later favourites, Raleigh and Essex, were less stable than Leicester and Hatton, no one could doubt their abilities: it was simply that their ambition over-reached them.

Robert Dudley, Earl of Leicester, by F. Hogenberg. Robert Dudley was a favourite of the queen's from the start of the reign, and was given the prestigious court position of Master of the Horse. In the early 1560s Elizabeth was widely reckoned to be in love with him, even though he was already married. Although his wife died in 1560, the suspicion that her death was too timely to be an accident made any idea of a royal marriage impossible. As a Privy Councillor he was a close and loyal servant for many years, and he was by her side at Tilbury in 1588 as the commander of her army. He died shortly afterwards.

THE ALTERATION OF RELIGION

The first business of the new reign was the settlement of religion – or the 'alteration of religion' as it was rather more aptly described at the time. Back in the reign of Edward VI, Stephen Gardiner had protested against swift religious change on the grounds that the Bishop of Rome 'wanteth not wits to beat into other princes' ears that where his authority is abolished, there shall, at every change of governors, be change in religion'. Edward's and Mary's reigns had both vindicated his warning, and Elizabeth's reign virtually turned it into a political principle. When James I came to the throne, the idea that religion changed with each new monarch was stated as a matter of fact. In the case of Elizabeth, there was no doubt about the direction of change. The only question was how far and how fast it would go.

A rather lukewarm and *politique* Protestantism, Elizabeth's own religion has always been something of an enigma. But an option for some sort of Protestantism was almost genetically programmed. As the daughter of Anne Boleyn she literally embodied Henry VIII's break with Rome. She was the eldest child of the English Reformation, even if it was as much the political as the theological inheritance that shaped her destiny. Anne herself had more than flirted with evangelical doctrines in her brief reign, and was enrolled among the Protestant martyrs by John Foxe in his account of the sufferings of the English Church (his *Acts and Monuments*, or 'Book of Martyrs' as it came to be known, which he published with a dedication to Elizabeth in 1563). Yet Elizabeth could hardly have remembered her mother, whom she had last seen being taken into custody in the precincts of Greenwich Palace early in 1536, when she herself was not even three years old. It was the circumstances of her birth, rather than any sentimental attachment to her mother's memory, that determined Elizabeth's religious stance. As the papacy had never recognised Henry's divorce as valid, while the king claimed that his marriage to Catherine of Aragon was against scripture itself, it was on the authority of the Bible alone, of the Bible as opposed to the Catholic Church, that Elizabeth based her very right to the throne, and in a sense her very right to life.

Had Elizabeth retained any kind of feeling for the Catholicism to which she had conformed unenthusiastically during Mary's reign, no doubt some deal could have been struck with the papacy to sort out the troubled question of her legitimacy. Yet Elizabeth was of the first generation to grow up out of communion with the Church of Rome, and therefore lacked that sympathy with the 'old religion' (as it was coming to be known) which still characterised the majority of her subjects. With no strong religious motive to seek the sanction of the Holy Father, there were three overwhelming reasons not to do so. Firstly, there were problems in English common law regarding the rights of inheritance of those born out of wedlock, problems which could not necessarily be resolved by papal dispensation – not strictly relevant to the inheritance of the throne, but with potentially nasty implications for it. From the Catholic point of view, Elizabeth could never be more than a legitimised bastard. From a Protestant point of view, which based its understanding of the forbidden and permitted degrees of marriage on the text of Leviticus, her birth could be reckoned legitimate before God and therefore in no need of further clarification before man. Secondly, to owe her throne to the grace of the Pope would be to recognise some sort of papal political supremacy. But from her earliest youth Elizabeth had heard the papacy's political claims dismissed as tyrannical usurpations. Henry VIII's father might have been content with a degree of dependence on papal grace, but this would never do for his daughter. Lastly, and worst of all, to be *deemed* legitimate would be to acknowledge her illegitimacy, to accept the social taint of 'base birth' which even the fullness of papal power could not purge from the proud hearts of Europe's nobility.

Whatever her religious views, they were not as strongly held as those of the Protestant exiles of Mary's reign, nor indeed as strongly held as those of Mary. Although Elizabeth had dragged her feet at first, and had never shown any real enthusiasm, she had conformed to the Mass under Mary. Mary had never conformed to the *Book of Common Prayer* under Edward. For zealous Protestants, the Mass was an act of blasphemous idolatry. Elizabeth's Protestantism was not of their stamp. Though, like Mary, no coward, unlike Mary she was not the stuff of which martyrs are made. That said, Elizabeth indulged in relatively risk-free gestures which indicated her real sympathies. When she finally bowed to the inevitable, and attended Mass, she complained throughout proceedings of a stomach-ache! The fine rosary which Mary gave her was never used or even worn: in Edward's reign, the rosary had become the badge of Mary's political affinity. In Elizabeth's reign, the rosary was once more banned. Later, Elizabeth clearly preferred the company of dutiful conformists such as herself – Cecil, Parker and Leicester – to the stiff-necked and hard-faced men who returned from abroad to fill most of the influential posts in her Church hierarchy, men like John Jewel (Bishop of Salisbury), Edmund Grindal (Bishop of London) and William Whittingham (Dean of Durham).

The theological flimsiness of Elizabeth's Protestantism is equally evident in her complete insensitivity to the Puritan myth of 'the Word'. When Grindal, by then Archbishop of Canterbury, urged upon her the importance of providing for the Church an adequate supply of learned preachers, she replied that the Book of Homilies – a volume of off-the-peg sermons for the less able clergy – was more than enough preaching for anyone. Not only was the doctrine of the Homilies, although Protestant, less then wholly satisfactory in Puritan eyes, but there was a more disturbing failure on her part to appreciate the importance of the preached word, the word preached from the heart, at the core of Protestant spirituality. Not that Elizabeth was averse to a good sermon. She had enjoyed a humanist training, and appreciated the art of rhetoric – and herself had a knack for the well-turned phrase. But her taste in preachers was revealing. She preferred the grandiloquence of Lancelot Andrewes, more obviously scholarly and rhetorical, to the plain style affected for the most part by more thorough-going Protestants. The preaching of Andrewes was closer to the baroque of the Jesuits (whose pulpit oratory enthralled the notoriously irreligious King Henry IV of France) than to the austere and affected simplicity of the Puritans. The sermon, even among devotees such as the Puritans, always had something of the stage about it. One suspects that it was amusement and intellectual pleasure, rather than spiritual enlightenment and edification, that Elizabeth most looked for from a preacher.

In many ways, however, Elizabeth's religion remains an enigma. She said that she would not open windows into men's souls. She certainly never opened any into her own. She was in religion, as in so much else, decisively ambiguous. All we can conclude from her ambiguity is that her religious life was not dominated by some consuming sense of gospel truth or divine love. Systematic ambiguity may be attractive to the postmodern mind, but was hardly compatible with the profound faith of a Luther, a Calvin, or a Teresa of Avila. It goes without saying that Elizabeth left nothing remotely resembling the spiritual diary so characteristic of the Puritan. Nor did she leave much else. Unlike her father, she was no amateur theologian, and she was content with a merely outward obedience. Her contempt for the fine points to which so many of her contemporaries devoted their lives is summed up in her comment to a visiting French ambassador: 'there was only one Jesus Christ and one faith, and all the rest that they disputed about but trifles'. Historians have endeavoured to affiliate her with this or that creed, deducing systematic religious principles from stray comments and anecdotes that have come down to us. Thus she brusquely ordered monks to take away their candles during her coronation, assuring them that she had enough light to see by: a gesture redolent of the Protestant critique of Catholicism as idolatry and a religion of empty ceremonies. Yet she retained a cross and candles on the altar of the chapel royal, to the intense annoyance of her chaplains and bishops, who argued with her long, hard and often over these 'dregs of popery', which they rightly saw as dangerous (from their point of view) not only in themselves but also in the hope which they instilled into the hearts of the disaffected. The woman who walked out of a Mass at the elevation of the blessed sacrament (thus advertising her essential solidarity with the Protestants who had been burned in Mary's reign after showing similar disrespect to the sacrament) nevertheless had the wording of the *Book of Common Prayer* amended in order to make it easier for the Catholics who had burned them to swallow the new communion (the amended wording was compatible with a Catholic understanding of the real presence of Christ in the sacrament).

What all the gestures really tell us, though, is that they are precisely that – gestures. They are not unconscious manifestations of Elizabeth's innermost thoughts and preferences, but carefully choreographed moves and shrewdly scripted soundbites designed to elicit particular responses from particular audiences at particular times. There was probably no better example on the stage of Tudor politics of someone who, as Thomas More had put it in his *Utopia*, knew how to improvise a part for herself in the drama unfolding around her. Elizabeth always played the appropriate part. Here and there we can cling on to something a little more solid. Her defence of church music is too lasting to be dismissed as a mere gesture. And her patronage of church musicians such as Thomas Tallis and William Byrd, who were notorious (if docile) Roman Catholics, shows that music could take precedence for her over both dogma and the requirements of obedience. Her musical taste was not without theological significance: the extremes of Protestantism represented by the Puritans and by the Reformation in Switzerland looked with hatred upon the ornate musical styles of the Renaissance as an idolatry of the ear, a distraction from the worship of God in spirit and truth, every bit as damnable as the images and stained glass which had once decorated the interiors of churches. Yet we look in vain to Elizabeth for a textbook rationale of church music. What we hear in the Anglican musical tradition, which she did more than any other single person to found, is a testimony to her taste rather than to her theology.

The alteration of religion, then, was the first business to be transacted in Elizabeth's first Parliament in 1559. One of the first surviving policy papers of the reign, entitled the 'Device for Alteration of Religion', sets out the context of the problem and the plan for change with such brilliant clarity that it can only represent the thinking of William Cecil himself. Shrewdly assessing the dangers both at home and abroad, the 'Device' proposes swift but judicious change:

> At the next Parliament: so that the dangers be foreseen, and remedies therefore provided. For the sooner that religion is restored, God is the more glorified, and as we trust will be more merciful unto us, and better save and defend Her Highness from all dangers.

Its plan seems, broadly, to have been followed. Even the 'Device', however, failed to anticipate the degree of opposition which the religious legislation would face. Although the exiguous record of parliamentary proceedings is difficult to interpret, what is beyond doubt is that the process was more contentious than any previous Tudor change of religion. Almost uniquely in the history of Tudor Parliaments, there was concerted and sustained opposition to government proposals. Several bills were either flatly voted down or else subjected to wrecking amendments by the House of Lords (the House of Commons was usually even more subservient than the Lords to the legislative proposals of the Crown). The content of these bills is largely a matter for conjecture. No drafts survive, and the one-line descriptions in the sketchy parliamentary journals do not provide a reliable basis for analysis. But they were unwelcome to the House of Lords, whose temporal peers were split almost evenly in religion, and whose spiritual peers, the bishops (all of them selected or at least re-appointed by Mary Tudor), were determined to fight every inch of the way.

The bishops had a second forum for dissent, which they also exploited to the full. Convocation, the representative body of the clergy, always sat at the same time as Parliament, and was manned by the bishops (the upper house) and representatives of every diocese (the lower house), who were for the most part drawn from the ranks of the deans, archdeacons and canons who administered the Church on the ground. In short, Convocation *was* the hierarchy of the Church of England. Led by Edmund Bonner, the Bishop of London (Cardinal Pole had died on the same day as Mary Tudor, and the see of Canterbury was therefore vacant), Convocation drew up and promulgated towards the end of February an uncompromising summary of Roman Catholic doctrine as the teaching of the Church of England. Never before had Convocation openly repudiated the religious policy of the Crown, and the government was clearly disturbed at the prospect of trying to pass religious legislation in the teeth of opposition from the entire hierarchy. Parliament was adjourned while the queen and her advisers worked out what to do next.

What was arranged was one of the familiar expedients of reforming governments in the sixteenth century, a public disputation on the relative merits of the old and the new religions, held in Westminster Abbey on 31 March. As the Crown held the ring, the reformers were able to define the terms and the topics of discussion. Rather than engage their opponents on such central issues as papal primacy, the sacrifice of the Mass, or the real presence, they chose instead to argue over the use of Latin in the liturgy, the administration of the chalice to the laity in communion, and the so-called 'private Mass'. In short, they shrewdly chose issues where they felt a better chance of victory, issues where the Catholic position depended crucially on the authority of the Pope and medieval tradition rather than on the intrinsic merits of the theological case. The Catholic party at the disputation was on the back foot from the start, and in fact the combat was never properly joined, as the two sides bickered fruitlessly over procedural technicalities – a situation which, as the Catholics were the ones complaining, made them look as though they lacked the stomach for a fight. Two of the Catholic bishops were arbitrarily imprisoned for their role in this debacle, and the Catholic party as a whole was to a certain extent discredited, especially in London.

Catholic resistance in the House of Lords was in consequence weakened. The spiritual peers were depleted in numbers, and the Catholics among the temporal peers were somewhat demoralised. When religious legislation came back to the Lords after the Easter break, it was in the form of two separate acts, one re-establishing the royal supremacy, the other re-enacting the *Book of Common Prayer*. The Act of Supremacy went through with the support of the temporal peers, only one of whom joined the ten bishops present in opposing it. The Act of Uniformity, however, was opposed by nine temporal peers as well as nine bishops, and passed by only three votes – with two bishops in custody, and with Goldwell (Bishop-elect of Oxford) and Feckenham (Abbot of Westminster) prevented from attending. This is not to suggest that there was any real risk of Elizabeth's Reformation being frustrated. Even if the bishops had all been present, all Elizabeth needed to do was to create a few new temporal peers. It was simply easier to stop a few spiritual peers voting.

One of the few unambiguous features of Elizabeth's religious position is her utter commitment to maintaining the settlement of the Church which was the first business of her first Parliament. The phrase 'Elizabethan Settlement' which in the twentieth century became attached to the achievement of 1559 could in many ways hardly be less appropriate. It is unlikely that anybody apart from the queen herself envisaged what was done as a 'settlement', with all the finality implied by that term. There had been too many sharp turns in religious policy in too few years for anyone to feel confident about stability. And if few expected it, still fewer hoped for it. Catholics hoped for another turn of fortune's wheel (as we can see from those countless parishes which held onto their Catholic liturgical gear for years after its use was made illegal), while Protestants hoped for further reformation to complete the construction of the new Jerusalem (as we can see from those revealing letters which leading Protestants sent to their co-religionists in Switzerland). 'Semper eadem', however, was Elizabeth's motto: nowhere more so than in her religious position after 1559. Time and again pressure for change bubbled up. First it came from her own bench of bishops, although their impotence even to remove that cross and those candles from her chapel gave them a healthy respect for her will, so that they encouraged their subordinates to raise the cry for reform. Subsequently it came from the lower clergy and even from enthusiastic laymen agitating in Parliament. Invariably it was resisted.

When many parish ministers threw off their vestments in the mid-1560s, demanding the right to celebrate the liturgy in little more than plain clothes, it was Elizabeth who compelled her Archbishop of Canterbury to impose uniformity and uniform upon them. Here she showed a characteristic blend of rigidity and cunning. Everyone agreed that vestments were 'things indifferent' (often described by the Greek word *adiaphora*). But while the zealous Protestants, soon to be known as Puritans, argued that therefore the authorities should not make such an issue out of wearing them, the authorities in their turn argued that the dissidents should not make such an issue out of refusing them. It was Elizabeth who chose to make vestments a test of obedience, and thus to invest an intrinsically marginal issue with great extrinsic significance. Yet her inflexible policy was shrewdly implemented. She held back from investing her personal authority and charisma in the matter, and compelled the unfortunate Matthew Parker, her Archbishop of Canterbury, to promulgate orders on the subject over his own name, thus diverting onto him the brunt of the reformers' ire.

Nor was there ever any prospect of Elizabeth yielding to the Puritan pressure for abolishing bishops and introducing 'presbyterian' Church government. Elizabeth's essential social conservatism would always have prejudiced her against such a policy, and probably her education confirmed that temperamental inclination. Roger Ascham tells us that her theological reading in her schoolroom days included the writings of Cyprian of Carthage, a bishop of the early Church whose letters and treatises firmly upheld the doctrine of what is sometimes called 'monarchical episcopacy'. No reader of Cyprian in her formative years was likely to feel much sympathy for the alternative model of collegiate church government worked out by Calvin and his followers: a model in which local churches were presided over by godly oligarchies which elected their pastor and controlled access to the sacrament of communion. She was always going to prefer the clear vertical lines of authority which characterised the traditional ecclesiastical hierarchy to the more horizontal patterns of power which typified Calvinist Church organisation, and were often associated with republican governments.

Agitation for presbyterianism first appeared around 1570, and periodically resurfaced thereafter in the 1570s and 1580s, in speeches in Parliament, in pamphlet broadsides, and in local initiatives to establish a semblance of presbyterianism on a voluntary basis. Elizabeth's favourite Archbishop of Canterbury, John Whitgift (the only clergyman ever appointed to her Privy Council), actually first won her favour by means of his lengthy controversy with England's leading presbyterian theoretician, Thomas Cartwright. Whitgift's fair enough observation that the presbyterian model was rich in potential for faction and divisiveness was precisely how Elizabeth herself saw it. There was more to Puritanism than presbyterianism, but the presbyterian inclinations of many Puritans helped consolidate Elizabeth's prejudice against the movement as a whole. She ordered her bishops to stamp out any ecclesiastical initiatives which smacked to her of disobedience. Many of her bishops sympathised with at least some elements in the Puritan programme. In December 1576, barely a year after his appointment as Archbishop of Canterbury, Grindal refused to implement her direct instructions to suppress 'prophesyings' (in essence, Bible-reading groups). As a result of his obduracy he was suspended from the exercise of his duties and deprived of the revenues of his see, remaining archbishop in name alone until his death in 1583. In Whitgift, Elizabeth found her ideal replacement for Grindal, and for the next twenty years he ruthlessly clamped down on Puritan activists and readily took the flak for her. This made him the particular butt of the 'Marprelate Tracts', a popular series of wickedly satirical pamphlets against the bishops published by a small group of outspoken Puritans in the years 1588–89. These tracts were in fact too successful for their own good. Not only were those responsible hunted down, but their irreverence towards authority enabled the bishops to exploit the traditional association between religious dissent and sedition in such a way as to discredit Puritanism with important sections of the political élite.

Among the reasons for Elizabeth's refusal to contemplate further religious change was her personal animus against the figure who was becoming the international godfather of Protestantism, John Calvin. For it was in Calvin's adopted home, Geneva, that John Knox, in the darkest moments of the Marian repression, had penned and published his notorious *First Blast of the Trumpet against the Monstrous Regiment of Women*, a pungent little treatise which generalised from the unsatisfactory policies of female rulers in England, Scotland and the Netherlands (Mary Tudor, Mary of Guise and Mary of Hungary, all of whom were at that time vigorously repressing heresy) and from a selective corpus of biblical evidence to construct a powerful theoretical case against the exercise of political authority by women.

This untimely tract appeared shortly before Elizabeth succeeded to the throne. Knox bore the brunt of her displeasure. When he sought to return to Scotland, Elizabeth would not let him so much as set foot in her domains, compelling him to take the slower and riskier sea route. Calvin also learned his lesson. Shortly after Elizabeth's accession he sent her a copy of his commentary on the Book of Isaiah, with a letter of congratulation. But William Cecil wrote back explaining that there was no chance of Elizabeth accepting the gift because she blamed Calvin personally

John Knox from a 1580 woodcut. The awesome prophet of the Scottish Reformation is sporting the patriarchal beard which from about 1550 became fashionable among Protestant ministers as a way of distinguishing themselves from the tonsured and generally clean-shaved priesthood of the Catholic Church. Elizabeth never forgave him for his *First Blast of the Trumpet against the Monstrous Regiment of Women* (Geneva, 1558).

for the publication of Knox's little effort. In vain Calvin pleaded that it was not he but the city council which controlled censorship in Geneva. This little equivocation deceived nobody. The damage had been done. Just as the 'obvious' Lutheran destiny of the English Reformation in the 1530s had been closed off by Henry VIII's ineradicable hatred for Luther, so now the equally 'obvious' Calvinist destination of the Reformation was closed off by Elizabeth's hatred for Calvin.

SCOTLAND

Religious concerns dominated the politics of Elizabeth's reign from start to finish. Elizabeth's regime was as keen as those of Edward and Henry before it to encourage the Reformation cause in Scotland as a means of closing England's back door to potential enemies. With Mary Queen of Scots married to the Dauphin Francis, the prospect that the French might invade through Scotland was a very real one, raised in the 'Device for Alteration of Religion' as one of the potential obstacles to be faced in returning the Church of England to the Protestant fold. When, a few months after the alteration of religion in England, Henry II's death in a jousting accident placed the young Dauphin on the throne of France as Francis II, the Scottish problem assumed menacing proportions. Francis was politically in the pocket of his wife's powerful uncles, the militantly Catholic Duke of Guise and his like-minded brothers. It was Guise who had retaken Calais, and now that the English were heretics as well as enemies, he would be doubly keen to renew hostilities against them. The response to the Scottish threat was essentially that adumbrated in the 'Device', namely 'to help forward their divisions, and especially to augment the hope of them who incline to good religion'.

In the meantime, and despite Elizabeth's obstructive attitude, John Knox had returned to Scotland in May 1559, and had fomented widespread religious unrest. In this troubled context, the Protestant 'Lords of the Congregation', a band of lords united by a formal bond to promote their religious cause through political action, moved to overthrow the French Regent of Scotland, Mary of Guise, in October. However, Scottish politics remained typically tumultuous, and the case for English intervention, which Cecil put forward in a policy paper of August 1559, was strong. Cecil argued that swift financial and military assistance to the rebel lords would be decisive in securing religious change in Scotland and breaking the French connection. In the religiously divided context of European politics, England and Scotland would be drawn together by their shared Protestant commitments, and their time-honoured enmity would be turned into lasting friendship.

Queen Elizabeth, however, was not so easily convinced, and the Scottish crisis of 1559–60 was the first of many episodes in which we can see the tortuous emergence of policy from the complex relationship between Elizabeth and her trusted chief minister and other advisers. Where Cecil's approach was a curious blend of religious principle and *realpolitik*, notable earlier in the reign for a real breadth of strategic vision, Elizabeth's was compounded of caution, parsimony and an ideology which privileged the values of kingship over the values of the gospel to the extent that they might compete. On those occasions when her instincts and Cecil's did not immediately converge, the result was hesitation. In this early case, the hesitation was compounded by the fact that Cecil, although clearly Elizabeth's chief minister, had not as yet established the dominant position on the Privy Council that he was to hold in later years. There were other, more cautious voices to whom the queen seemed inclined to listen, maintaining that the dire financial straits of the Crown ruled out intervention in Scotland. She herself now first displayed the reluctance she often showed later for interfering in the domestic affairs of other kingdoms. She had a high view of the duties of obedience which subjects owed to their princes. This had, after all, been the relentless message of English preaching throughout her childhood, and was at the core of the whole concept of the royal supremacy. So she was far from relishing the evident hypocrisy in encouraging the subjects of other monarchs to commit what she condemned as mortal sin in her own.

The resurgence of the Regent's party in Scotland, which retook Edinburgh in November, brought matters to a head. Cecil had already extracted some grudging financial aid for the lords. Now direct military assistance was called for. But Elizabeth remained so set against it that Cecil asked to be relieved of the burdens of office. Only this threat, it seems, changed her mind. First her navy and then, in March

1560, an army of a few thousand men went into action on behalf of the Protestant faction in Scotland. The forces engaged were hardly adequate to the task, but fortune smiled on the English. Religious tensions in France prevented effective aid from that quarter, making the English contribution decisive. William Cecil himself was sent north to Scotland to negotiate a peace, and his task was facilitated by the death of Mary of Guise on 11 June. The Treaty of Edinburgh, signed on 6 July, removed almost all French troops from Scotland and excluded Frenchmen from high Crown office. The Lords of the Congregation took over, and in August 1560 pushed a Protestant Reformation through Parliament, repudiating the papacy, suppressing the monasteries, and prohibiting the Mass. There was no clear doctrinal statement – but then England itself had not yet seen the Thirty-Nine Articles. However, with John Knox dominant in the kirk, a fully Calvinist settlement was only a matter of time. The solution was not ideal from the point of view of England and of Elizabeth. There was no royal supremacy, and while bishops were not actually abolished, they were marginalised. Moreover, the death of Francis II in December 1560 made Mary Stuart's eventual return inevitable, which in turn posed a new threat to the stability of the settlement. Nevertheless, the Protestant regime in Scotland had nowhere to turn for support other than England.

The triumph in Scotland sealed Cecil's place at the heart of Elizabeth's government. Although Elizabeth, as a monarch and a woman, continued to see the world from a very different perspective from his, she would never treat his advice with disdain, and for the rest of his long life (he died in 1598) no one challenged his primacy in policy advice.

The complex interplay of religion and politics was just as evident in the second foreign policy venture of Elizabeth's reign, an attempt to exploit growing religious conflict in France in order to regain Calais. In 1562 the Protestant party in France, known as the Huguenots, sought English financial support in the civil war which everyone could see was coming. By the Treaty of Hampton Court (August 1562), England agreed to provide men and money in return for the cession of Dieppe and Le Havre (then known in English as Newhaven) until such time as Calais was handed back. Elizabeth was more enthusiastic for this venture than she had been for the Scottish expedition. Again, this was a matter of the royal perspective. Elizabeth shared to the full her sister's sense of national disgrace at the loss of Calais, calling it 'a matter of continual grief to this realm'. She was therefore understandably attracted by the dream that she might 'have this our Calais returned to us', not just for honour but for the sake of enhancing still more the contrast between herself and the late Mary Tudor. Cecil, on the other hand, was less keen, already on record as judging Calais a drain on the exchequer and its loss a blessing in disguise. Support for Elizabeth came from her favourite, Robert Dudley, whose brother Ambrose, Earl of Warwick, was put in command of the troops which occupied Le Havre and Dieppe in October 1562.

This time, events vindicated Cecil's scepticism. Whereas in Scotland the English intervention could be presented as aid in the struggle for liberation, in France it was manifestly predatory, notwithstanding the religious dimension. Once a peace was brokered between Catholics and Huguenots, both sides turned against the old enemy. Le Havre surrendered in summer 1563, showing how difficult it would have been to hold Calais against the might of France. If the Le Havre adventure consolidated Cecil's position by bearing further witness to his sound judgement, it also confirmed Elizabeth's fundamentally non-militarist prejudices. Not for another twenty years would royal troops cross the Channel. During that time, the only military actions that Elizabeth sanctioned were against her own rebellious subjects, once in England, repeatedly in Ireland.

ELIZABETH'S POLITICAL STYLE

The love of gesture and the concern for image which emerge from an analysis of Elizabeth's apparently 'revealing' actions and sayings on the subject of religion offer us the key to her political character. For these same traits were almost always evident in her actions and sayings, whatever the subject. While we can learn something from this, we must be properly humble and realise that we can learn very little more than Elizabeth wished us to learn – and that often these lessons are rather suspect. The queen could be hard to read. Late in her reign an ambassador commented on how, during their conversation, she would often digress from the subject in hand. But he was unsure whether this was done deliberately, in order to gain time, or was simply an unselfconscious part of her character. Life at Elizabeth's court was carefully stage-managed. The formal manner in which she sometimes greeted foreign ambassadors and visitors was designed to impress them with her wealth, power and security. The splendidly decorated Presence Chamber in her palace, with its throne beneath a cloth of estate to denote her royal rank, the well-built young gentlemen guarding the door, the handful of elegant noblemen and ladies in waiting or maids of honour disporting themselves gracefully around it, and one or two grave councillors on hand to ensure that the proceedings were properly recorded – and of course at the centre of it all, the person of the queen herself, striking and attractive in her youth, bewigged and heavily made-up in her later years, but always gorgeously attired in dresses remarkable for the richness of their cloth, the complexity of their design, the finesse of their workmanship, and the brilliance of the jewels which adorned them – all this carefully co-ordinated display invariably sent the right message to the bedazzled visitor.

There were less formal exercises as well. One ambassador commented on how Elizabeth made her entrance on one occasion in an especially dignified manner, expressly so 'that I might see her while she pretended not to see me'. Special scenes might be staged for the benefit of ambassadors and their foreign masters. Thus, early in the reign, Elizabeth's oldest companion, Kate Ashley, threw herself on her knees before the queen in the Presence Chamber, upbraiding her for her familiarity with Dudley and urging her to make an honest woman of herself by marriage. Notwithstanding Ashley's years of intimacy with Elizabeth, it is hard to see her making quite so bold without some strong steer from above. For the scene gave Elizabeth the pretext to explain herself and to defend her good name and her favour for Dudley. Many years later, when the negotiations for a possible marriage between Elizabeth and the Duke of Anjou were underway, Leicester himself took the starring role in a remarkably similar scene. He appeared before the queen and, with otherwise incredible audacity, demanded whether or not she was still a virgin. It can hardly be thought that, with Elizabeth at the height of her powers, he would have dared question (or even challenge) her in such an intimate matter without her express instructions. But the point was of course to set French minds at rest about the relationship between the queen and her favourite early in the reign. Had Leicester himself slept with her, he would not have needed to ask!

We can detect the hand of the director behind these scenes by comparing them with those plainly unscripted scenes in which unwelcome gestures were made by her subjects, and she in turn was invited to respond with gestures that were far from her purposes. When Sir Richard Shelley, a young Catholic gentleman, dared to cast at the feet of the queen as she walked in her Whitehall gardens a petition seeking a

Queen Elizabeth at the opening of Parliament. In the immediate foreground the Commons stand at the Bar and present their Speaker.

limited toleration for her Catholic subjects, she did not seize upon the opportunity to dispense mercy as St Louis of France had once dispensed justice, beneath the oak tree, to those who brought him their griefs and grievances. Shelley was put under arrest, thrown into gaol, and left to rot.

Parliament was another target of the queen's carefully planned displays of personality. She inherited her father's ability to win round that occasionally wilful and noisy institution. But where he had overawed with his physical presence, Elizabeth employed the power of words, skilfully varying her tone between gentleness and wrath. Although entire history books have been written to document the rise of 'opposition' to Elizabeth in Parliament, in fact Elizabeth managed her Parliaments effectively enough. The only serious opposition she ever faced there was over religion, in 1559, and that was soon overcome – and her largely episcopal opponents were soon relieved of their seats in the House of Lords. Far from Parliament opposing Elizabeth, it was far more often that she opposed Parliament. In the course of her reign, many bills failed to become statutes because she took against them and denied them the royal assent. And while this was sometimes because they were politically offensive to her (as with certain proposals for harsher treatment of Catholics), it also seems that at times she did it simply to show who was in charge. Upon other occasions, Elizabeth found herself in receipt of unwanted advice, especially from her loyal House of Commons. The underlying problem here was her status as a woman. It was impossible for a chamber full of politically aware and opinionated gentlemen not to feel that, on a whole range of issues, from religion to economic regulation, they knew better than she did, and it was equally hard for them to deny her the benefit of their superior wisdom.

The occasional imprisonment of recalcitrant MPs, however, combined with the judicious treatment (now conciliatory, now contemptuous) of delegations from the Commons enabled her to maintain an adequate working relationship with Parliament (the Lords, her 'cousins' by contemporary etiquette, were never a cause for concern after 1559). At times Elizabeth was excessively anxious about the tendency of the Commons to infringe her 'prerogative' by debating matters of high policy without her authorisation. But the high view of kingship which underlay this anxiety was by no means an inexplicable foible. It was simply her memory of the kingship of her father. Like Mary, she knew that she could never have quite the hold over her subjects that he had attained. But she did rather more than Mary to emulate him as far as she could. She was always proud of her physical resemblance to him, evident in her bearing and her red hair. And she frequently invoked his memory, his example and his legacy in her public comments – most famously in her speech to the troops at Tilbury during the Armada campaign, where the 'heart and stomach of a king' which she claimed were hidden in her own 'weak body of a woman' were most certainly the heart and stomach of Henry.

Elizabeth used her femininity to great effect in the political arena. Of course, it did not exactly compensate for the defect of her birth – not her illegitimacy but her sex. Her repeated comments about her father and her evident pride in being his daughter show that she was a woman who lived always with the consciousness of not being a man. But she made the best of it. Courtly love was the language of her court. She expected as a matter of course to hear from the lips of her male favourites and servants effusions fit for Renaissance sonneteers or nineteenth-century romantic novelists. Throughout her life she fished shamelessly for compliments when conversing with men. The string of handsome and charming youths who shook a nice leg at a dance would not have disgraced a Hollywood starlet. When men such as Leicester found themselves out of favour, they earned their recovery by amorous letters or small talk which became more extravagant as the ageing queen's charms faded ever further. The conventions of courtly love, in which the social precedence of men over women was inverted by the image of the woman as the dominant, even tyrannical, partner in relationships, and that of the man as the strong made weak and dependent by passion, furnished a handy metaphor for the political inversion in which those involved found themselves, and helped make the unprecedented situation a trifle less unfamiliar.

MARRIAGE AND THE SUCCESSION

There has long been debate over whether or not Elizabeth ever had any intention of marrying. Historians have differed over this, as over much else concerning Elizabeth, precisely because she herself was once more deliberately obscure and ambiguous about her intentions. Even at the start of her reign, when foreign princes jostled for the privilege of marriage to Europe's most eligible spinster, there were hints of ambivalence circulating around the queen's court. The rumour that Elizabeth had some physical incapacity for marriage is frequently reported from the earliest days, as are comments from Elizabeth's own lips in favour of virginity and against marriage in general and childbirth in particular. Dr Huick, her personal physician, who had known her many years, reckoned in the 1560s that she was physically incapable of sexual relations. On the other hand, at much the same time a committee of physicians judged her fit to bear children. Many years later, when she was forty-five and in the midst of negotiations for a marriage with the Duke of Anjou, another committee of physicians and ladies in waiting convinced Cecil that there was no reason why Elizabeth should not, even at this improbable age, bear a child. But despite their privileged knowledge of Elizabeth's bodily functions, the sceptical historian might observe that, if the truth really was otherwise, neither of these committees had much reason to report it. Elizabeth was notoriously sensitive to what she chose to see as aspersions upon her beauty and charm – the Earl of Leicester's secret marriage to Lettice Knollys was interpreted as one such affront – and might not have reacted too well to aspersions upon her essential femininity, notwithstanding her own explicit contempt for marriage and childbirth.

If there was not in fact a physical incapacity for marriage, it has been suggested, then perhaps she had some sort of psychological hang-up about it, although opinions differ as to whether this went back to her experiences in the household of Sir Thomas Seymour – which today would be classified as child abuse – or was simply a result of jealousy and frustration or indeed of sexual orientation. What is clear is that Elizabeth reacted extremely badly to marriage or even contemplation of marriage on the part of men who were close to her. Sometimes this can be put down to political rather than personal considerations. Members of the royal family were not allowed to marry without the consent (in effect, without the arrangement) of the sovereign. Thus when in the 1560s Lady Catherine Grey married Edward Seymour, Elizabeth's reaction – to throw them both in gaol – was no different from that of her father to the marriage of Lord Thomas Howard and Lady Margaret Douglas in the 1530s. The Duke of Norfolk's plan to marry Mary Queen of Scots comes into the same category. Even though Mary was not Elizabeth's subject, it was clearly incumbent upon the duke to inform his queen of his intentions, and the expectation of refusal which understandably deterred him from broaching the issue need not have rested upon any perception of the queen's emotional hostility to marriage.

Nevertheless, Elizabeth's peculiar reactions to marriage extended beyond the blood royal to almost any marriage contracted by men or women of her court. Her favourites almost invariably concealed their marriages from her as long as possible, a subterfuge which inevitably exacerbated her wrath when the marriages inevitably came to light. After the row following Leicester's second marriage, he was in due course forgiven and restored to favour. But his wife was never again allowed to come to court. Similar stories of royal rage at the marriages of courtiers or maids of honour could be almost endlessly duplicated. One victim remained in disgrace so long that he died in prison. Elizabeth's bishops and clergy also suffered from her attitude to marriage. She refused to allow the wives of bishops to accompany their husbands to court, and as long as she remained on the throne, the law permitting the marriage of priests, which had been repealed by Mary, was not restored to the statute book. It certainly looks as though Elizabeth had a rooted dislike for the concept of matrimony.

Doubts or speculations about the queen's sexual orientation, however, may be easily laid to rest. Whatever her attitudes to marriage and sexual intercourse, she manifestly enjoyed the company of men. Her relationship with Robert Dudley in the early years of her reign appeared to court and council alike as nothing less than courtship. The complex rituals of flirtation and courtly love with which she often surrounded her dealings with men at court and on the council likewise reflected conventional assumptions about relations between the sexes, besides providing a convenient grammar and vocabulary with which to negotiate the existential discomfort for noble adult males of finding themselves in the unaccustomed position of dependence upon and service to a woman. Their situation could be rendered more palatable by being decked out as that of lovers seeking the favour of some damsel out of a chivalric romance. Hence the renewed vogue for chivalric and Arthurian literature which arose in Elizabethan times (and soon fell out of fashion thereafter, remaining in obscurity until rescued in the age of romanticism and the neo-gothic),

Elizabeth's falcon downs a heron. Illustration from George Turberville, *The Book of Faulconrie or Hauking* (1575), p.81. The books of Gascoigne and Turberville were issued as a pair and are usually found bound within a single cover. Although neither book explicitly states that the princely lady in the illustrations is meant to be Queen Elizabeth, the Tudor roses on the liveried servants in the scenes make her identity obvious.

Below left & right: Illustrations from George Gascoigne, *The Noble Arte of Venerie or Hunting* (1575), pp.90 and 133. Right: Elizabeth enjoys a picnic during a hunt. Left: the huntsman presents Elizabeth with a knife to make the first cut in butchering the deer.

seen at its most elaborate in the complex allegories of Spenser's unfinished Protestant epic, *The Faerie Queene*.

If, in her relationships with her more handsome courtiers, Elizabeth indulged in that language of formal flirtation which scholars call 'courtly love', she has nevertheless gone down in history as the 'Virgin Queen'. Although base rumour and the more malicious tongues of her Catholic enemies were quick to impugn her virginity, especially in the early years when her intimacy with Robert Dudley was an open secret, there has never been any serious reason to question her boast. For Elizabeth to have lost her virginity before marriage would have been an intolerable political risk. Kings and princes might sow their wild oats: royal bastards were nothing more than testimony to royal virility. But the sexual double standard was firmly in place in Tudor England, and for a queen to bear an illegitimate child would have been political suicide, earning her the fatal contempt of her own nobility. Mary Queen of Scots provided Elizabeth with an object lesson in this respect. Mary's tangled matrimonial and sexual career certainly did nothing to cement the loyalty of a traditional aristocracy. Elizabeth's relationship with Dudley aroused enough resentment as it was. There is no telling what the Duke of Norfolk, or even the impeccably loyal Earl of Sussex, might have done if Elizabeth had borne Dudley's love-child.

For all the peculiarities and inconsistencies of Elizabeth on the subject of her own marriage and on marriages contracted in her court circle, it would be risky to attempt long-distance psychoanalysis in search of the explanation. Her own objections to marriage are expressed in thoroughly rational terms, ranging from her own disinclination to the married state to her clear perception of the political problems attendant upon marrying a foreign prince. The Tudor age was not sentimental about marriage, and Elizabeth was shrewd enough to draw reasonable conclusions from what she saw around her. Her own mother's marriage had ended on the block, and the rest of her father's matrimonial record would hardly have filled her with enthusiasm for the holy state. The one wife of Henry's with whom she had established a close relationship, Catherine Parr, had died in labour. Her elder sister's marriage was a palpable disaster. Nor was her cousin, Mary Queen of Scots, conspicuously well served by the immature boy, the feckless youth, and the reckless adventurer with whom she successively linked herself. Leicester's first marriage, another failure, had ended in obscure tragedy. Elizabeth herself knew well enough the authority that contemporary opinion vested in husbands over their wives, and was probably reluctant to imperil her sovereign position by submitting herself to any man in any degree. Mary Tudor had looked on marriage as her destiny. Elizabeth certainly did not, and given her inclinations and her experience, her decision not to marry was in many ways a coolly sensible one.

MARY QUEEN OF SCOTS

The question of the succession was further complicated by Mary Queen of Scots, who had been a threat to the stability of the Elizabethan regime from the very start, when she quartered the arms of England with those of Scotland and France in what was an implicit claim if not to the throne then at least to the succession. For the rest of her tragic life, the English crown was the supreme object of her desire, and her aspirations were among the crucial influences on Elizabethan politics and on Elizabeth's personal life. Time and again, however, events conspired to frustrate her legitimate hopes and less worthy ambitions. English victory in Scotland in 1560 ensured the success of the Reformation there, and fatally weakened the position of her Scottish allies and French relatives. Yet that was not too much of a problem as long as she was married to the king of France, for ultimately the might of France would have been thrown into the balance to avenge the English insult to French honour. But the death of her husband, the unmanly Francis II, was a more telling blow. Not only was her own power drastically reduced, but so was the influence of her Guise cousins in French politics. Suddenly, Scotland was all that was left to a woman who had dreamed of bequeathing no less than four kingdoms: England, France, Scotland and Ireland. With nothing to be gained from remaining in France, she returned in 1561 to what was almost a foreign country, herself more French than Scottish in tastes and manners. Here, her policy was simple: to angle for recognition of her claim to the English succession. For her at least, in Dr Johnson's famous words, there was no nobler prospect than the high road that leads to England.

What Mary most sought from Elizabeth was some explicit acknowledgement as heir presumptive. However, she was tacitly excluded from the English succession under the terms of the 1544 Act of Succession, which was still in force. Not that this counted for much. The same exclusion obviously extended to her son, James, and it did not stop him from taking the English throne in 1603. There can be no doubt that, in purely hereditary and customary terms, her claim to the throne was the strongest: she was descended from Henry VIII's elder sister, Margaret. And had the matter ever come to a head, she might well have been able to vindicate her claim against the statutorily based but hereditarily inferior claims of the Greys, descended from Henry's younger sister Mary. If the history of the Tudors had shown anything, it had shown that the express wills of princes and parliaments were as nothing beside the force of arms and the consensus of the people about the rights of heirs. But Mary never showed herself a shrewd politician: unlike Elizabeth she wore her heart on her sleeve, and had little of her English cousin's talents for dissimulation, equivocation and obscurity. She had a certain difficulty also in distinguishing fantasy from reality. Thus she simply refused to believe that Henry VIII's will and the 1544 statute had excluded her from the succession, and repeatedly demanded to be shown an authenticated copy. Some of Elizabeth's problems lay here. Only an Act of Parliament could formally have guaranteed the succession of Mary, and the Parliaments which convened under Elizabeth were unlikely to sanction the succession of a Catholic. Moreover, Elizabeth had her own reasons for leaving the question of her successor wrapped in indecent obscurity. She knew from her own experience under Mary Tudor how the person of the heir to the throne became a focus for plots and opposition. Suspicious to the very core of her Tudor being, she had no desire to whet the assassin's knife with hope.

Mary Stuart's few years in power were characterised by an ineptitude and miscalculation which not only failed to win her the throne of England but also lost her that of Scotland. Her policy was always inconstant and often impenetrable. Her unpredictable changes of attitude towards her nobility and her idiosyncratic position over religion alienated substantial sections of political opinion in Scotland. Perhaps the most remarkable thing is that, as late as 1568, she could still muster enough support to fight a civil war: a tribute not to her own talent, although she seems to have had a remarkable personal charisma which enabled her to win over the most improbable enemies, but to the endemic vendettas of Scottish noble politics, which ensured that whoever was in power would never lack for rivals. More characteristic was her failure to appreciate even this fundamental reality of Scottish politics, which led her to take refuge in England (of all places) after her defeat in that war. The shrewd option was simply to concede the demands of her foes and patiently rebuild her position, as she had done before. Instead, she staked – and lost – everything on a wild throw of the dice, fleeing to England in the hope of securing political and military support from Elizabeth: from Elizabeth, the parsimonious and peace-loving Protestant, and the one person in the world who had everything to gain from Mary's exclusion from politics. Thus began nearly two decades of residence in England during which her status declined gradually from that of an honoured if slightly troublesome guest through house arrest to an irksome and unpleasant confinement (in the hands of a singularly obnoxious Puritan zealot) as public enemy number one, living on sufferance, and finally to her execution amidst public rejoicing.

The handling of Mary neatly illustrates the strengths and weaknesses of Elizabeth's character and policy. From the start Elizabeth respected her cousin as a fellow sovereign. To that very limited extent, then, there was something in Mary's dream of support. Elizabeth felt too exposed herself to look with equanimity on the dispossession of a neighbouring sovereign by a clique of ambitious noble malcontents. On the other hand, her instinct for political survival prevented her from granting the personal interview on which Mary pinned her hopes. Perhaps Elizabeth feared lest she fall victim to the renowned charm of the Scottish queen. Perhaps she was worried that Mary's tarnished reputation in matters of sexual relations and political manoeuvres might reflect upon her own (which had, after all, suffered enough from her unconsummated, if not always entirely innocent, affair with Robert Dudley). Mary was suspected of serial adultery and conspiracy to murder. Most probably, Elizabeth feared the political consequences of giving second place at her court (and no lower place could have been accorded to a visiting sovereign) to someone who certainly had a record for plotting and intrigue. Thus Mary was kept firmly and safely at arm's length.

On the other hand, Elizabeth resisted long and hard the clamouring crescendo for Mary's execution. This had begun in 1569, for Mary's arrival had provoked within a year a plot to liberate her and overthrow Elizabeth and her political and religious establishment. The reliably Protestant Parliaments of Elizabeth called for Mary's execution with monotonous regularity – often at the instigation of the Privy Council. Perhaps Elizabeth's reluctance to bow to this pressure showed some appreciation of how closely Mary Stuart's present position resembled her own former position under Mary Tudor back in the 1550s, when Mary was being pressed by a group of her councillors to seal her political achievement with Elizabeth's blood. Yet perhaps also we can see, between the reluctance to allow Mary to come to court and the refusal to adopt the Machiavellian solution to a very real political problem, Elizabeth's own political limitations. Between reason and honour Elizabeth was putting Mary into an intolerable situation, virtually driving her into precisely the sort of intrigues that Elizabeth most feared. Faced with the growing certainty of life imprisonment, not only without trial but without even the shadow of justice (as a sovereign, Mary was not even subject to Elizabeth's jurisdiction), it was only to be expected that Mary would conspire to bring about the only event that could possibly lead to her release – Elizabeth's death. Finally, Elizabeth was perfectly well aware how it would look if she consigned Mary to the scaffold. The action would inevitably be presented as one of cruelty and tyranny and inhumanity – as of course it was.

Mary's arrival immediately destabilised the still shaky structure of Elizabethan politics. For that old-fashioned section of the English nobility which wished to settle the doubts over the succession, which resented the political hegemony of William Cecil, and which regretted the divisiveness of the religious situation, Mary Queen of Scots actually looked more like a solution than a problem. As Elizabeth's reluctance to marry was increasingly apparent, the notion of marrying off Mary to an English nobleman seemed to some people the best of all possible worlds. And England's premier nobleman, the Duke of Norfolk, was happily an eligible middle-aged widower at that precise moment. The match held out the prospect of the succession secured to an English heir (Mary had proved that she could have children), the Elizabethan Church of England guaranteed by the duke (a confirmed if moderate Protestant), and the Catholics reconciled to a Catholic queen (and presumably enjoying a fair degree of toleration). Mary and Norfolk had agreed the marriage by the end of 1568, and spent 1569 working on English aristocrats and foreign ambassadors to try and give their plan unstoppable momentum. But Norfolk and his allies shied away from broaching their plan with Elizabeth, and eventually it was she who, when the rumours became impossible to ignore, broached the subject with him, extorting a confession from him and brusquely commanding him to abandon any idea of going through with the marriage. Elizabeth had no intention of sanctioning Mary Stuart's claim to the throne, still less of strengthening her political position by allowing her to marry the richest man in her kingdom. Besides which, everyone knew that this marriage would leave Cecil's political position untenable, and Elizabeth had no intention of dismissing her chief councillor.

Norfolk had invested too heavily in his hopes to put them aside at the mere word of the queen, and retired in dudgeon to consider his options – which included raising the standard of rebellion. In the end, his nerve failed him, but two of his allies, the Catholic Earls of Northumberland and Westmorland, decided to make their move without his support, calling out their retainers in the name of the old religion and marching southwards with the intention of taking control of the person of the Scottish queen. Their plot was doomed from the moment that Mary herself was whisked away to the safety of the Midlands, and their army melted away as the Earl of Sussex marched northwards at the head of vastly superior forces. The rising of the northern earls was put down with greater cruelty than any other Tudor rebellion. In the wake of the Pilgrimage of Grace, Henry VIII had demanded the execution of a man in every village north of the Trent, but the then Duke of Norfolk had wisely mitigated his severity in practice. After this much less serious rebellion, Henry's solution seems to have been implemented by his daughter. Perhaps as many as 800 men were hanged, although Elizabeth claimed 'we have always been of our own nature inclined to mercy'. Cruelty to the little people, however, was mixed with an astonishing indulgence towards the main culprit, the Duke of Norfolk. His grandfather would never have dared show the degree of disobedience to Henry VIII which he had shown to Henry's daughter. But equally, Elizabeth herself was far less ready than her father to destroy her greatest subject. For all her insistence that she was every inch as much a monarch as her father, Elizabeth could do nothing about the cultural disadvantage conferred on her by her sex, and the relationship between sovereign and nobility could never be the same under a woman as under a man.

Norfolk, however, pursued his own destruction with unwonted steadiness of purpose. Released from custody in August 1570, he was soon deep in intrigue with Spanish and papal agents once more, still with a view to marrying Mary. Little more than a year later he was back in the Tower, and in January 1572 he was convicted of high treason. Even so, it was four months before Elizabeth could be persuaded to sign his death warrant. Elizabeth was nothing like as ready as her father to set the heads of her nobility rolling around Tower Hill.

THE CATHOLIC PROBLEM

The northern earls had rallied their troops under a Catholic banner – quite literally, for it was the banner of St Cuthbert, traditionally housed at the shrine in Durham Cathedral, the banner under which the men of the north were accustomed to march against the Scots. This reminded Elizabeth and Cecil of the political risks inherent in religious division. Their public line, though, was to maintain that religion was just a pretence to conceal the rebels' real objective, 'the subduing of this realm under the yoke of foreign princes'. The lesson was hammered home by the untimely decision of Pope Pius V to excommunicate and depose Elizabeth as a heretic and a tyrant. The papal bull announcing this sentence, *Regnans in Excelsis* (known, like all papal bulls, from its opening words), appeared in February 1570, just as the last embers of revolt were being stamped out. Henceforth it was possible to argue that no good Catholic could be a loyal subject of the queen. This specious line of argument was invoked over the next twenty years to justify ever stricter penal laws against Catholics, laws which often in effect defined aspects of Roman Catholic faith or worship as high treason. The process began almost immediately in the 1571 Parliament, where calls for the execution of Mary Stuart and Norfolk were accompanied by frenzied proposals for dealing with 'papists' – who were increasingly seen as the 'enemy within'. Reconciling and being reconciled to the Roman Catholic Church were made treasonable offences, and the possession of Catholic devotional objects which had received papal blessing became liable to the penalties of 'praemunire' (forfeiture of goods and imprisonment at Her Majesty's pleasure). A bill to levy heavy fines on Catholics who refused to take communion in their parish church failed only because Elizabeth herself exercised the royal veto. One of the few religious bills to which Elizabeth did give assent in that Parliament was an act requiring all clergy holding benefices in the Church of England to subscribe to the Thirty-Nine Articles (the summary of its doctrine which had been agreed by Convocation in 1563) – thus making it harder for closet Catholics to stay inside or infiltrate the ministry of her Church.

Religious and political tension increased throughout the reign, but most rapidly from 1580, when a new initiative by the Catholic refugee community in Europe began to bear fruit: training priests abroad and sending them back as missionaries. The mission to England in 1580–81 of two Jesuits, Robert Parsons and Edmund Campion, reinvigorated the Catholic community, struck fear into their dedicated Protestant opponents and astounded the nation in general. Touring the land and evading their pursuers for months, they reconciled hundreds of Catholics before Campion was captured and Parsons fled the country. Campion, having been tortured, was tried and executed under the old treason law, along with some other priests. But the charges were not especially convincing, and now that the Catholics had some appealing martyrs to set against the Protestant martyrs made famous by John Foxe, they were quick to celebrate them in print. The guiding spirit of the Catholic refugees abroad, William Allen, published his *Brief History of the Glorious Martyrdom of Twelve Reverend Priests, Father Edmund Campion and his Companions* in 1582, and William Cecil thought it worth his while to write a reply, *The Execution of Justice in England* (1583).

Amidst the panic inspired by the mission of Campion and Parsons, new measures against Catholics were multiplied and, more to the point, were purposefully implemented. By the 1590s, thousands upon thousands of 'recusants' (as those who refused to attend Church of England services were known) were being regularly mulcted of huge sums, while hundreds of Catholics, both priests and those who sheltered them, were being imprisoned, banished, or even executed. About 120 Catholic priests were executed over the next twenty years, most of them under new laws which simply declared it treason to have been ordained as a Catholic priest

Parsons and Campion from George Carleton, A *Thankfull Remembrance of Gods Mercy in the Deliverance of the Church and State in the reigns of Elizabeth and James I* (1627), p. 59. A typical piece of English propaganda, implying that Roman Catholic monasteries were training camps for religious terrorists plotting against Elizabeth I's life. The document in the priest's hand is meant to be literally a 'licence to kill' (it reads 'Pope's licence'), on the grounds that the papal excommunication of Elizabeth in 1570 released Catholics from their allegiance to her.

abroad. But in an age when religion was the most important issue in the political arena, arguments about whether the executions were for political or religious reasons were essentially verbal. Those who lobbied in Parliament for harsher measures were not bothered about such distinctions. Nor were Catholics unduly worried by this quibbling. English Catholic victims were given a prominent place in a pictorial martyrology published in 1588 by Richard Verstegan, the *Theatre of the Cruelties of the Heretics of Our Times*.

Elizabeth's claim that she did not seek to open windows into men's souls was looking increasingly threadbare. Yet, to be fair, repression was imposed upon her almost as much as upon her Catholic subjects. The Catholics held Cecil chiefly to blame for their miseries, and although in early modern Europe there was a polite preference for blaming ministers rather than monarchs, for once there is much to suggest that they were right. Cecil's papers for the 1580s and 1590s are full of bright ideas for tightening the screws on Catholics, from imposing the oath of supremacy on laymen to taking away the children of recusants for re-education. The 1571 bill which Elizabeth vetoed was powerfully urged in the Commons by Thomas Norton, one of Cecil's closest political allies, and in the Lords by Cecil himself. It might be thought that Elizabeth was simply diverting the flak for this policy onto Cecil, as she diverted the flak for the repression of Puritans onto her Archbishops of Canterbury. Yet while we have good evidence for her role in commanding her bishops to act against the Puritans, the evidence with regard to the Catholics points in the other direction. Elizabeth's ministers were the driving force, led by Cecil and egged on by Francis Walsingham (appointed Secretary in 1573), whose profoundly anti-Catholic attitudes were shaped by his experience as ambassador in Paris, where he had witnessed the horrors of the Massacre of St Bartholomew's Day. They even manipulated the information which was supplied to her in order to build up the Catholic threat as far as they could. Only thus could they induce her to implement even a selection of the imaginative sanctions they worked out. This is not to set up Elizabeth as some sort of model of toleration. Had she wished to grant toleration to Catholics, there was little to stop her. Her demand for outward obedience to her religious settlement was uncompromising. But she was more sensitive than her chief minister to the accusation of persecuting men for their religion.

Although most Catholic victims suffered under laws which simply redefined their religion as treason, the widespread fear of 'popery' was by no means groundless. The later sixteenth and early seventeenth centuries saw a series of high-profile political assassinations, usually of Protestants by Catholics, sometimes of Catholics by Catholics: Admiral Gaspard de Coligny in 1572, Prince William of Orange in 1584, Duke Henry of Guise and Cardinal Charles de Guise in 1588, Henry III of France in 1589, and Henri IV of France in 1610. Add to this that some Catholic theologians were prepared to justify tyrannicide, and there was genuine reason to fear for the queen's safety. Catholic plots against her were regularly brought to light by Walsingham, who had built up a formidable network of spies and informers. However, few Catholics participated in the plots. Most Catholics bent over backwards, with a disconcerting spinelessness designed to put their loyalty to the person of Elizabeth beyond any doubt: a testimony to the power of the Tudor myth, and to the growing symbolic power of the English state (it is towards the end of Elizabeth's reign that the term 'state' begins to be used in English in something approaching its modern political sense). In 1585, Catholic loyalists petitioned the queen, in vain, in these terms:

> We do protest before the living God that all and every priest and priests, who have at any time conversed with us, have recognised your Majesty their lawful and undoubted queen... And if we knew or shall know in any of them one point of treason or treacherous device or any undecent speech... we do bind ourselves by oath irrevocable to be the first apprehenders and accusers of such.

At the time of the Armada, a group of Catholic noblemen approached the government and offered, in return for the relaxation of recusancy fines, to raise, equip and maintain in the field at their own expense a troop of horsemen for the defence of the realm. Under the circumstances, Cecil was predictably reluctant to authorise the formation of a Catholic private army, and was strongly opposed in principle to any relaxation of the penal laws, so the offer was rejected. But when he composed the official account of the defeat of the Armada, he gleefully included the whole story in order to emphasise to Catholics abroad the total loyalty of the Tudor queen's subjects (even while insisting at home on the intrinsic treachery of those same Catholic subjects, in order to justify his fiscal and punitive grip on them).

THE BREAK WITH SPAIN

The increasing pressure on Catholics in the later 1570s and 1580s was imposed upon the queen on account of the worsening international situation, which was to culminate in open war between England and Spain. This was certainly not a conflict that Elizabeth wanted. As with so much in her life, her actions were driven by circumstance, and policies were forced upon her. The emerging conflict itself was not primarily a religious war, yet the religious gulf between Catholic Spain and Protestant England was what drove the reorientation of English foreign policy by which a new enmity with Spain was substituted for the traditional enmity with France. It was the combination of this religious division and the clash of interests between England and Spain in the Netherlands (and to a lesser extent on the high seas) that led inexorably to conflict.

Philip II of Spain had serious problems in the Netherlands, one of his hereditary territories, where Lutheran, Anabaptist and Calvinist brands of Protestant reformation had by the 1560s made significant inroads among one of Europe's most urbanised and educated populations. Of course, Catholicism also retained a very considerable following. But the fragmented nature of local political authority in the Netherlands often impeded effective repression of religious dissent (except when backed by overwhelming and expensive military force), with the result that at many times there was almost a free market in religion. Philip wished to eliminate religious diversity in the province. Any sustained attempt to do this was likely to be bad for trade as well as for Protestantism, and English interests in the Netherlands were primarily in trade, and secondly in solidarity with their Protestant co-religionists. Refugees from the Netherlands were often allowed to settle in England, where 'strangers' churches' (churches providing worship according to foreign rites) were sometimes made available to them.

While English attempts to muscle in on Atlantic trade in the 1560s led to distant battles with Spanish vessels, these marine equivalents of border incidents, involving privateers rather than the queen's navy, did not seriously upset relations between the two kingdoms. However, the seizure of Spanish bullion in December 1568, when treasure ships en route for the Netherlands had to take refuge at Southampton from storms and pirates, might at other moments have been tantamount to a declaration of war. This sudden move, indeed false move, is somewhat out of keeping with Cecil's usual caution and Elizabeth's habitual hesitation. Cecil, who was mostly responsible, was driven by a deep-seated suspicion of Spain arising from his strongly anti-papal (if theologically simple, even naïve) version of Protestantism. Elizabeth's consent, if indeed it was properly obtained before the treasure was taken ashore, seems to have been motivated more by the prospect of some easy financial gain. As the bullion had not yet been delivered to the Netherlands, it could still in some sense be regarded as the property of the Genoese bankers who were lending it to Philip II, so her government was in a strong position to negotiate a loan on favourable terms. The Spanish reacted quickly, perhaps over-reacted, by impounding English ships, and trade between England and the Netherlands broke down. In the event, things did not turn out as badly for England as they might have done. Trade returned to normal in about a year, and while the evident hostility of the English government led to Spanish complicity in the Northern Rising of 1569, and in the plots focusing on Mary Queen of Scots, the financial costs inflicted on both sides did long-term damage only to the Spanish in the Netherlands. The Duke of Alva's mission to 'pacify' the Netherlands was impeded at a crucial moment by the English coup.

The contacts of the Spanish ambassador with the rebel earls in 1569, and his involvement in the Ridolfi plot the following year, led to his dismissal from court and return home. Diplomatic relations between the two countries ceased for a few years. Again, this damaged Spain more than England. More disaffected subjects of Philip from the Netherlands took refuge in England, among them pirates who harried Spanish shipping in the Channel. Ironically, it was an English decision in 1572 to curtail their hospitality to these 'Sea Beggars' that led them to raid Brill in search of a base back on their home territory – an event which sparked off rebellion throughout Holland and Zealand. Philip's problems with the Netherlands had moved onto a new and more troubling level. Despite Elizabeth's protestations of sympathy with the Spanish predicament – as ever, she had a gut reaction against any kind of rebellion – many of the Dutch refugees in England were permitted to rush home to join the rising. For the rest of the decade, Elizabeth and her ministers could enjoy the spectacle of successive Spanish governors floundering in the murky waters of Dutch politics, while the Protestant Reformation, in the form of Dutch Calvinism (sufficiently close to the Church of England in theology, although not in Church government) made headway. Meanwhile, English privateers harried and plundered Spain's Atlantic shipping.

Spain's problems in the Netherlands were an open invitation to France, which had for centuries striven to expand into the confusing patchwork of civic privileges and feudal principalities which lay on her northern borders. For a brief moment, some of Elizabeth's advisers even contemplated an offensive alliance with France against Spanish interests there, as in their turn the young king of France, Charles IX, and his mother, Catherine de Medici, flirted with the Huguenot princes and nobles with a view to reducing the power of the Guise dynasty. The brief moment passed when the flirtation turned unexpectedly into a bloodbath. At the instigation of Catherine de Medici, the Huguenot leaders were assassinated at the French court in the 'Massacre of St Bartholomew's Day' (24 August 1572), and the Catholic people of France, following the royal lead, butchered Huguenots in towns and cities across the country.

The massacre was one of the decisive moments in English as well as French history. It probably shocked English Protestants even more than the rising of the Northern Earls in 1569, and it vindicated the very worst suspicions and fears of the bloodthirstiness and untrustworthiness of 'papists'. There were, inevitably, renewed calls for the execution of Mary Queen of Scots. Spanish repression of Protestants in the Netherlands and Catholic massacres of Huguenots in France now looked very like a conspiracy, and minds harked back to the meeting of Catherine de Medici with the Duke of Alva at Bayonne in 1565. The Protestant imagination was particularly open to the apocalyptic, and this was the kind of thing they expected to herald the end of the world. More to the point, it heralded a new phase in the civil wars of France. Spain could act in the Netherlands with less fear of French interference. The cause of the Reformation was under threat, and many in England saw it as their mission to succour their co-religionists abroad. In seeking to understand the English Protestantism of Elizabeth's reign (though not that of Elizabeth herself), it is crucial to realise that the bishops and theologians of the Church of England identified their cause with that of continental Calvinism, even if Elizabeth was far from agreeing with them.

The paradox of Elizabethan diplomacy in the 1570s was the need to maintain, as far as possible, good relations with the Catholic power which had perpetrated the massacre, while simultaneously maintaining good relations with the Huguenots. England's only card, now looking a little dog-eared, was the queen's marriage. The suggestion was that she might marry Francis, the youngest brother of the French king. Francis, Duke of Alençon and later (once his elder brother Henry became Henry III of France in 1576) Duke of Anjou, came closer than anyone else to securing Elizabeth's hand in marriage. It is still difficult to believe that Elizabeth ever had any intention of going through with it, but, as Spanish fortunes in the Netherlands revived in the later 1570s, under the vigorous generalship of Alessandro Farnese, Duke of Parma and Piacenza, the political value of friendship with France drove the negotiations on.

Political opposition to the Anjou match in England made Mary Tudor's marriage to Philip of Spain look popular. Pamphlets were published against it, argued in violent and apocalyptic terms. To the fear of a foreign prince was now added fanatical hatred of his religion. The best-known opponent of the marriage is John Stubbs, whose *Discovery of a Gaping Gulf* laid out the arguments in lucid and lurid terms. Elizabeth had reacted furiously on previous occasions when Parliament had dared debate her marriage and the succession, regarding their interference as an infringement of her prerogative. Her reaction to the colossal impertinence of

George Gascoigne depicted presenting a book to Queen Elizabeth. She is seated in her Chamber of Presence on a throne beneath a 'cloth of estate', a formal sign of her royal status.

being told what to do, in public, by a Puritan commoner from Norfolk, was savage. Stubbs and his printer were prosecuted under a statute from the previous reign, and were sentenced to lose their right hands. The silence of the crowd as this sentence was executed – Stubbs bravely waved his stump and shouted 'Long live the queen' before fainting from shock – was widely interpreted as a vote of sympathy for the victim. The Spanish ambassador thought the people would rise up if the marriage went ahead. His knowledge of the people may have been restricted to London, but London mattered. As some lawyers reckoned the statute under which Stubbs's sentence was imposed was no longer in force, and as the arguments which Stubbs deployed reflected remarkably closely those being urged against the marriage by members of the Privy Council, the impetus behind the prosecution and the execution of this cruel punishment can only have come from the queen herself – a rare false move from a woman who was so skilled in public relations.

Mary's council had at least been decently divided over her marriage. Elizabeth's was almost unanimous in its disapproval. The only exception was the Earl of Sussex, a councillor of the old guard, who did not share the hatred and fear of 'popery' which consumed most of his colleagues. He had always wanted to see Elizabeth married and the succession secured, and when you had as many Catholic relatives as he did, you were not scared by the prospect of a Catholic king. However, while Elizabeth relied upon his unshakeable loyalty (it was he to whom she entrusted the suppression of the rebellion in 1569), she was not overly attentive to his opinion. The Anjou match reached its crisis in 1579, when Anjou was granted the privilege, rare among her hopeful foreign suitors, of an invitation to England and to court. In fact, Anjou came and left in August without a cast-iron decision, but with the distinct impression that the queen was favourable. Yet it remains hard to see Elizabeth's display of enthusiasm for the marriage as anything other than a ploy. Anjou was an ugly and ungainly little man. Though she treated him with every sign of affection during his visit, he was simply not her type – she liked handsome, dashing, athletic men like Leicester, Hatton, Raleigh and Essex.

The intricate politics of Elizabeth's change of heart will be endlessly debated. But it seems likely that, in a move typical of her governmental technique, she wanted to shift the blame for her own unwillingness to marry onto her councillors. She wanted them to beg her not to marry Anjou, before graciously conceding in a way which would make it their fault, not hers, that she had never married. In the event, they called her bluff. Shortly after Anjou's departure, they undertook, despite their misgivings, to do their best to implement her will. By the New Year, she was backing away from the marriage, and her councillors and ambassadors were busy disengaging her from whatever commitments she might be thought to have entered into. Queen and council had stared each other out, and the queen had blinked first. In fact, negotiations were kept open for a year or two, and Anjou made a second visit to England in the hope of rescuing his blighted prospects. But whatever favour Elizabeth might show him was discounted in her private dealings with her councillors, who now knew that she had no intention of going through with it, and helped her play the game to its conclusion – Anjou's departure, with some suitable financial compensation, in February 1582.

WAR WITH SPAIN

It was only towards the end of the 1570s that the cold war between England and Spain started to heat up. Spanish resurgence in the Netherlands from 1578 onwards was bad enough, but worse was to come. In 1580 the direct line of succession to the throne of Portugal expired, and on a long shortlist of potential heirs, Philip II probably had the best claim. There was a Portuguese candidate, but he was a bastard, and it was difficult at that time for the illegitimate to appeal to *légitimisme*. Overwhelming force secured the succession for Philip, and thus brought under his control the vast financial resources of Portugal's trade and overseas empire. With fresh resources came fresh ambition, and Philip's agents plotted in Rome, France and England with Elizabeth's disaffected Catholic subjects and with the militantly Catholic Guise faction in France. Vast strategic schemes were devised for the invasion of first Scotland and then England, with a view to substituting Mary Queen of Scots for Elizabeth. At home in England, plans to assassinate Elizabeth were unmasked with a regularity that was at times suspicious. But Francis Walsingham's network of informers and double agents served him well, even if they often crossed the boundary between detection and entrapment.

Elizabeth in her turn gave ever more open support to the war at sea being waged by privateers such as Francis Drake, whom she knighted on board the *Golden Hind*, moored on the Thames, in April 1581 upon his return, laden with Spanish booty, from his circumnavigation of the globe. With English aid to the Portuguese pretender, Don Antonio, and Spanish aid to rebels in Ireland, the two countries drifted towards a war which almost everyone saw as inevitable. The new ways of the world were signalled in the absence of any formal declaration of war. Yet when Drake sailed for the West Indies in autumn 1585 with a fleet of over twenty ships, he did so under a commission from the queen which made his expedition an act of war.

The Dutch had for some time been angling for more than moral support from England, and the fall of Antwerp to Farnese in 1585 brought the situation to a critical point for Elizabeth's government. Despite her misgivings about war, her councillors prevailed upon her to intervene directly. Under a treaty signed in August at Nonsuch Palace, the Earl of Leicester led a force of several thousand men to assist Philip's enemies in the Netherlands. This represented an important shift in policy for the queen. Since the ill-fated expedition to Le Havre in 1562–63, she had held out against invitations or advice to send troops into foreign theatres. As a queen, she had little enough to gain from war. Kings and nobles, educated in and motivated by a tradition of chivalry and martial prowess, could seek glory in conquest, in battle, even up to a point in defeat. For all the cynicism of More's *Utopia*, and for all the pacifism of a fashionable intellectual like Erasmus in his widely read essay on the proverb *dulce bellum inexpertis* ('war is sweet – if you're not in it'), the space which sixteenth-century chronicles still gave to detailed accounts of military preparations and actions reminds us that for many men of that time, war was in effect the highest form of politics. Once kings went to war, cost was no object (although at times it might become an insuperable obstacle, as it had for Henry VIII in 1525). Elizabeth had a very clear sense of the cost, and a shrewd sense that such benefits as there might be would mostly redound elsewhere. She hesitated long before agreeing to go to war (there had been pressure for this since the later 1570s). And she hesitated long before appointing Leicester to lead the expedition.

The Earl of Leicester might have been genuinely committed to the protection of Dutch Calvinists and Dutch liberties. But he saw the expedition to the Netherlands as his guarantee of a place in the history books. Elizabeth was well aware of this, and also of the danger of entrusting too many troops to one of her subjects. So she kept a close eye on his conduct in the Netherlands. Militarily, there was little splendour in the grubby business of besieging or defending the forts and walled towns with which the country was dotted. Leicester slowed, but did not halt, Farnese's advance. He certainly lacked the resources, and probably also the skills. Politically, there were temptations aplenty, and Leicester succumbed, accepting the invitation of the Dutch to become their Governor-General in January 1586. Elizabeth was livid at what she saw as his presumptuous self-elevation to a sovereign status vying with her own. After some characteristic changes of mind, she compelled him to resign the title.

THE DESTRUCTION OF MARY QUEEN OF SCOTS

The chief concern of domestic policy through the 1580s (apart, of course, from the military and financial preparations for war) was the 'enemy within', the Roman Catholics, and above all Mary Queen of Scots, who might so easily become a focus for their discontent. The sometimes hysterical fear of Catholic plots peaked in one of the most extraordinary episodes of the reign, the making of the 'Bond of Association' in 1584, an episode which paradoxically revealed both the deep devotion of the English people to their queen and their increasing preparedness to act collectively without her lead. Inspired by the assassination of William of Orange on 10 July 1584, but conditioned by the series of plots against Elizabeth's life which were continually being uncovered, the Bond of Association was, as its title suggests, a contract or agreement of a group of people to pursue common objectives. The objectives were the protection of the queen's life and, in the event of her suspicious or sudden death, vengeance to the death against the perpetrators and beneficiaries of the deed. Modelled to some extent on the kind of political bonds and covenants which commonly figured in Scottish politics, it is a public document unique in English history for binding its signatories to commit murder under specified circumstances:

> we do not only vow and bind ourselves... never to allow, accept or favour any such pretended successors, by whom or for whom any such detestable act shall be attempted... but do also further vow and protest, as we are most bound, and that in the presence of the eternal and everliving God, to persecute such person or persons to the death with our joint and particular forces, and to take the uttermost revenge on them that by any possible means we or any of us can devise...

The subtext of the bond was the importance of keeping Mary Queen of Scots off the throne at all costs in order to defend the Protestant establishment. What is most significant about the bond is its popularity. Drafted in October by the Privy Council, and circulated by them on a county by county basis for signature by the nation's political élite, it rapidly succeeded in attracting signatures not only from most of the gentry and civic patriarchs of England, but also from vast numbers of enthusiastic men of the 'middling' and 'lower' sorts. It became a nationwide expression of loyalty. Better than anything else it symbolises the change in the religious temper of the nation since 1559. Although under peer pressure it was even signed by some Catholic gentlemen here and there, and although equally some Puritan gentlemen with acute consciences held back from promising to commit murder, this explicit contract to destroy Mary Stuart simply could not have been conceived in the 1560s, when so much of the English élite remained Catholic at heart, nor promulgated in the 1570s, when hatred of 'popery' was not yet the common coin of English culture. The Bond of Association was the index not simply of a Protestant country, but of a country which would do almost anything to prevent a Catholic from taking the throne. The tone of the document was mitigated in the Parliament which met over the winter

Lopvs compounding to poyson the Queene

IN NOMINE DOMINI incipit Omne Malum.

The Rebellion of Northu: & Westm:

The treacherous practise of Don Jo: of Au:t

Stucely encouraged by P: & K: of Sp: rayseth rebell:

Desmonds bloody practise approued

Babington with his Complices

oman Catholic plots against Elizabeth, as seen in part of an engraving by Cornelius Danckwerts, entitled
Thankfull Remembrance of Gods Mercie, which was issued to accompany the 1625 edition of George
arleton's book of the same title. At the top: Dr Lopez, Elizabeth's physician, who was executed in 1590
ving been convicted on scanty evidence of attempting to poison the queen. In the central panel: Pope Pius
who excommunicated Elizabeth on 25 February 1570, releasing her subjects from all oaths of allegiance
her; Don John of Austria, to whom the crown of Ireland was offered in 1577 by James Fitzgerald;
r Thomas Stukeley, who secured papal and Spanish support for a campaign in Ireland; and the Earl of
esmond, whose tenants and clansmen forced him into revolt in 1579. At the bottom: the Babington Plot,
hich aimed at the assassination of Elizabeth and her replacement by Mary Queen of Scots.

Hi mihi sunt Comites quos ipsa pericula ducunt

In quo quis peccat
In eo punitur.

Babington with his Complices in Sᵗ Giles field

The Babington Plot, from George Carleton's *Thankfull Remembrance*, p. 100. In 1586, the Derbyshire gentleman Anthony Babington was the central figure in a plot to liberate Mary Queen of Scots and assassinate Elizabeth. The confidence in success which led him to commission a group portrait of the conspirators was misplaced. Sir Francis Walsingham's spies had penetrated the conspiracy and all the correspondence between the plotters and the captive queen passed across his desk. In due course Babington and the rest were rounded up. They were executed on 20 September 1586. The real significance of this plot was that it enabled the Privy Council to overcome Elizabeth's reluctance to sanction a definitive solution to the problem posed by Mary.

of 1584–85. Elizabeth herself was far from entirely happy with the gung-ho rough justice proposed in the original bond, and the subsequent statutory version provided for a semblance of legal process, in the form of a commission of enquiry to precede any vengeance.

In the event, lynch law was not needed. Pressure for the execution of Mary Queen of Scots, which had been building up since 1570, became irresistible in the context of all-out war with Catholic Spain, especially as Philip II was now cultivating links with Mary's French relatives, the ultra-Catholic Guise dynasty. Mary sealed her own fate when she became entangled in the Babington plot to secure her liberation and Elizabeth's assassination. Francis Walsingham, who controlled Mary's communications with the outside world, allowed her to believe that she had a secure link to a group of youthful Catholic adventurers led by the Derbyshire gentleman Anthony Babington. The whole conspiracy was so deeply penetrated by Walsingham's men, and his access to its communications so total, that apologetic claims that Mary in fact had no knowledge of the plot to kill Elizabeth are not untenable. That she was, at the least, cruelly entrapped is undeniable. Moreover, if her consent to the plot was full and informed, she might be allowed some plea of self-defence, in that the Bond of Association had put beyond any doubt the determination of the English establishment to take her life. Once the plot was exposed, Mary was tried in a special court of English nobles. Elizabeth knew perfectly well how posterity would view any decision to execute Mary, and convened Parliament in October 1586, either to consider alternatives or, more realistically, to spread the burden of guilt. Parliament added to the pressure which the Privy Council was exerting behind the scenes, and Elizabeth was impelled reluctantly, hesitantly, but inexorably, towards signing the death warrant. Even then she hesitated about executing it, and it was her Privy Council, on its own initiative, which finally despatched it. Mary was beheaded on 8 February 1587. Even Elizabeth's closest adviser, William Cecil, was in disgrace for weeks afterwards, but most of her wrath fell upon her unfortunate Secretary, William Davison, whose career was destroyed by his role in this affair.

THE SPANISH ARMADA

English intervention in the Netherlands achieved one thing. It provoked Philip II into direct action against England, partly as revenge, partly as crusade, and partly as a means of knocking England out of his Dutch problem. His decision to launch an amphibious assault against England was a fateful one. Preparations for the vast expedition occupied most of 1587, and were set back by Drake's famous raid on Cadiz. But the Armada set sail in summer 1588, and, notwithstanding persistent harrying in the English Channel from the large, experienced, superbly equipped and brilliantly led English navy, it made its way to its rendezvous off Calais. There the deficiencies of Philip II's strategy became painfully apparent, as Farnese's invasion barges could not get out to join Medina Sidonia's deep-water fleet without exposing themselves to the guns of the smaller and nimbler English and Dutch vessels. The fleet at anchor was stampeded by English fireships, and then scattered by the prevailing winds. Attempting to return home by circumnavigating the British Isles, about half the Spanish ships were sunk or wrecked by storms or enemy fire. Thousands of men were lost, dozens of ships. The English victory was total, their losses negligible.

Much of Elizabeth's reputation has been built upon her display of courage in 1588, when the landing of Spanish troops, the terror of western Europe, seemed imminent. Her appearance at the muster of her forces at Tilbury, when she made

Dextra Excelsi fecit salutem.

The Invincible Armado in 88.

Above: The Spanish Armada off the French coast. From George Carleton's *Thankfull Remembrance*, p. 144. By the 1620s, when this pamphlet was published, the 'Protestant wind' here shown blowing along the Channel was already a fixture in the national mythology

Below: Chart of the course of the 'Invincible Armada'.

FRANCISCVS DRAECK NOBILISSIMVS EQVES ANGLI

Right: Sir Francis Drake's circumnavigation of the globe and daring naval (or piratical) exploits earned him fame throughout Europe. Known to Spaniards as 'el dragón', Drake became for a time the bogeyman for the Spanish, as Napoleon ('Boney') did for nineteenth-century England.

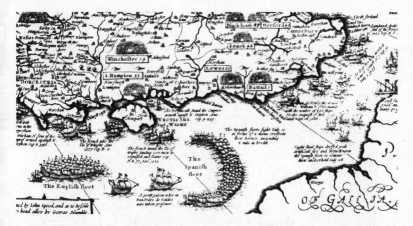

Section of John Speed's map of the route of the Armada, 1588–89, indicating the formation the Armada held as it sailed up the English Channel, and some of the action as the English employed 'fire-ships' to break it up while at anchor off Dunkirk.

her famous address to the troops, was an inspiring moment in the national myth. Although Elizabeth's army, commanded by Leicester, was large, it was arguably fortunate that it was not put to the test. The superiority of Spanish troops and tactics on land was probably as marked as the superiority of English ships and tactics at sea. But for an island power, that was the right way round, so the English victory cannot be put down solely to good fortune, however important the role of poor strategy and dire weather.

The defeat of the Armada was the high point of Elizabeth's reign. England had seen off the most powerful invasion force launched against her since the Norman Conquest, and if this was as much because of the weather as because of the strength of the nation's defences, so much the better in an age which interpreted the chances of wind and weather as the judgements of the Lord. As far as the English at the time were concerned, their victory came down to divine providence and defensive prudence. It was God's favour to England in general, and to Elizabeth in particular, which explained his providence. Victory was celebrated in verse and music, art and literature and chronicle. Elizabeth herself appeared as the saviour of her people.

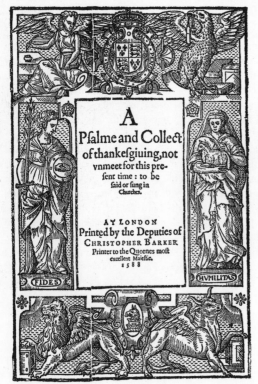

Above: Preaching at Paul's Cross, London. Londoners flocked to hear sermons at the open-air pulpit in the cathedral churchyard. On Sunday 24 November 1588, a stately procession escorted Elizabeth to the cathedral for an official service of thanksgiving for victory over the Armada, which included a sermon preached from this pulpit by John Piers, Bishop of Salisbury.

Left: Title page of a thanksgiving service issued in 1588 for use in churches to celebrate the defeat of the Spanish Armada.

THE IRISH CONFLICT

There is no indication that Elizabeth herself ever had the faintest idea about what was going on in Ireland, but the 'Irish Problem' was apparent to her advisers from the start. That problem was, as the 'Device for Alteration of Religion' pointed out, that:

> Ireland also will be very difficultly stayed in their obedience, by reason of the clergy that is so addicted to Rome.

Since the 1530s, traditional Irish Catholicism had been driven, thanks to the English Reformation, into a potent alliance with incipient Irish nationalism. Elizabeth realised, of course, that royal authority was under threat. No Tudor was slow to detect treason. But whether she could appreciate the situation in anything other than the crude polarity of obedience and rebellion is unlikely.

English troops campaigning in Ireland during the sixteenth century. Protestant England feared Catholic Ireland would be used as a 'back door' by European Catholic powers. Signs of Irish rebellion were confronted with great force. The mainland authorities instigated a policy of Protestant 'plantation' areas in Ireland, of which the plantation of Ulster (1608–11), largely populated by Scots, was the most effective.

What was going on in Ireland was the familiar interaction of politics and religion which dominated Tudor politics in general. But whereas the strength of personal monarchy smoothed the path of the Reformation in England, and in Wales patriotic affection for the Tudors combined with aspirations for a share in the security and spoils of the Tudor regime to the same effect, in Ireland almost everything was against the Reformation from the start, or rapidly turned out that way. English authority had never reached far beyond the Pale, and even within it the Tudor regime faced increasing problems, often because of mismanagement. While the royal supremacy was accepted relatively easily, the dissolution of the monasteries had been only partial. Irish religious orders, many of them inspired by 'observant' ideals of renewal, proved more durable than their English counterparts – although their survival was itself as much to do with the distance and ineffectiveness of royal authority as with any innate moral qualities of the Irish monks and friars.

As for the Protestant Reformation introduced under Edward VI, this never became law in Ireland. And when the zealous English Protestant John Bale was made bishop of Ossory (an appointment which confirms that the Duke of Northumberland had a keen sense of humour) and put on one of his violently anti-Catholic plays, he was unceremoniously hounded out of town (and, when Mary came to the throne, out of the island and the queen's realms). The restoration of Catholicism under Mary (to the extent that it needed to be restored, which was not far) relieved the Irish from only one of the irksome restraints of English rule. The attempt to use privately funded colonisation, rather than publicly funded conquest, as a cheap way of exporting English political and social culture to Ireland was actually begun in Mary's reign. The fact that the new colonies and boroughs of the 'plantations' specifically excluded native Irish people meant that the process was all too obviously being conducted at their expense rather than for their benefit.

Elizabeth's sole initial concern with Ireland was to introduce the Protestant Reformation there. But the Reformation which was carried through the Dublin Parliament early in 1560 by the Earl of Sussex, Lord Lieutenant of Ireland, was being sown on untilled ground, and found it hard to put down roots. Much of Ireland was entirely outside English control, though none of it out of reach of English punitive expeditions. Ireland was a perpetual drain on English resources. Elizabeth was never prepared to put in the kind of money which might have sufficed to introduce the English model of government to which English policy aspired. It is doubtful anyway whether England actually had the resources which would have been needed for the job. The aims of policy were variously to prevent and suppress rebellion, and to keep out or expel foreign powers. The overriding priority was to prevent Ireland from becoming a threat to England. At times, notably in the 1590s, even this modest objective required funding on a huge scale.

As Anglo-Spanish relations deteriorated in the 1570s, Philip II looked to foment unrest in Elizabeth's backyard. It was a small force of Spanish and Italian mercenaries which sparked off the rebellion of the Fitzgeralds of Munster in 1579. The rebellion was largely defeated within a year, but the English troops ravaged the province for

English troops on the march in Ireland. The Irish found little mercy at English hands. Lord Deputy Grey boasted of how, in his two years in Ireland in the early 1580s, he had executed nearly 1,500 Irishmen of some rank, besides 'innumerable' churls.

years before capturing and killing the head of the Fitzgeralds, the Earl of Desmond, in 1583. When, in the 1590s, weak government by successive Lord Deputies fuelled the ambition of the Earl of Tyrone and he launched a rebellion, Philip II was once more ready to assist. The English government was cornered into seeking the military reduction of the entire island. This reluctant conquest was eventually achieved early in 1603, thanks to the efforts of Elizabeth's last Lord Deputy, Charles Blount, Lord Mountjoy. Elizabeth's problems with Ireland were at an end, but English problems with Ireland were barely beginning.

THE EARL OF ESSEX

English politics in the 1590s was dominated by the figure of the queen's new favourite, Robert Devereux, Earl of Essex. William Cecil remained her chief minister until his death in 1598, and his son Robert Cecil, groomed for succession by his father and recruited to the Privy Council as Secretary in 1591, imperceptibly took over the reins. Yet it was Essex who bestrode the scene, though he proved a meteoric

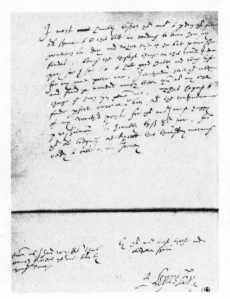

The last letter of Robert Dudley, Earl of Leicester, to Elizabeth I, 29 August 1588. Dated at Rycott, and signed 'by your Ma[jestie]s most faythful and obedyent servaunt, R. Leycester,' the writer would 'know how my gratious la[dy] doth and what ease of her late paine she findes... For my wone poore case, I contynew styll your medycyn... thus hoping to finde perfect cure at the Bath... I humbly kyss your foote.' Six days later Leicester was dead.

rather than a colossal figure. Succeeding in effect to the place vacated in 1588 by the death of Leicester, his stepfather and patron (having already succeeded him as Master of the Horse in 1587), Essex was the more talented and ambitious of the two, but also arguably the less stable. Like Leicester, he yearned for military glory: indeed, he was said to be 'entirely given over to arms and war'. Unlike Leicester, he was to be given a serious chance of winning it. Forbidden by the queen from joining the naval expedition against Lisbon, he went anyway, and was summoned back in short-lived disgrace. Denied leadership of an expedition to France in 1589, he was awarded his first command on another such expedition in 1592 – without notable success. His return at least saw him promoted to the Privy Council, but military ambition was once more fanned by the opportunity of leading another seaborne assault against Philip II, this time a raid on Cadiz, in 1596.

Essex's raid was in itself something of a success. Cadiz was sacked, and it was not his fault that he was not able to add a Spanish treasure fleet to the plunder. Yet this time his return exposed the gulf between masculine and feminine estimates of military glory. Loot was of more interest to Elizabeth than honour in battle, and hardly any was brought back. For her, the expedition was simply another loss-making venture. From this time, his relations with the queen began to deteriorate. Elizabeth grew doubtful about his pride, ambition and jealousy, while Essex saw the relentless rise of Robert Cecil in the Privy Council as a threat to his own position. Leicester had accepted the primacy of the father, but Essex resented the successes of the son. The conflict between the 'sword', the old concept of the nobility as

Portrait engraving of Francis Bacon. Bacon's early advancement came thanks to the patronage of the Earl of Essex, but Essex's strenuous and tactless efforts to have him made Attorney General in 1593 offended Elizabeth I (who appointed Sir Edward Coke) and not only hampered Bacon's prospects but damaged Essex's credit.

based in military service to the Crown, and the 'pen', the new concept of service in administration (which in France came to be called the 'robe'), was exemplified in their rivalry. Another voyage against the Spanish in 1597 brought Essex no change in his fortunes, as it once more failed to intercept the treasure fleet. His temper was not improved by discovering, on his return, that Robert Cecil had secured the profitable post of Chancellor of the Duchy of Lancaster. Elizabeth managed to coax him out of his despondency by bestowing upon him the office of Earl Marshal, one of the very highest titles at her disposal.

It was Ireland which led to Essex's undoing, as to that of many other English politicians. First, his underlying weaknesses reappeared in a quarrel between him and the Cecils during 1598 over who should be the new Lord Deputy of Ireland. In a personal interview with Essex, Elizabeth made it plain that she was taking the Cecils' advice. Furious, Essex turned his back on her – a mortal insult to her royal status. She slapped him, and he reached for his sword. Although bystanders prevented this ugly scene from going any further, Essex stormed out, proclaiming that not even from Henry VIII himself would he have accepted such treatment. He was wrong, of course. Nobody had ever tried anything like that in front of Henry VIII, and to have done so would have meant certain and rapid death.

As affairs in Ireland went from bad to worse, Elizabeth's government was faced with the necessity of despatching overwhelming force to suppress the rebellion there. This time, there was no quarrel about whom to put in charge. Essex was the only credible choice, and the offer was one that, for all his misgivings, he simply

O.Sydney worthy of tryple re. nowne, For playing tho maytours that troubled the crowne. 1581.

The reception of Sir Henry Sidney (Elizabeth I's Lord Deputy in Ireland) by the mayor and aldermen of Dublin, upon his return to the city after a victory over rebels. It was during Sidney's two terms of office as deputy that the English government's policy towards the Irish turned decisively towards martial law and ever more brutal repression.

Conscientia: mille: testes

Tyrones false Submission afterwards rebelling.

Hugh O'Neill, Earl of Tyrone, formally renewed his allegiance to Elizabeth at the hands of Lord Deputy Russell in Dublin in 1594. Nevertheless, within the year he was in rebellion, and with Spanish support went on to wage war against the queen for nine years.

could not refuse. He had always wanted a major command, though he had wanted it in the glamorous European theatre, not among the bogs and woods of the 'other island'. Crossing to Dublin in April 1599 with the largest army ever sent to Tudor Ireland, he rapidly showed that he was no Farnese. He did not know what to do, and he did not know how to hold his army together. His position weakening, he ignored his clear instructions to attack the Earl of Tyrone and in September opened unauthorised negotiations which resulted in a truce. Without permission to abandon his command he then hurried home to justify his actions. Elizabeth was prepared to condone neither his disobedience nor his failure. He was put under house arrest, stripped of his offices and rusticated. His incompetence was thrown into relief by the achievement of his successor, Lord Mountjoy, who, over the next couple of years, with inferior resources to those lavished upon Essex, methodically crushed the rebels, destroyed a substantial expeditionary force sent from Spain and secured Tyrone's surrender.

Essex, however, would not accept his fate. Putting together a motley array of disaffected soldiers, ambitious and underfunded younger sons, and even some hopeful Catholics, as well as one or two more substantial but still marginal figures, he sought to launch a coup in February 1601. If he could not win the queen's favour, he proposed to extort it. The coup as it unfolded can seem almost mindless in retrospect. Starting from his town house in the Strand with barely 200 men, he headed into London with a view to raising popular support for a march on the court complex. It is hard to see how he hoped to succeed.

The answer probably lies in the recent example of another disaffected but popular military hero (and although Elizabeth and her council had now seen through Essex's pretensions, the aura of the popular military hero still hung about him). The Duke of Guise had seized power in Paris back in 1585 in much this fashion, as the Paris mobs rallied to his cause and swelled the few hundred men with which he had started his march upon the French court. But if Essex had read his modern history, he had not read closely enough. Guise had launched his coup against a massively unpopular monarch, in a city where his network of support was dense, in the context of intermittent but bitter civil wars which were fuelled by religious hatred. Essex, in contrast, overplayed a weak hand. His was a falling star and Elizabeth still commanded enormous popular loyalty. Londoners were bemused but unmoved by Essex's appeals, and he gave himself up. Briskly tried for treason, he was beheaded on 25 February.

THE 1590s

Although the instability of her last favourite was the political problem which confronted Elizabeth most personally in the 1590s, it was far from the most serious. Naval war with Spain, intervention in France on behalf of Henry IV (whose claim to the throne was contested by the militant Catholic faction there, with Spanish backing), and the repression of rebellion in Ireland placed intolerable financial strains upon her regime. These were intensified by years of poor harvests, and by their inevitable accompaniment: epidemic disease.

Demographically, the disasters of the 1590s were second only to those of the 1550s. Economically, things may even have been worse, although her councillors remembered the lessons of the 1540s and 1550s, and at least resisted the last temptation of debasing the currency. Partly because of that self-denial, the financial position of the Crown had never been worse in the Tudor era. Long-term inflation had reduced the real value of customs duties and, together with almost systematic under-assessment of the wealth of the nobility and gentry, had massively eroded the real yields of direct taxation. The one novel financial expedient of the period, selling

When Elizabeth visited the Earl of Hertford at Elvetham in 1591, he arranged splendid outdoor entertainments around a small ornamental lake in the shape of a half-moon, specially dug for the occasion. The entertainments, including pageants, songs, verses, fireworks and banquets, filled the three days of her visit. In this picture of the scene, Elizabeth is shown seated beside the left horn of the moon on a throne beneath a cloth of estate.

or issuing trade monopolies, not only compounded the economic dislocation but for a while soured Elizabeth's relations with her Parliament. The domestic strains of foreign war and economic crisis in turn undermined law and order, and the Privy Council was having to meet on a daily basis to cope.

All this, added to the uncertainty over the succession, might have amounted to a crisis every bit as bad as that of 1558. Yet the severity of the problems serves chiefly to highlight the extraordinary success of Elizabeth and her government in defending and governing the country through these difficult years. There was neither a baronial nor a popular revolt. Essex's attempted coup in 1601 made him look ridiculous. What held the country together was a combination of nationalism, Protestantism, and loyalism, focused on the person, or perhaps on the image, of Elizabeth herself.

THE MYTH OF ELIZABETH

The image of Elizabeth which did so much to hold the country together through the crisis of the 1590s was built upon the foundations of monarchical ideology which had been laid by her predecessors, notably Henry VII and in particular Henry VIII. The general Tudor myth of the monarch as the sole bulwark against anarchy was given particular expression in the person of Elizabeth. Moreover, it was an image which was built up gradually and deliberately through the reign. Elizabeth herself was always concerned with the public face of her words and actions, and she chose and designed them carefully in order to put across favourable impressions of herself. Hence her care to distance herself as far as possible from unpleasant or unpopular proceedings. It was the bishops who had to suppress unwanted manifestations of Puritanism. It was her councillors and servants who had to bear the brunt of responsibility for executing Mary Queen of Scots. It would be going too far to see her as a practitioner of 'spin' along the lines of modern political media manipulation. But she showed something of the same concern with her image.

There was positive image-making as well as a shrewd management of the negative. The progresses which presented the queen to her subjects, although confined within the English heartlands of the south and east, were filled with civic receptions and public entertainments which put across positive images of Elizabeth as a Protestant paragon, a dispenser of justice, a bringer of peace and a defender of the realm. Themes such as these ran through the splendid entertainment laid on by the Earl of Leicester at his great castle of Kenilworth for a royal visit in 1575. With fireworks and water features, music and pageants, this was one of the most spectacular shows of the Tudor era. It took months to prepare, and was recorded for posterity in a pamphlet written by one of Leicester's clients. Official propaganda was by no means unknown, but alongside it there was a barrage of printed material produced by well-wishers of various kinds: hack writers in search of reward, clergy out for preferment, minor officials in search of promotion and public office. And in between the official propaganda and the private enterprise variety were a host of

'A Hieroglyphic of Britain', which John Dee himself designed as the frontispiece to his *General and Rare Memorials Pertayning to the Perfect Arte of Navigation* (1577). John Dee (1527–1608), alchemist, geographer, mathematician and astrologer to the queen, wrote the *Arte of Navigation* as a manifesto for Elizabethan naval imperialism. He explains in the text (p.53) that the frontispiece shows the British Republic (or commonwealth) 'on her Knees, very Humbly and ernestly Soliciting the most Excellent Royall Maiesty, of our Elizabeth (Sitting at the helm of this Imperiall Monarchy; or rather, at the helm of this Imperiall Ship, of the most parte of Christendome...)', and that above is a 'Good Angell', sent by God to guard the English people 'with Shield and Sword'. Elizabeth steers her vessel towards the Tower of Safety, atop which stands Victory, ready with a wreath to crown her.

The Red Cross Knight from Edmund Spenser's *The Faerie Queene* (3rd edition, 1598). This vast chivalric epic, one of the supreme artistic achievements of the cult of Queen Elizabeth, was designed as an allegory of the political and religious struggle between Protestantism and Catholicism.

further publications, many of them hugely influential, which struck the same notes. John Foxe's 'Book of Martyrs', the *Acts and Monuments*, issued in successive and expanding editions, may have been international in its scope and intention, but its readers drew from it a national myth in which Elizabeth – presented by Foxe as a woman denied her martyr's crown only by a special and greater providence of God – played a decisive role.

Elizabeth's court, too, played its part in presenting a glorious picture of the queen to her people. From the ordinary offices of its daily life and the regular ceremonies of the Chapel Royal to the set-pieces of Accession Day celebrations and tournaments (which emerged in the 1570s) and grand state processions, there was usually something to impress the visitor to London and Westminster. Audiences for such displays might consist largely of Londoners, foreign dignitaries and visiting country gentry – but it was a socially, and perhaps also a statistically, significant fraction of the population which at some time or other saw the queen in her splendour. The portraiture and poetry in which the creation of the queen's image is seen at its most sophisticated, most of which was produced and circulated within the context of the

Above: Portrait of Richard Tarlton. Tarlton was introduced to Elizabeth I through the Earl of Leicester and became immensely popular as one of the Queen's Players, specialising in the dramatic jigs popular at the time.

Left: Detail from a portrait of Elizabeth I. Elizabeth was often depicted holding a sieve. This was an allusion to the Roman tale of Tuccia, a Vestal Virgin whose virginity was impugned. Tuccia vindicated her honour by carrying water from the Tiber to the Temple of Vesta in a sieve, without spilling a drop. The 'sieve portraits' are thus among the clearest assertions of the cult of England's 'Virgin Queen'.

court, was inevitably accessible and comprehensible only to a restricted audience. But simpler messages about the queen were widely disseminated.

Parliament gave the queen and her councillors a national stage on which to perform. Although, in accordance with its role, Parliament served as a sounding-board for the grievances of the people (especially those of the gentry and civic leaders who populated the House of Commons), the long historiographical tradition which has seen Parliament as a forum for growing 'opposition' to the Crown in Elizabeth's reign has fundamentally mistaken the nature and purpose of the institution at that time. It was there to vote taxation, to help enact legislation, and to offer advice to the Crown. Elizabeth got the laws she wanted and got tax, although often not as much as she wanted. She tended perhaps to get rather more advice than she wanted, which was where most of the tensions arose between her and the House of Commons. But few members of her Parliaments would have wished to classify themselves as 'opposition' in the sense in which the term is used today. To oppose the monarch was to be at best a disobedient subject, at worst a traitor or a rebel. The Catholic bishops opposed the religious settlement in 1559 – and all but one were subsequently deprived of their bishoprics. Most of the trouble Elizabeth had with her Parliaments was over unwelcome advice: on further religious change; on the succession; on Mary Queen of Scots; on foreign policy; on how to deal with Catholics. Often enough, troublesome MPs were mouthpieces or stalking-horses for Elizabeth's own Privy Councillors, using Parliament as an extra forum for urging their policies upon the queen. As a woman she inevitably suffered, in a way that a competent king usually would not, from the casual assumption by the men of her council and indeed of her Parliaments that they knew more of the ways of the world than she did.

Despite her imperious way with unwanted advice, Elizabeth knew how to charm her Parliaments. Her responses to delegations from the Commons were carefully scripted and widely reported. In Lords and Commons, her councillors were tireless in putting over the themes of peace, Protestantism and prosperity as the fruits of her rule. And when grievances became acute, as in the intense agitation against monopolies around 1600, she knew how to make concessions graciously and to maximum effect. Parliament was, in short, an important 'point of contact' between Crown and country.

Above all, the daily and weekly liturgical offices of the Church of England drummed home a message of obedience and loyalty, from the daily prayers for the queen to special services of thanksgiving for her accession or for deliverance from dangers. With the 'Homily against Disobedience and Wilful Rebellion' regularly read in parish churches across the land, the duties of the subject were constantly reiterated. And with the royal coat of arms prominently displayed in those churches, where paintings of the crucifixion or the Last Judgement had once had their place, the sacred status of the Crown was unmistakably proclaimed to everyone.

Elizabeth worked at her contemporary image in ways in which previous monarchs had worked at their memory. The media, the court, Parliament and the Church all played their part in creating that image, which had a more lasting impact

The 'Procession Picture', an idealised representation, as Sir Roy Strong argues, of the glories of Elizabeth's court. Six Knights of the Garter walk before the queen, who rides on a triumphal chariot beneath a canopy borne by four courtiers. Gentlemen Pensioners guard the route. In the foreground stands the Earl of Worcester, who, as Master of the Horse, was the manager of court life and ceremonial.

on posterity than the memorials on which other monarchs spent so heavily. Her reign was a great age for building, and saw some of the greatest houses in the land go up: for example, Hardwick Hall and Burghley House. It was also a great age for foundations: grammar schools and almshouses were established in towns across the country, and one or two colleges in Oxford and Cambridge. Yet Elizabeth, unlike her four Tudor predecessors, built and founded nothing (with the partial exception of the collegiate church at what we still call Westminster Abbey, which she 'founded' at no real cost to herself after she had closed down the actual monastery). Of their palaces and colleges and hospitals and religious houses, some have survived and some have fallen. But her portraiture and literature have, ultimately, proved more durable than their architecture.

THE DEATH OF ELIZABETH

Elizabeth died at Richmond in the early hours of 24 March 1603. A London diarist with a friend at court reported her death in the following words:

> This morning, about three o'clock, Her Majesty departed this life, mildly like a lamb, easily like a ripe apple from the tree, *cum leve quadam febre, absque gemitu* [with a slight shiver, without a groan]. Dr Parry told me that he was present, and sent his prayers before her soul. I doubt not but she is amongst the royal saints in Heaven in eternal joys.

It was not all as serene as the publicity implied. Despite her great age – only a small minority saw their seventieth year in those days – and despite having undergone severe illnesses at several points, Elizabeth was not reconciled to dying. What proved to be her final illness set in late in 1602 and thereafter her decline was steady. Even her mind began to weaken, though not to the extent that she allowed the physicians to hasten her end with their quack remedies. Unable to eat much, unwilling to sleep, her last days were difficult. Today we would say that she had a strong will to live.

John Whitgift was Elizabeth's favourite Archbishop of Canterbury. He not only shared her sturdy disapproval of Puritans, but also remained, like the queen, unmarried. Elizabeth never approved of clerical marriage, and seems actively to have disliked the wives of her married bishops.

Tudor England was more intimate with death, in all its forms, and the classical and medieval notion of the 'good death' was still widely held. Yet neither Elizabeth's religion nor perhaps her preferred stoic philosophy provided her with consolation in her last days. Nor were there the social consolations of friends and family. She had outlived friends and favourites, contemporaries and juniors. Leicester had died in 1588, Cecil in 1598, and she had signed Essex's death warrant just two years before. It is said that she was hit particularly hard by the death in February 1603 of her old friend and cousin Catherine Carey, Countess of Nottingham (wife of Lord Howard of Effingham). Elizabeth's reluctance to face death was of a piece with that reluctance to face the inevitable which she had often shown in her royal career. It is symbolised in her failure to make a will.

Reports from her deathbed vary hugely in their details. According to one, she asked Whitgift to pray for her. According to the recollections of one of her ladies in waiting, Lady Southwell, she sent him packing with the comment that he and his kind were nothing but 'hedge-priests'. Lady Southwell's testimony betrays her own Catholic inclinations, and may therefore be suspected at least of embroidery in its desire to tell a good story against the Church of England. On the other hand, the words she puts on Elizabeth's lips seem to carry the familiar lash of the royal tongue. This same report includes another story which bears all the hallmarks of authenticity. The succession to the throne had by now been wrapped up by Robert Cecil's secret diplomacy with James VI. Yet even now her hopeful councillors sought some kind of answer from her on this, the oldest unanswered question of her reign. Believing her unable to speak, they offered to run through a list of candidates and asked her to lift a finger if she wished to approve one. Various names, including that of the king of Scots, left her unmoved. But at the name of Lord Beauchamp, a male descendant of the Grey line, she burst into life: 'I will have no rascal's son in my seat, but one worthy to be a king'. Yet she literally would not lift a finger to solve the problem. Hesitating to the end, she lost consciousness a little later in the day, and died in the night.

6

THE LEGACY OF THE TUDORS

When the last of the Tudors expired in 1603, the passing of the dynasty evoked mixed feelings. The Tudors had presided over one of the most radical periods of change in the history of the kingdom, change accompanied by unprecedented levels of judicial terror and torture. In terms of international politics, England was arguably no weaker at the sunset of the Tudor dynasty than it had been at its dawn. English interventions in European politics had been barely more effective in the 1590s than in the 1490s. But ultimately this was simply a problem of scale. A nation of around 3 million people was in no position to wage war effectively against the traditional enemy, France, with a population at least 10 million greater and with vastly superior natural resources. Henry VIII's expansionist policies had hit the fiscal wall in 1525, and succeeded in the 1540s only in dissipating the spoils of the Church and smashing the national economy. It was only the internal divisions of France in the later sixteenth century that enabled England to achieve modest foreign policy successes with minimal military commitments on the continent. And in the 1590s the costs of suppressing a rebellion in Ireland once more stretched royal finances to breaking point. The hardships of that decade were such that, for all the myth of Elizabeth, her death came as something of a relief. There was always more public concern with the accession of a new monarch than with the death of the old one, and the accession of James I, which soon brought with it the blessings of peace, meant that there was relief as well as regret at the passing of the Tudors. It was only as Stuart government ran into problems of its own that the days of the Tudors in general, and of Elizabeth in particular, began to be recalled as an age of special splendour.

However, the constitutional position of the English monarchy was probably stronger than it had been at any time since the Norman Conquest. The Crown's power over the kingdom had intensified throughout the century, though neither inevitably nor invariably. Equally, though, the power of the central machinery of government which the Tudors had established piecemeal for various short-term political objectives (the nationalisation of the Church, the suppression of rebellions, the elimination of religious dissent) had grown to a degree which made it an effective tool not only in the hands of a strong monarch, but also to a certain extent in the absence of one. The ease with which a foreigner, and a Scotsman to boot (to call somebody a Scot could be grounds for an action for slander in Tudor England), took the throne in 1603 owed a great deal to the smooth operation of this well-oiled machine.

Admittedly this machine needed a king to function, but when the obvious supply ran out in 1603, it was able to recruit one with a minimum of fuss and inconvenience. This shows some considerable advance even since 1553, when the machine had made a similar, if riskier, attempt to shape the succession to suit itself. In 1553 Mary had been able to strike back. If the governing apparatus had looked elsewhere in 1603, it is hard to believe that James would have been able to do anything about it. Over the next century or so, that governing apparatus was to show itself equal to the task of kingmaking in 1660, 1689 and 1714. In the meantime it also learned the neat trick of ridding itself of unsuitable applicants. To that extent at least, the state was an emergent reality in late Tudor England: the fruit of, more than anything else, the recurrent uncertainty about the succession which plagued the century and overshadowed its politics. On the other hand, there remained important limits to the power of that state. Taxation remained a matter of national consent, expressed though Parliament, and the Tudor regime's capacity to tax the wealthy actually declined in the second half of the sixteenth century. To some extent this might be seen as the ruling class's price for supporting the Reformation. It is certainly the case that the nobility and gentry did very well out of the Tudor regime through co-operating with its assault on the Church. But the Tudor failure to achieve significant and lasting fiscal reform or stability left government policy a potential hostage to a tax-paying class whose parsimony was exceeded only by that of Elizabeth herself.

England was politically stable as well as constitutionally strong when Elizabeth died. The last rebellion had been in 1569, and had been put down with almost ridiculous ease. There may have been a handful of Catholic plots and the occasional food or enclosure riot, but there was to be no further rebellion until 1642. The Tudor dynasty had come to the throne at the end of the longest period of civil war in English history. It ended in the midst of the longest period of civil peace England had ever experienced. Seventy years were to pass without an aristocratic revolt. Although we have now learned not to view medieval politics as a story of intrinsic conflict between king and barons, the fact remains that recurrent conflict, whatever its cause, disturbed the basic political consensus. The Tudors had permanently changed the relationship of the nobility to the Crown, and when rebellion returned in the 1640s, for all its debts and appeal to the past, it would be a very different kind of rebellion from anything ever seen before.

The great legacy of the Tudors to the history of England, then, was the emergence of the nascent English state. Within a few years of Elizabeth's death, a court preacher (William Barlow, Bishop of Rochester) was able to refer quite unselfconsciously to 'our Church and State' in the sense in which we still use those words today. His predecessor a hundred years before, John Fisher, would have thought 'our Church' universal rather than national, and would probably have needed the word 'state' carefully explained to him.

This emergence of the 'state', however, was not so much a dynastic achievement as a by-product of dynastic weakness. It was the vulnerability of the succession which called forth the 'state'. The royal supremacy in the Church of England, the omnicompetence of statute, the revival of Parliament, the institutionalisation of the Privy Council – all these constitutional developments arose directly from the succession problem or else from its attempted solutions. The succession was the running sore of the century: in 1502, when the death of Prince Arthur raised the spectre of the Wars of the Roses; in 1533, when Henry VIII's divorce and remarriage – an attempted solution to the succession crisis – led to sweeping changes in the English constitution; in 1553, when the state apparatus endeavoured to divert the succession for its own ends; in the 'exclusion crisis' of the 1580s, when the state apparatus envisaged war to the knife to prevent the succession of Mary Queen of Scots; in 1603 itself, when the state apparatus obtained the secure succession it desired in the person of the Stuart King James VI of Scotland. It is worth noting that the argument used to place legal obstacles in the path of Mary Stuart's succession (the exclusion of the Stuart line under the Act of Succession of 1544) was passed over in embarrassed silence in 1603. But then it was Mary's Catholicism that was the real problem, and James's Protestantism was enough to outweigh any technical problems. If England was to some degree a 'monarchical republic' (as Patrick Collinson has called it) by the time the last of the Tudors went to her grave, it was the constitutional changes, political manoeuvres and unconstitutional expedients scrabbled together in the face of recurrent succession crises that had made it so.

FURTHER READING

This sampling from recent writing on Tudor history is meant to serve two purposes. First of all, it suggests where readers might profitably turn if they wish to pursue in greater depth subjects touched upon in this book. Secondly, it gives a fair idea of the secondary sources which have done most to shape my own account of the Tudors. It is not in any sense a comprehensive bibliography of Tudor history, but most of these books themselves include ample bibliographies which sum up the previous work on their subjects. Most of the works mentioned below are by professional academic historians, and most of them have written much more than is mentioned here. While they are often writing primarily for students and for professional colleagues, they are always more interesting and usually more readable than much of what passes for 'popular' history on the shelves of bookshops and public libraries. The close studies of particular themes and topics are probably not for the 'general reader', but the biographies and narratives most certainly are. Indeed, readers should be advised that although a generation ago academic history writing was often deliberately technical and at times impenetrable in its jargon, clear and readable prose is now the norm in the profession. This is not true of those who cultivate the exotic blooms of fashionable 'theoretical perspectives' such as postmodernism, postcolonialism, and the rest of a whole bundle of notions which have been jocularly summed up as 'posterior analyticism'. But among those actually interested in writing about the human past, clarity and even elegance prevail.

Two books stand out as introductions to Tudor England: John Guy's *Tudor England* (OUP, 1988) and Susan Brigden's *New Worlds, Lost Worlds* (Penguin, 2000) – the latter extending its view to the other Tudor kingdom, Ireland. In addition, Penry Williams, *The Later Tudors: England, 1547–1603* (OUP, 1995) is a comprehensive and up-to-date survey of the second half of the period. Steve Hindle, *The State and Social Change in Early Modern England, c.1550–1640* (Palgrave, 2000) is a perceptive blend of political and social history which reminds us that dynasties and reigns are not the only useful chronological divisions. For the earlier period, a lucid thematic analysis of politics and government can be found in S.J. Gunn, *Early Tudor Government, 1485–1558* (Macmillan, 1995).

Further Reading

The standard biography of Henry VII remains S.B. Chrimes, *Henry VII* (London, 1972; new edn, Yale, 1999), though it may be superseded by Sean Cunningham, *Henry VII* (Routledge, 2007). The Bosworth campaign is well handled in *The Making of the Tudor Dynasty* by R.A. Griffiths and R.S. Thomas (Alan Sutton, 1985). Christine Carpenter's devastating critique of Henry in *The Reign of Henry VII*, ed. B.J. Thompson (Paul Watkins, 1995) is required reading for all Tudor historians, as is her *The Wars of the Roses* (CUP, 1997). T.B. Pugh's analysis of Henry VII's relations with the English nobility in *The Tudor Nobility*, ed. G.W. Bernard (Manchester UP, 1992) is fundamental to understanding the reign, as are the many contributions of J.R. Lander, especially his *Government and Community: England 1450–1509* (Arnold, 1980), and more recently his *English Justices of the Peace, 1461–1509* (Alan Sutton, 1989). The Tudor matriarch, Lady Margaret Beaufort, has been definitively treated by M.K. Jones and M.G. Underwood in *The King's Mother* (CUP, 1992).

The standard biography of Henry VIII is also now of almost venerable age. J.J. Scarisbrick, *Henry VIII* (London, 1968; new edn, Yale, 1997) remains a pleasure to read, but it is time for a new synthesis – which is not provided by the string of biographies to have appeared in the meantime. In the meantime, David Starkey's *The Reign of Henry VIII: Personalities and Politics* (2nd edn, Collins & Brown, 1991) adds some new dimensions. David Starkey's *Henry: Virtuous Prince* (Harper, 2008) is the first instalment of a long-awaited biography. The many surveys of Henry's six wives have been eclipsed by David Starkey's *Six Wives: the Queens of Henry VIII* (Chatto & Windus, 2003), which has completely rewritten several crucial episodes, besides shedding much new light on Henry himself. Anne Boleyn has attracted far more attention than Henry's other wives. E.W. Ives, *Anne Boleyn* (Blackwell, 1986; new edn 2004) is particularly good, and can be supplemented with the stimulating study by Retha Warnicke, *The Rise and Fall of Anne Boleyn* (CUP, 1989), even if her conclusions have not won general assent.

Henry's servants have been well served, especially in recent years. Peter Ackroyd's *The Life of Thomas More* (Chatto & Windus, 1998) combines scholarship with insight, and is an excellent introduction to the vast literature on Henry's most talented and controversial councillor. John Guy's excellent *Thomas More* (Arnold, 2000) revises not only some old myths but also, more usefully, all the recent ones. *Thomas Cromwell, Tudor Minister*, by B.W. Beckingsale (Macmillan, 1988), is the best attempt at a biography, but the minister who arguably had a greater impact on English history than any other Tudor subject is still best approached through the monographs of the late Sir Geoffrey Elton: *The Tudor Revolution in Government* (CUP, 1952), *Policy and Police* (CUP, 1972) and *Reform and Renewal* (CUP, 1973), as well as the relevant chapters of his collected *Studies in Tudor and Stuart Politics and Government* (3 vols, CUP, 1974–83), and his textbook, *Reform and Reformation: England 1509–1558* (Arnold, 1977). S.J. Gunn, *Charles Brandon, Duke of Suffolk* (Blackwell, 1988) is a model study of an early Tudor nobleman. Henry's bishops have also done well. P.J. Gwyn's *The King's Cardinal* (Barrie & Jenkins, 1990) is contentious and controversial as well as thorough – a shame that it is overly long and poorly produced. The collection of essays edited by S.J. Gunn and P.G. Lindley, *Cardinal Wolsey* (CUP, 1991) is an indispensable supplement and corrective to Gwyn (Simon Thurley's contribution on Wolsey's domestic building works is particularly important). Diarmaid MacCulloch's *Thomas Cranmer* (Yale, 1996) is simply definitive, but not simply a biography: it is also a masterly survey of much of the political and religious history of England in the 1530s and 1540s. Glyn Redworth's *In Defence of the Church Catholic* (Blackwell, 1990) and Maria Dowling's *Fisher of Men* (Macmillan, 1999) introduce two of the episcopal supporting cast, Stephen Gardiner and John Fisher.

The political history of Henry's reign has also been explored in a wide range of specialised studies, such as Helen Miller, *Henry VIII and the English Nobility* (Blackwell, 1986) and S.E. Lehmberg, *The Reformation Parliament* (CUP, 1970). The collection of essays edited by Diarmaid MacCulloch, *The Reign of Henry VIII* (Macmillan, 1995), illuminates most aspects of Henrician politics (R.W. Hoyle's contribution on 'War and Public Finance' is particularly important). The greatest crisis of the reign, the Pilgrimage of Grace, is now better understood then ever before thanks to Michael Bush, *The Pilgrimage of Grace* (Manchester, 1996), and especially to R.W. Hoyle, *The Pilgrimage of Grace and the Politics of the 1530s* (Oxford, 2001).

W.K. Jordan's two massive volumes on Edward VI – *Edward VI: the Young King* and *Edward VI: the Threshold of Power* (Allen & Unwin, 1968 and 1970) – remain massively unsatisfactory hagiography. The traditional wisdom about the Dukes of Somerset and Northumberland which they enshrine has been devastatingly revised by M.L. Bush, *The Government Policy of Protector Somerset* (Arnold, 1975) and David Loades, *John Dudley, Duke of Northumberland* (OUP, 1996). Jennifer Loach's posthumously published *Edward VI* (Yale, 1999) is excellent as far as it goes, but too obviously unfinished. The best insight into Edward himself comes from MacCulloch's *Tudor Church Militant* (Penguin, 2000). Stephen Alford's *Kingship and Politics in the Reign of Edward VI* (CUP, 2002) adds considerably to our understanding of the reign. Dale Hoak, *The King's Council in the Reign of Edward VI* (CUP, 1976) focuses on one of the main instruments of Tudor government.

The recent historiography of Mary Tudor has been dominated by the writings of one scholar, David Loades, whose *Mary Tudor* (Blackwell, 1989) and *The Reign of Mary Tudor* (Ernest Benn, 1979) are the only place to start. Anna Whitelock's *Mary Tudor: England's First Queen* (Bloomsbury, 2009) gives the most up-to-date account. Jennifer Loach, *Parliament and the Crown in the Reign of Mary Tudor* (OUP, 1986) is one of the most searching explorations of Marian politics. The fullest biography of any public figure of her reign is Thomas F. Mayer's controversial *Reginald Pole* (CUP, 2000).

Biographies of Elizabeth are thick on the shelves, and there is sadly little to choose between most of them. However, David Loades, *Elizabeth I* (Hambledon, 2003) stands out from the crowd; and Wallace MacCaffrey's *Elizabeth I* (Arnold, 1993), focusing more on political than personal issues, is the judgement of a scholar whose life's work has been devoted to the exploration of the politics of the reign in a series of influential monographs. David Starkey's *Elizabeth: Apprenticeship* (Chatto & Windus, 2000), which wears its learning lightly and addresses a wide readership with a sparkling style, offers some genuinely new insights into the political formation of the last Tudor monarch, giving a sense of what might be done for Elizabeth's whole life if the story was rewritten from the ground up. Carole Levin's *The Heart and Stomach of a King: Elizabeth I and the Politics of Sex and Power* (University of Pennsylvania Press, 1994) is a stimulating reflection on how Elizabeth coped with the problem of being a female ruler in a man's world. Christopher Haigh's thematic study, *Elizabeth I* (new edn, Longman, 2001), is a *tour de force*, persuasively and wittily written, and packed with acute analysis of the queen and of the politics of her reign. G.R. Elton's *The Parliament of England, 1559–1581* (CUP, 1986) entirely and convincingly rewrote this hitherto badly misunderstood passage of English history.

The lives of Leicester, Essex, and other leading men of Elizabeth's court have been endlessly retold, in biographies often as undistinguished and indistinguishable as those of their sovereign. However, Paul Hammer's *The Polarisation of Elizabethan Politics* (CUP, 1999), the first instalment of a comprehensive account of Robert Devereux, Earl of Essex, taking the story down to 1597, is a penetrating insight into both the world of the new nobility created by the Tudors and the later politics of the reign. There is a great deal in the two studies by Conyers Read, *Mr Secretary Cecil and Queen Elizabeth* and *Lord Burghley and Queen Elizabeth* (Jonathan Cape, 1955 and 1960), but William Cecil awaits a definitive biography. In the meantime, M.A.R. Graves, *Burghley* (Longman, 1998) is a useful students' introduction, while Stephen Alford's *The Early Elizabethan Polity: William Cecil and the British Succession Crisis, 1558–1569* (CUP, 1998) shows what can be done, giving a profound and persuasive analysis of Cecil's policy. Elizabeth's bishops have not attracted anything like the interest shown in their predecessors, with the shining exception of Patrick Collinson's *Archbishop Grindal, 1519–1583* (Jonathan Cape, 1979). Collinson's article 'The Monarchical Republic of Queen Elizabeth I', which appeared in the *Bulletin of the John Rylands Library* 69 (1987), pp. 394–424, opened an entirely new window on the politics of Elizabethan England. The war with Spain, and in particular the Armada campaign, have a vast literature. Colin Martin and Geoffrey Parker, *The Spanish Armada* (Hamish Hamilton, 1988) is the best place to start. Important aspects of the 'myth' of Elizabeth are explored in Frances Yates, *Astraea* (Routledge & Kegan Paul, 1975) and Roy Strong, *The Cult of Elizabeth* (Thames and Hudson, 1977).

There are biographies galore on Mary Queen of Scots, but without doubt the best is John Guy, *My Heart is My Own* (Fourth Estate, 2004). The case against Mary is forcefully argued by Jenny Wormald, *Mary Queen of Scots: a Study in Failure* (George Philip, 1988), while some more favourable interpretations can be found in the collection of essays edited by Michael Lynch, *Mary Stewart: Queen in Three Kingdoms* (Blackwell, 1988).

The most important social and political development of the Tudor period was the Reformation, on which the literature is vast. Felicity Heal, *The Reformation in Britain and Ireland* (OUP, 2004) and Christopher Haigh, *English Reformations* (Oxford, 1993) are the best overall narratives currently available. Eamon Duffy's

The Stripping of the Altars (Yale, 1992) is a moving account of the destruction of the old religion, while Norman Jones, *The English Reformation* (Blackwell, 2001) offers a fresh look at the construction of the new. Eamon Duffy takes a new look at Mary's restoration of Catholicism in *Fires of Faith* (Yale, 2009). There are many studies of the local impact of the Reformation, most of them articles in academic journals. Among the books, the best are Susan Brigden, *London and the Reformation* (OUP, 1989), and Caroline Litzenberger's study of Gloucestershire, *The English Reformation and the Laity* (CUP, 1997). Eamon Duffy's *The Voices of Morebath* (Yale, 2001) gets even closer to the grass roots with a microscopic examination of the Reformation in a rural parish. Brisk introductions are available in Richard Rex, *Henry VIII and the English Reformation* (Macmillan, 1993) and Diarmaid MacCulloch, *The Later Reformation in England* (2nd edn, Palgrave, 2001).

Setting the Tudors and their England into the wider context of the interrelated history of Britain and Ireland as a whole has been one of the most fruitful paths in recent research, pioneered by Brendan Bradshaw and Steven G. Ellis in *Conquest and Union: Fashioning a British State, 1485–1725*, ed. S.G. Ellis and S. Barber (Longman, 1995), and *The British Problem, c.1534–1707*, ed. B. Bradshaw and J. Morrill (Macmillan, 1996). Working within this perspective, S.G. Ellis's *Tudor Frontiers and Noble Power* (OUP, 1995) offers the most innovative view of Tudor politics published in the last decade. For the history of the other nations the best starting points are: S.G. Ellis, *Ireland in the Age of the Tudors* (Longman, 1998); Jenny Wormald, *Court, Kirk, and Community: Scotland 1470–1625* (Arnold, 1981); and Glanmor Williams, *Renewal and Reformation: Wales, c.1415–1642* (OUP, 1993). Mark Nicholls, *A History of the Modern British Isles, 1529–1603* (Blackwell, 1999) is a fine narrative synthesis.

LIST OF ILLUSTRATIONS

Integrated Illustrations

1550 1600.

Page 127, top: Queen Mary's instructions to Lord Russell, Lord Privy Seal. © Jonathan Reeve JRCD3b20p998.

Page 127, bottom: Passport for Richard Shelley to travel to Spain, signed 'Philippus' and 'Marye the quene'. © Jonathan Reeve JRCD3b20p999.

Page 129: Philip II of Spain, engraving by F. Hogenberg, 1555. © Jonathan Reeve JR188b4p823 1550 1600.

Page 135: Title page from the 1570 edition of John Foxe's *Acts and Monuments*. © Jonathan Reeve JR985b20p1003 1500 1600.

Page 136: The burning of Bishop John Hooper at Gloucester. © Jonathan Reeve JRCD2b20p1004 1550 1600.

Page 137: Edmund Bonner (Bishop of London, 1539–59) as Protestants saw him thanks to Foxe's *Book of Martyrs*. © Jonathan Reeve JR239b7p321 1550 1600.

Page 138: The burning of Hugh Latimer and Nicholas Ridley at Oxford. © Jonathan Reeve JRCD2b20p1005 1550 1600.

Page 149: Prayers written out by Elizabeth (then aged twelve). © Jonathan Reeve JR221b5fp286 1550 1600.

Page 150: The Entrance of Queen Elizabeth. © Jonathan Reeve JR201b5p21 1550 1600.

Page 151: A sketch of Elizabeth in one of the commonest of her portrait poses, holding a fan. © Jonathan Reeve JR978b65p61 1500 1600.

Page 153: Robert Dudley, Earl of Leicester. © Jonathan Reeve JR203b5fp4 1550 1600.

Page 161: John Knox from a 1580 woodcut. © Jonathan Reeve JRCD3b20p1041 1550 1600.

Page 165: Queen Elizabeth at the opening of Parliament. © Jonathan Reeve JRCD3b20p1019.

Page 169, top: Elizabeth's falcon downs a heron. © Jonathan Reeve JR172b4p740 1550 1600.

Page 169, middle & bottom: Illustrations from George Gascoigne, *The Noble Arte of Venerie or Hunting* (1575). © Jonathan Reeve JR173b4p741 1550 1600 and JR125b2p535 1550 1600.

Page 176: Parsons and Campion from George Carleton, *A Thankfull Remembrance of Gods Mercy in the Deliverance of the Church and State in the reigns of Elizabeth and James I* (1627). © Jonathan Reeve JR207b5p50 1550 1600.

Page 181: George Gascoigne depicted presenting a book to Queen Elizabeth. © Jonathan Reeve JR143b3fp186 1550 1600.

Page 185: Roman Catholic plots against Elizabeth, as seen in part of an engraving by Cornelius Danckwerts, entitled *A Thankful Remembrance of Gods Mercie*. © Jonathan Reeve JR129b2p601 1550 1600.

Page 186: The Babington Plot, from George Carleton's *Thankfull Remembrance*. © Jonathan Reeve JR204b5p9 1550 1600.

Page 188, top: The Spanish Armada off the French coast. © Jonathan Reeve JR216b5p148 1550 1600.

Page 188, middle: Sir Francis Drake. © Jonathan Reeve JR191b4p830 1550 1600.

Page 188, bottom: Chart of the course of the 'Invincible Armada'. Courtesy of Jonathan Reeve JR988b4p836 1500 1600.

Page 189: Section of John Speed's map of the route of the Armada. © Jonathan Reeve JR984b20p1069 1500 1600.

Page 190, top: Preaching at Paul's Cross, London. © Jonathan Reeve JR209b5p68 1550 1600.

Page 190, bottom: Title page of a thanksgiving service issued in 1588. © Jonathan Reeve JR242b7p405 1550 1600.

Page 191: English troops campaigning in Ireland during the sixteenth century. © Jonathan Reeve JR214b5fp138 1550 1600.

Page 193: English troops on the march in Ireland. © Jonathan Reeve JR214zb5fp138 1550 1600.

Page 194: The last letter of Robert Dudley, Earl of Leicester, to Elizabeth I. © Jonathan Reeve JR986b20p1088 1500 1600.

Page 195: Portrait engraving of Francis Bacon. © Jonathan Reeve JR226b5fp406 1550 1600.

Page 196, top: The reception of Sir Henry Sidney (Elizabeth I's Lord Deputy in Ireland) by the mayor and aldermen of Dublin. © Jonathan Reeve JR197b4p921 1550 1600.

Page 196, bottom: Hugh O'Neill, Earl of Tyrone. © Jonathan Reeve JR213b5p116 1550 1600.

Page 198: Entertainments at Elvetham, 1591. © Jonathan Reeve JR211b5p104 1550 1600.

Page 200: 'A Hieroglyphic of Britain'. © Jonathan Reeve JR174b4p743 1550 1600.

Page 201: The Red Cross Knight from Edmund Spenser's *The Faerie Queene* (3rd edition, 1598). © Jonathan Reeve JR194b4p856 1550 1600.

Page 202, top: Portrait of Richard Tarlton. © Jonathan Reeve JR149b3fp258 1550 1660.

Page 202, bottom: Detail from a portrait of Elizabeth I. © Jonathan Reeve JR993b65p 1500 1600.

Page 204: The 'Procession Picture'. © Jonathan Reeve JR200b5pii 1550 1600.

Page 205: John Whitgift. © Jonathan Reeve JR983.

Colour Sections

1. A portrait miniature of Henry VII, from the Bosworth Jewel. The Royal Collection © 2008, Her Majesty Queen Elizabeth II RCIN 420012.

2. Lady Margaret Beaufort above the gate at Christ's College, Cambridge. Courtesy of Elizabeth Norton and the Amberley Archive.

3 & 4 Pair of portraits of Henry VII and his queen, Elizabeth of York. The Royal Collection © 2008, Her Majesty Queen Elizabeth II RCIN 404743. The Royal Collection © 2008, Her Majesty Queen Elizabeth II RCIN 403447.

5. Edward IV, father of Henry VII's queen, Elizabeth of York. The Royal Collection © 2008, Her Majesty Queen Elizabeth II RCIN 403435.

6. Richard III. The Royal Collection © 2008, Her Majesty Queen Elizabeth II RCIN 403436.

7. The family of Henry VII with St George and the dragon. The Royal Collection © 2008, Her Majesty Queen Elizabeth II RCIN 401228.

8. Arthur, Prince of Wales, Henry VII's eldest son who died in 1502. The Royal Collection © 2008, Her Majesty Queen Elizabeth II RCIN 403444.

9. Margaret Tudor, Henry VIII's elder sister and Queen of Scotland. The Royal Collection © 2008, Her Majesty Queen Elizabeth II RCIN 401181.

10. Henry VIII c.1535. The Royal Collection © 2008, Her Majesty Queen Elizabeth II RCIN 403368.

11. Laughing child, possibly Henry VIII, c.1498. The Royal Collection © 2008, Her Majesty Queen Elizabeth II RCIN 73197.

12. Richmond Palace as built by Henry VII. Courtesy of Jonathan Reeve JR945b20p788 1500 1550.

13. Catherine of Aragon, Henry VIII's first wife. The Royal Collection © 2008, Her Majesty Queen Elizabeth II RCIN 404746.

14. Catherine of Aragon. The Royal Collection © 2008, Her Majesty Queen Elizabeth II RCIN 421499.

List of Illustrations

INDEX

More Tudor History from Amberley Publishing

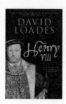 

Tudor History from Amberley Publishing

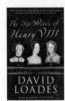

THE TUDORS
Richard Rex

'The best introduction to England's most important dynasty'
DAVID STARKEY
'Gripping and told with enviable narrative skill... a delight'
THES
'Vivid, entertaining and carrying its learning lightly'
EAMON DUFFY
'A lively overview' **THE GUARDIAN**

£9.99   978-1-4456-0700-9   256 pages PB 143 illus., 66 col

CATHERINE HOWARD
Lacey Baldwin Smith

'A brilliant, compelling account' **ALISON WEIR**
'A faultless book' **THE SPECTATOR**
'Lacey Baldwin Smith has so excellently caught the
atmosphere of the Tudor age' **THE OBSERVER**

£9.99   978-1-84868-521-5   256 pages PB 25 col illus

MARGARET OF YORK
Christine Weightman

'A pioneering biography of the Tudor dynasty's most
dangerous enemy'
PROFESSOR MICHAEL HICKS
'Christine Weightman brings Margaret alive once more'
THE YORKSHIRE POST
'A fascinating account of a remarkable woman'
THE BIRMINGHAM POST

£10.99   978-1-4456-0819-8   256 pages PB 51 illus

THE SIX WIVES OF HENRY VIII
David Loades

'Neither Starkey nor Weir has the assurance and command
of Loades' **SIMON HEFFER, LITERARY REVIEW**
'Incisive and profound. I warmly recommend this book'
ALISON WEIR

£9.99   978-1-4456-0049-9   256 pages PB 55 illus, 31 col

MARY ROSE
David Loades

£20.00 978-1-4456-0622-4
272 pages HB 17 col illus

MARY BOLEYN
Josephine Wilkinson

£9.99 978-1-84868-525-3
208 pages PB 22 illus, 10 col

JANE SEYMOUR
Elizabeth Norton

£9.99 978-1-84868-527-7
224 pages PB 53 illus, 26 col

HENRY VIII
Richard Rex

£9.99 978-1-84868-098-2
192 pages PB 81 illus, 48 col

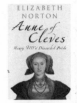

THOMAS CROMWELL
Patrick Coby

£20.00 978-1-4456-0775-7
272 pages HB 30 illus (20 col)

ANNE BOLEYN THE
YOUNG QUEEN TO BE
Josephine Wilkinson
£9.99 978-1-4456-0395-7
208 pages PB 34 illus (19 col)

ELIZABETH I
Richard Rex

£9.99 978-1-84868-423-2
192 pages PB 75 illus

ANNE OF CLEVE
Elizabeth Norton

£9.99 978-1-4456-0183-0
224 pages HB 54 illus, 27 col

Available from all good bookshops or to order direct
Please call **01453-847-800 www.amberleybooks.com**